George Young

Manitoba Memories

Leaves From my Life in the Prairie Province, 1868-1884

George Young

Manitoba Memories
Leaves From my Life in the Prairie Province, 1868-1884

ISBN/EAN: 9783744724333

Printed in Europe, USA, Canada, Australia, Japan

Cover: Foto ©Thomas Meinert / pixelio.de

More available books at **www.hansebooks.com**

MANITOBA MEMORIES

LEAVES FROM MY LIFE IN THE PRAIRIE PROVINCE, 1868-1884.

BY

REV. GEORGE YOUNG, D.D.,

Founder of Methodist Missions in the Red River Settlement.

WITH INTRODUCTION BY

REV. ALEXANDER SUTHERLAND, D.D.,

General Secretary of the Missionary Society of the Methodist Church.

With Portraits and Illustrations.

TORONTO:
WILLIAM BRIGGS,
Wesley Buildings.

MONTREAL: C. W. COATES.   HALIFAX; S. F. HUESTIS.

1897.

Entered, according to Act of the Parliament of Canada, in the year one thousand eight hundred and ninety-seven, by WILLIAM BRIGGS, at the Department of Agriculture.

INTRODUCTION.

MANY a book has been published for which no good reason could be assigned, but this book is not of that class. Many manuscripts might have been consigned by publishers to the waste-basket or the flames and the world have been none the poorer; but to have withheld these "Manitoba Memories" from the public would have been a distinct and serious loss. Methodists would have lost some pages of inspiring autobiography, as well as the story of the planting of Methodism in the great North-West; Christians who can rise above the low level of denominational shibboleths would have lost the profit which comes from studying the movements of other divisions of the Lord's army than their own; patriots would have lost the record of some of the most stirring scenes in the founding of our Western Empire; and coming historians of both Church and State would have lost a veritable mine of materials of the highest value.

Only a single chapter is devoted to the author's autobiography, but the glimpses it affords of his early life serve the good purpose of bringing the reader into sympathy with the man and his work. From this starting point we follow him with sympathetic interest through the valedictory services at Toronto, before setting out with his companions for their distant mission fields; the long and toilsome journey over the hundreds of miles of unsettled prairie that intervened between St. Cloud and Fort Garry; the difficulties which beset his early ministry, growing in part out of the sparseness of population, the long distances between the settlements, the scarcity and cost of supplies, and, last but not least, the bigotry of some who claimed a monopoly of religious teaching, poorly qualified though they might be to supply it. But all these were successively overcome, and the reader cannot fail to rejoice in the success which ultimately crowned the labors of this devoted missionary and those who succeeded him in the work.

The part of these "Memories" which will most deeply stir the hearts of loyal Canadians, irrespective of name or party, is that which covers the revolt of the half-breeds under Louis Riel in 1869. In this book we have a simple narrative of the facts, recorded by an eye-witness whose well-known reputation for integrity, veracity and uprightness precludes any suspicion of unfairness. The narrative in its simplicity, directness, circumstantial details and evident freedom from mere partizan bias, bears the stamp of truthfulness upon its face, and the future historian will find in it materials which he can use with unhesitating confidence. The beginning of the troubles; the persistent attempts of Riel to fan the passions of the ignorant half-breeds (which a word from the Hierarchy could have checked, had it been spoken); the seizure of Fort Garry and the imprisonment of loyal Canadians; the escape of some and the recapture of part of them; the climax of crime and cruelty in the cold-blooded murder of Thomas Scott; the enforced exodus of the loyal element until order was restored by the triumphal entry of the forces under General Wolseley—all these occurrences are detailed with simple but graphic power, and supply information of intense interest and permanent value.

Following the stirring chapters on the Riel rebellion, the author turns again to the peaceful scenes of missionary labor and the planting of the Methodist Church. "The First Manitoba Missionary Conference," when Drs. Punshon and Wood, and John Macdonald, Esq., (all of whom have since joined the "great majority") met the missionaries of the North-West, is sketched chiefly in the language of contemporaneous records, and Dr. Lachlan Taylor's journey through the "Great Lone Land" is given in the words of the Doctor's own journal and report. The history of the early educational movement is an interesting chapter, and so is that which details two dissimilar missionary journeys in 1874 and 1875. The second of these journeys was in the winter season, through an uninhabited wilderness, and gave our author some experience of the toils and hardships of missionaries in the far North. But to follow the remaining chapters in detail would exceed the limits properly assigned to an Introduction, and I must refer the reader to the book itself for further information.

A work such as was done by George Young and his associates in the North-West does not bulk very large in the public eye at the time. Theirs was emphatically the work of laying foundations, and this is a work which has to be done quietly, and, for the most part, out of sight; but its importance to the superstructure to be built thereupon cannot be overstated. That these men planned wisely and built solidly, the results abundantly testify. Not often is it given to pioneers to see the full fruit of their labors; but it is matter of profound satisfaction that the man who, under God, planted the seeds of Methodism in the Prairie Province, has lived to see and help to gather the wonderful harvest that sprang from his sowing. Some men have monuments in dead marble, reared long after they have passed away; George Young has his monument to-day in the living Methodism of the great North-West.

A. SUTHERLAND.

METHODIST MISSION ROOMS,
    Toronto, May 10th, 1897.

PREFATORY.

THE writer of this volume desires to intimate to its readers that in its preparation and publication he has simply yielded to the solicitations of many friends, as well as to the request of the members of the Manitoba and North-West Conference embodied in the following resolution:

Moved by Rev. G. R. Turk, seconded by Rev. Dr. Sparling—

"That we have read with pleasure the letters of the Rev. George Young, D.D., which have recently appeared in the *Christian Guardian*.

"Because of his intimate association with the early history of this country, Dr. Young is specially qualified to impart information which can be obtained from no other source, and which will be of great interest and importance to coming years. We, therefore, as a Conference, express the hope that Dr. Young may see his way clear to place the information contained in the letters in permanent book form. Also, that a copy of this resolution be forwarded to Dr. Young by the Secretary of this Conference."

My readers will suffer another prefatory remark:

I have given a more detailed account of some of the events narrated than would be deemed advisable but for the fact that hitherto they have not, to my knowledge, appeared in print, or when they have were so interblended with the fictitious as to be deservedly discredited by their readers. I will also add, that in consenting to prepare this volume I was influenced somewhat by the strong probability that it would be read by a goodly number of our young people whose birth has taken place since the times when these recorded events transpired, and who may not so much as have heard of their occurrence.

To such, and all others who may consult these pages, I herewith give the assurance that I have not in the least drawn upon my imagination in their preparation, but in all cases where the incidents given or the events described have not been matters of personal experience or observation, I have drawn my information from what I deem reliable sources.

CONTENTS.

Chapter I.
An Autobiographical Sketch. (1821–1868) . . . 11

Chapter II.
Valedictory Services 29

Chapter III.
The Forthgoing of the Missionary Party . . . 54

Chapter IV.
Perplexities and Encouragements Interblending . . 67

Chapter V.
The Arrival of an Efficient Helper 90

Chapter VI.
Troublous Times 100

Chapter VII.
Escaping for Life 117

Chapter VIII.
The Climax of Crime and Cruelty . . . 131

Chapter IX.
Post-Mortem Indignities, etc. 148

Chapter X.
An Enforced Exodus 163

CONTENTS.

CHAPTER XI.
A Notable Military Expedition 174

CHAPTER XII.
The Triumphal Entry, and What Came of It . . . 186

CHAPTER XIII.
The Building of Our First Grace Church . . 200

CHAPTER XIV.
The Fenian Raid of 1871—A Fizzle and a Farce . . 212

CHAPTER XV.
The First Manitoba Missionary Conference . . . 230

CHAPTER XVI.
Dr. Lachlan Taylor's Wonderful Tour Among the Missions in the "Great Lone Land" 250

CHAPTER XVII.
Our Early Educational Movements in Manitoba . . 268

CHAPTER XVIII.
Two Missionary Journeys into the Interior . . 280

CHAPTER XIX.
My Last Hand-Shake with an Heroic Missionary . . 302

CHAPTER XX.
Returning to Ontario 317

CHAPTER XXI.
My Second Appointment to Mission Work in Manitoba . 328

CHAPTER XXII.
My Third Appointment to Mission Work in the North-West 343

MANITOBA MEMORIES.

CHAPTER I.

AN AUTOBIOGRAPHICAL SKETCH.

(1821-1868.)

HAVING been spared to pass the seventy-fifth milestone in my life's pathway, and to enjoy fifty-seven years of membership in the Methodist Church and fifty-five years of preacher life, it would seem as if the requests of many friends that I should give a brief sketch of some, at least, of my many recollections of events and experiences of bygone years, were not altogether unreasonable.

To the chapters following this much larger space will be given, as it is judged that my Manitoba memories will be regarded as of more general interest than those by which they were preceded, and which will therefore be more briefly recorded, and even in many cases barely summarized.

The two births of which I have been the subject occurred at the following dates: The first on the last day of the year 1821, and the second in October, 1840. In the first I entered the life that now is; by the second I was introduced into "the household of faith," and became a child and an heir of God and a "joint-heir with Christ." My ancestors, who were of the old U. E. Loyalist stock, emigrated from the States and settled in those parts of the County of Prince Edward still known as East and West Lake respectively, considerably more than a hundred years ago. When but nineteen years of age my mother became the subject of three experiences such as have come to but few in so quick succession—a happy young wife, a stricken widow, and an anxious mother—and all during the months of the year 1821. My early days were passed with my mother in the old homestead with her parents, who, being Methodists, accounted it a privilege to open their home for public worship and as a resting-place for the weary itinerants of those pioneering times.

Some of my earliest recollections are of the names and appearance of those zealous servants of the Most High. This is especially the case with one whom I can never forget—the Rev. Geo. Ferguson, an ex-soldier bought out of the army by the Methodists—a man small of stature, but large of heart, and all aflame with love to God and zeal for His glory, whose energetic and persistent efforts in pulpit and prayer-meeting exercises were greatly blessed in the conversion of multitudes of those early settlers. The one incident in connection with this consecrated man's ministry of which I have the most vivid recollection was the placing of his hands on my head and earnestly beseeching God to bless and save "the little fatherless boy." Will not "the effectual fervent prayer of a righteous man avail much?" After many years of devoted service in the itinerancy, and when he was literally a "worn-out" preacher, the name of this saintly man was placed on the list of superannuates, where it remained until he was transferred to the ranks of the immortals.

Another distinct recollection I have of early childhood days was that of hearing in the class-room, to which my mother led me, the earnest and frequent singing of the hymn beginning with "A charge to keep I have," which was so deeply impressed on my mind even then as to become ineffaceable. To this day I rarely read or hear it announced in worship without being reminded of those messages which it bore to my mind in the times long gone by.

After many years of widowhood my mother became the wife of Mr. Thomas Bowerman, whereupon we removed to a new home, in a much more sparsely settled part of the country, where for several years my educational opportunities were both few in number and poor in quality. Schools were distant, teachers incompetent, text-books ill adapted, and opportunities for study few and far between, so that my chances for getting an education were in striking contrast with those now enjoyed by our highly favored youth, whether in city or country. Helping to clear up land, to till soil difficult of tillage, ploughing, harvesting, threshing, teaming, and caring for stock, generally occupied my attention and called into exercise my energies during the years most favorable for close work in school or college. Very true, much of this was in a degree educative, though it tended to the training and developing of muscle rather than mind. Still it was not entirely valueless in its bearings upon my future, inasmuch as it brought me such practical knowledge as subsequently availed me much, by producing in me such a purpose of self-help as I have been thankful for ever since.

I will relate just here what I have ever regarded as a very remarkable instance of Divine interposition, which occurred prior to my conversion. Our barn was built on a hill side, the timbers on the upper side resting on a foundation built but little above the ground, while on the lower side they rested on posts some twelve or fourteen feet in height, the basement becoming a shelter for the stock in wintry weather, while the upper stories contained grain, threshed or unthreshed, hay, etc. Early one stormy morning, while I was engaged in feeding the cattle in the basement stables, a terrific wind storm, a veritable tornado, struck the building, and by its marvellous force crushed the entire structure to the earth, as if had been but a child's playhouse. Hearing the crash of the falling and breaking timbers, I was instantly prompted to fall on my knees and pray. Responding immediately to the prompting, the prayer of the penitent publican was earnestly uttered, and, I fully believe, instantly answered. In a moment all was over, and stillness and darkness reigned where I was, the broken timbers having so encompassed me and the mows of hay and wheat so completely covered me that both light and sound were entirely excluded, while I was as free from injury as before the crash occurred.

My first thought was that I had been so buried beneath the large quantities of hay and grain which I knew had rested on the timbers above and must have fallen along with them, that escape would be impossible; but a vigorous effort resulted in a few minutes in making an opening through which light streamed and out of which I rushed, without either scratch or bruise. Then it was that I discovered that in my kneeling to pray I had avoided the falling beams and other timbers, now so piled upon each other on either side and for about three feet above my head as to leave a space about a yard square—the only space discernible where I could have escaped being crushed to death. Had I been disobedient to the prompting and remained standing, I must have been instantly killed. Whence came that prompting to kneel and pray—was it from within or from above? Was it of blind chance that those falling timbers were so piled on each other and at such distances as to ward off the supports of the mow of hay and grain, and thus shield me completely from any injury whatever? Of the many who came that day to view the ruins all seemed, as they took in the situation, to regard my escape as miraculous, and many unhesitatingly declared it to be so. How could they do otherwise? Has the God of Almightiness so laid aside His ability or His right to so direct and control and counterwork the great forces of Nature, which are but of His ordaining, as to involve the miraculous? I believe in God as Preserver as well as Creator, and that it was He and He alone that "redeemed my life from destruction."

When the rebellion of 1837, known as Mackenzie's rebellion, broke out, and a call came for volunteers to aid in its suppression, my loyalty led me to respond to the call, and joining a company of dragoons under the captaincy of E. D. S. Wilkins, Colonel Landon commanding the regiment, I came under military rule in the service of Queen and country. For the purpose of guarding Presque Isle Harbor, and also, I suppose, of dissuading any in that region having disloyal proclivities from making demonstration in that direction, we were stationed, with two or three companies of infantry, in the village of Brighton, where barracks were secured for the men and stables erected for the horses. Here we remained—except when out on duty in carrying despatches or patrolling—engaging daily in parades for drill in horsemanship, sword exercise, etc., etc., during our six months of service. This also was, in a way, an educative process of some value to me in after years when horse, saddle and saddle-bags became so closely associated with me in my circuit work. My soldier-life was no benefit to me, however, religiously; yet I am profoundly grateful for the restraining grace which saved me from being drawn into those excesses which proved the ruin of some of my comrades in the service.

I now come to that more important event, my second birth, which took place in October, 1840,

AN AUTOBIOGRAPHICAL SKETCH.

following a season of deep conviction which the Holy Spirit wrought in me through the use of means of His own choosing. A young friend of mine was suddenly stricken out of life under circumstances which seemingly afforded no opportunity for preparation for the great change. At the burial, as we stood by the open grave, an earnest, godly neighbor, an exhorter, was moved to speak such words of warning as greatly impressed all who heard them, and also proved the means of awakening to many of the associates of the deceased young man. My spiritual emancipation took place not many days thence, in connection with a series of special services in our newly-erected little school-house, which soon became the birthplace of many awakened souls. Almost immediately after this blessed incoming of life and light and peace, I was moved to seek, by testimony and exhortation, to persuade others to become reconciled to God, so that now nearly fifty-seven years have elapsed since I began to exclaim, "Behold the Lamb of God." At the close of the services referred to, with many others, I united with the Church and received baptism from the Rev. Lewis Warner, who gave me my first quarterly ticket, which I still hold, and which reads thus: "To do good and communicate forget not, for with such sacrifices God is well pleased." That Scripture, coming to me as it did, was as a message from heaven. As the weeks passed by, I was induced to take part in prayer and fellowship meetings, and occasionally to give an exhortation and "lead the meeting." Deeply conscious of my need of the requisite qualifications even for such exercises, I applied myself to the study of such commentaries, sermons and biographies, etc., as came within my reach, frequently devoting thereto the three or four hours which preceded the dawn. In the meantime, though still engaged in farm work, I assisted in revival services in adjacent neighborhoods, as best I could. In order that I might have educational advantages such as I had not hitherto enjoyed, I attended the Grammar School in Picton for a season, and was privileged in boarding at the parsonage and receiving assistance such as I much needed from our minister. In due course I received license as a local preacher, and being recommended by the Quarterly Official Meeting in Picton to the District Meeting, was thereby recommended to the Conference, after due examination, to be received on trial as a candidate for our ministry.

Sabbath, June 12th, 1842, was one of the many red-letter days in my life which I shall ever remember. On that day for the first time it was my privilege to enjoy the solemnities of a Conference Sabbath, and to me the privilege was great beyond description. First of all was the early and "old-time" love-feast, which was followed by the ordination sermon by President Green on "The Great Pentecostal Revival," and the ordination service. Then the three o'clock service and an eloquent sermon by Rev. G. R. Sanderson on "Glorying in the cross of Christ only." Then at seven o'clock another excellent and powerful discourse from Rev. Dr. Ryerson, on "The excellency of the knowledge of Christ," which helped to prepare us for, as it was followed by, the holy communion. No one will marvel when I state that these services one and all left an impression on my mind which can never be effaced. One, and only one, of the gifted preachers of that Sabbath continues in the Church militant at this date—I refer to Rev. Dr. Sanderson, who was my superintendent in 1845-46 in the Adelaide Street charge, Toronto, and subsequently our Editor and Book Steward, etc.

On the following day (Monday, June 13th) the Conference in the old Picton chapel (as we called it) closed, and my name having been read off for my first appointment, as assistant to my faithful and zealous friend, Rev. S. C. Philp, sen., who is yet on this side of the river, but "waiting for the boatman," I made haste to get my few belongings in the way of an outfit for my future life as an itinerant into shape; to say good-bye to my friends, and to set out, with horse, saddle, bridle and valise, a few clothes and a few books, for the somewhat distant field of labor, the old Oxford Circuit.

And now to summarize, as want of space will not allow of anything more extended. I will mention the fields of labor to which I have been assigned from year to year. The positions I have been permitted to occupy have been duly reported in the Annual Minutes, and need no mention from me, further than this simple statement. My circuits have been as follows: Oxford, Chatham, London (as a supply),

Brantford, Toronto, St. Catharines, Gatineau and Hull, Hamilton and Glanford, London (again as a supply), Niagara and Drummondville, Belleville, Montreal, Brantford, Kingston, Quebec, Toronto (Richmond and Queen Street Churches). At this point, however, I will diverge somewhat to make special reference to the appointment which the

REV. HENRY WILKINSON.

Conference gave me in 1848 as the colleague of Rev. Henry Wilkinson, Superintendent of the Hamilton Circuit.

I had made the acquaintance of my now sainted brother while he was President of Conference and Chairman of Toronto District, and had a very high estimate of his abilities, both as preacher and administrator, and also of his deep piety as well as his uniform kindliness, for which, and other reasons, I was greatly pleased with my appointment. Henry Wilkinson was a true out-and-out Methodist, and as a minister a long way above mediocrity in spirituality, zeal, industry, moral courage and faithfulness to his charge, as well as in his preaching ability and usefulness. It was a great blessing to me to be associated so closely with him in circuit work, and to enjoy a most friendly and free correspondence with him through the years of his after life. After leaving Hamilton, London, Toronto and Yonge Street Circuit enjoyed his services, until, literally worn out with hard work and the bearing of heavy responsibilities, he rested from his labors in the little parsonage at Eglinton, and went away to be "forever with the Lord." His mortal remains, with those of his more recently sainted wife, rest where so many of those formerly associated with him in the ministry are resting, in the crowded Necropolis in Toronto.

From the obituary which appeared in the Minutes of Conference of 1863, I have gleaned the following facts: In 1862 he was appointed to the North Yonge Street Circuit, and entered upon his work with his usual earnestness and activity. But he unhappily overrated his physical ability, and was soon laid upon what proved to be the bed of death. The second Sabbath previous to his death he preached three times, renewed tickets in two classes and conducted a fellowship meeting, though unable all day to take any food.

The Rev. James Elliott says: "I saw him on the afternoon previous to his death. He remarked, 'I suppose it is all over with me now; but it is all right.' Being greatly exhausted, he said, 'Poor humanity!' And then, as if passing suddenly in thought from the present to the glorious future, he exclaimed, 'Glorious humanity!' He repeated with deep feeling the verse of the hymn ending with,

> "'When Jesus doth His blood apply,
> I glory in His sprinkled blood.'

He responded with great energy to my petitions in prayer, and rejoiced with joy unspeakable. On the following morning he finished his race in holy triumph and passed to his reward, in the fifty-eighth year of his age and thirty-first of his ministry." He rests from his labors, and his works do follow him. Would that we had a hundred such men on the walls of our Zion to-day.

On the 13th of July, 1848, my marriage with the wife of my youth, Miss Mary Alsy Holmes, daughter of the late Rev. Ninian Holmes, took place, the Rev. Samuel Fear officiating. Our first parsonage home was a small frame building just erected by the circuit on the plank road leading from Hamilton to Caledonia, and in the neighborhood of the Glanford Chapel. During our term on the Hamilton Circuit the field was divided, Hamilton City being set off as a city charge, while the country, with several appointments added, formed a circuit for two men. I was left in that charge, but, as it turned out, only for a few months, when the Conference authorities removed me to London to fill a vacancy occasioned by the appointment of the Rev. S. S. Nelles to the presidency of Victoria College, a position which he held for thirty-seven years, discharging its manifold and onerous duties most acceptably to the Church and efficiently in the estimation of all who were most deeply interested in the prosperity of the University.

At the time of his removal from London he was but in his third year of ministerial labor, and the twenty-seventh year of his age. The appointment to such a responsibility of one so youthful was altogether extraordinary, but neither the position of the College nor the man thus appointed was of the ordinary. I became acquainted with him in his early home at Mount Pleasant in 1844, while he was still a student in the University of Middleton, and enjoyed his friendship, and often his society, through the subsequent years of his ever-increasing popularity until he rested from his labors. The testimony borne by the Rev. Professor Reynar, in his beautiful and most appropriate memorial address at the funeral, contained these words, "He was a man of many books, like John Wesley; but he was at the same time like Wesley—a man of one Book." On his death bed he said to his wife, "I have studied much and read many books, but there is no book like *the Book*, and there is no name like Jesus." When he was near death he sent back a message to the students as they were about to assemble for College prayers: "Give the boys my love and thank them for having been so thoughtful and kind," and requested them also to sing in their worship the first five verses of Cowper's familiar hymn, "There is a fountain filled with blood." That dying request indicated the rock foundation on which his faith rested.

A few brief extracts from a letter from Principal Douglas, which was read at a memorial service held in Kingston, must bring to a close my remarks regarding this my beloved and now sainted brother. "As a preacher, Dr. Nelles was distinguished among his peers. His ministry was not remarkable for evangelistic fervor, but it was analytical, marked by the discussion of philosophical principles, full of scientific allusions, and occasionally graced by singular brilliance in illustrative power. It had special charm for the thoughtful and cultivated amongst his hearers. The Christian character of Dr. Nelles was the crowning secret of his power. The transparent rectitude, the unsullied purity, the single-mindedness of the man inspired confidence wherever he was known. His sudden departure came like a thunderclap out of a clear sky. The end was worthy of the man. Intellect, scholarship, and wide experience of life, all bowed in sweet resignation to the Will Divine, and with the restfulness of a little child he reclined on the bosom of Jesus and went to 'the rest that remaineth for the people of God.' Yet a little while and we too shall hope to join him in singing the new song through the glad forever. May this be our beatitude when 'life's fitful dream is o'er,' and we hear 'the bells of the Holy City and the chimes of eternal peace.'" And that "little while" thus referred to by Dr. Douglas in his eloquent testimony to the gifts and great worth of his friend, came in due course before seven full years had passed—Dr. Nelles having rested from his weariness on the 23rd of October, 1887, the anniversary of his birth sixty-four years before; while Dr. Douglas entered upon the everlasting rest of the saints for which he longed, on the 10th of February, 1894. Who can doubt that their re-union in "the Holy City" became a blessedly realized fact at that date? May it be ours, with all their loved ones, to meet them again, and where there shall be no darkness, no pain nor any such limitations to holy service, as they both endured in this life.

The death of my mother, who had suffered long from that weakening, wasting and most depressing disease, consumption, occurred during my second year in Brantford. From an extended obituary prepared by her minister, and which appeared in the *Christian Guardian* soon after her death, I will make a few such extracts as I may deem appropriate:

"Our departed sister was an Israelite indeed. Her conversion to God took place under the ministry of the Rev. Solomon Waldron. She was a woman of superior judgment, a constant and unfailing friend, a kind and affectionate mother, an obliging neighbor, and a liberal supporter of the cause of God; above all, she was a devoted and exemplary Christian. Her zeal, patience, resignation and enlightened piety rendered her a pattern worthy the imitation of all her surviving friends. On visiting her soon after my arrival on the circuit, I found her sinking rapidly, and speaking to her of her future prospects, she replied with emphasis, 'I am calmly trusting my all on Jesus. He is my sure foundation.' For several days before her death she was enabled to rejoice continually. Among her last triumphant utterances were these words, 'All is well! All is well!' and her message to her son, the Rev. George Young, then in Brantford, 'Tell him, should he not come till I am gone, that I have gone to rest.' And then at the last, calling her children together for her parting words, she exhorted them to 'meet her in heaven.' Thus in the full assurance of a blessed immortality she joyously received her dismissal out of this life and passed within the veil, on October 8th, 1860, in her fifty-seventh year."

> "O, may I triumph so
> When all my warfare's past,
> And dying, find my latest foe
> Under my feet at last."

And now I have to record a hitherto unanticipated change in my position and work in the Church of my early choice. It came about in this wise: The Rev. Geo. McDougall, recently from his mission-field in the Rocky Mountain regions, had, in the autumn of the preceding year, attended the meeting of the Missionary Board, held in the town of Whitby, and by his stirring representations of the great need of the heathen and others occupying those regions, so deeply impressed and enthused the members of the Board as to lead them to decide upon more vigorous

AN AUTOBIOGRAPHICAL SKETCH.

efforts to promote the evangelization of these benighted thousands. He also made a strong appeal for the establishment of a mission in the Red River Settlement, now a part of Manitoba, which he felt sure would ere long become the home of many of our Canadian Church members and adherents, and where there was already a population of ten or twelve thousand, including natives and foreigners, many of whom were insufficiently supplied with the ordinances of religion. The result of his earnest appeal was that the Board unanimously decided upon the opening of the mission as soon as a suitable selection could be made from among those who might volunteer for that work, and a committee consisting of Revs. Dr. Wood, Dr. Taylor and Geo. McDougall, and Mr. John Macdonald, was appointed to make the selection and report to the Board. As the weeks and months passed by I had many opportunities of conversing with Mr. McDougall in relation to the field and the work to be undertaken, and also of consulting with Dr. Wood, and was led, after gaining the consent of my wife, to volunteer to go forth as the Church's first missionary to the Red River country. My offer was immediatly accepted by the committee, and as soon as practicable the Conference Special Committee released me from my responsibility as Chairman of the Toronto District and superintendent of the circuit, and appointed me to the far-away settlement in question. Many of our friends in the various stations we had occupied—Toronto, Quebec, Kingston, and others—were much exercised in mind, in view of our withdrawal from the home field and appointment to regions so remote, and where they feared we should meet with privations and hardships such as we were scarcely equal to; still they refrained from opposing the appointment. The preparations requisite for our departure and journey involved much that was perplexing and wearisome. Horses and harness, and waggons and tents, and clothing suitable, and a small outfit for housekeeping, had to be purchased and put in shape for transportation, and many friends were to be seen and parted with.

At length the last Sabbath of my ministrations in the Richmond Street West Church, for no one knew how long, came, and I preached a valedictory sermon from Exodus, 33rd chapter and 15th verse, which was followed by a most solemn and a largely attended communion service in which several ministers participated, among whom was the Rev. Dr. Ormiston, of the Presbyterian Church. A very gracious influence attended throughout, which I regarded as indicative of the Divine approval of our undertaking. During the week, a memorable one to many of us, valedictory services of special interest were held. A further reference will be made in the chapter following.

CHAPTER II.

VALEDICTORY SERVICES.

THE farewell missionary gatherings took place on the 7th and 8th of May and were very largely attended. In making a record of these I cannot do better than to incorporate much of what was reported in the *Guardian* and *Globe* of those dates.

From the "Christian Guardian" of May 13th, 1868:

"On Thursday evening last a valedictory service of extraordinary interest was held in the Richmond Street Wesleyan Church, in connection with the departure of the Revs. G. Young, E. R. Young and P. Campbell, the missionary band appointed to labor in the great North-West. By seven o'clock, the hour appointed for commencing the service, the immense building was crowded to its utmost capacity, presenting a most magnificent spectacle. Not only was the Methodism of Toronto fully represented in the gathering, but from adjoining districts east and west large numbers came thronging in, affording good evidence that the flame of missionary zeal was still burning in the heart of Methodism as warmly as when Wesley went forth in the spirit of the well-known motto, 'The world is my parish.' There was also a good representation of sister denominations, affording pleasing evidence of kindly feeling, and of deep interest in the missionary work.

RICHMOND STREET CHURCH.

VALEDICTORY SERVICES. 31

"On the platform were seated the Rev. James Elliott, President of the Conference; Rev. W. Morley Punshon, M.A., Rev. Drs. Wood, Taylor, Green, Ryerson, Jeffers, Cocker and Jennings; the Revs. Geo. Young, Geo. McDougall, E. R. Young, and P. Campbell, the missionaries for the Red River and Saskatchewan Districts; Revs. Wm. Pollard, R. Jones, S. Rose, G. Cochran, R. Whiting, Wm. Young, J. G. Manly, F. H. Marling, E. H. Dewart, John Carroll, A. Sutherland, and John Macdonald, Esq., and A. W. Lauder, Esq., M.P.P.

"The President took the chair at seven o'clock, and opened the exercises by reading the 35th chapter of Isaiah. He then gave out the 446th hymn, after which the Rev. R. Jones led in prayer.

"The Chairman then called on the Rev. Dr. Wood, General Superintendent of Missions, to addresss the audience. The doctor said it was twenty-six years since James Evans went to the great North-West, and so faithfully did he labor that scarce any part of the vast territory could now be found where that devoted missionary had not preached the Gospel. Mr. Evans was well-known as the inventor of the 'syllabic characters,' into which the Word of God had since been translated, and which was much better adapted to the Indian tribes than the ordinary Roman characters. Through the labors of Mr. Evans, and others who had succeeded him, thousands in that far-off region had been brought to Christ. Evans and Rundle were the first missionary laborers in the Hudson Bay Territory. Rundle's health having failed, he was compelled to leave the work; but it should be recorded as a remarkable evidence of the power of Divine grace, that the Stoney Indians, among whom he (Mr. R.) had labored, retained their knowledge of Divine truth for seven years, during which time they were without a missionary. Last

November the Missionary Committee had resolved to send a missionary to Red River, and another to the Blackfeet Indians, the most warlike and savage tribe on the great plains, and one to Norway House, to supply the place of the Rev. C. Stringfellow, who returns to Canada. He would refer to but one point more. The authorities of the Church might have appointed any one of our six hundred ministers to this field, but they preferred to wait, and watch the leadings of Providence in the selection of men. Those upon whom the selection has fallen had the entire confidence of the Missionary Committee.

"The Rev. E. R. Young was then called upon. He said there were times when it was impossible to give utterance to all the feelings of the heart, and this was one of them. He felt this movement was of the Lord, and he hoped, by God's blessing, to do some good. He would urge upon all, 'pray for us.' It was hard to say good-bye, but he was sure God would more than make up what they might sacrifice for Him. He was sure of one thing,—those who had been appointed to this work would not talk annexation. He would again ask the prayers of God's people that they might be made a blessing.

"The Rev. P. Campbell was next introduced. It was thirteen years since he obtained salvation. It had been previously impressed upon his mind that if he obtained salvation he would have to preach the Gospel. He was not willing to do this; but the impression returned again and again that he could not obtain salvation until he was willing to go anywhere at God's command. When he yielded the point he found salvation. Eleven years ago he was called into the work of the ministry, and God had blessed him with some success. When he heard Brother McDougall's statements at Whitby last year, he felt his desire to engage in the missionary work revive, and he resolved, should the Church appoint him, he would go. He had no desire but to preach Christ. He expected difficulties, but he had counted the cost, and trusted in the promises. He felt it hard to bid good-bye to parents and friends, but he was cheered by the prospect of meeting them again in a brighter and happier world. He felt that God's presence would compensate for the breaking up of social ties. He prayed God for a prosperous journey, and that he might be a useful minister of Jesus.

"The Chairman gave out the hymn commencing, 'On all the earth thy Spirit shower,' which was sung.

"The Rev. George Young was then called upon, and was received with applause. He said it was with great difficulty he had brought himself to say even a few words. In 1840 he gave his heart to Christ, and had never regretted the step. Some years after he was led to give himself to the work of the ministry, and he had never regretted that step. A few weeks ago he yielded to the request of the Church to enter upon this missionary work, and since that decision he had not experienced one moment's regret. His future was in God's hands. He could not tell how long he might labor in the mission field; but he had consecrated himself to God, body and soul, and by God's grace he would keep the offering upon the altar. He expected the Divine presence all through their prospective journey. He had a request or two to make. They (the missionaries) wanted the prayers of their Christian friends. He hoped the Missionary Committee would not think them slow if they did not report progress every few weeks, nor extravagant if the figures looked somewhat formidable. He hoped by God's blessing to return in the course of years, and report in person what the Lord had done for them.

"Rev. G. McDougall was the next speaker. He did

not feel disposed to ask sympathy on account of privations in missionary work; he considered it the highest honor that could be conferred upon him. He could not help thinking of the altered circumstances of his brethren. In a few weeks Brother Young would be gathering sticks for his camp-fire; but then he would be in the apostolic succession. (Laughter and applause.) Brother E. R. Young and Brother Campbell would soon be setting their nets for fish at their missions, and they would therefore be in the apostolic succession too. (Laughter and cheers.) The last time he stood in this church, Dr. Stinson and James Spencer were present,—now they were both gone. They (the missionaries) had a long and dangerous journey before them, but God would take care of them. He hoped they would soon have to ask for more men for that field.

"John Macdonald, Esq., was then called upon, and warmly greeted. He said this was an evening never to be forgotten. If we enjoyed advantages not inferior to those enjoyed in any part of the world, was it too much to say we were indebted for them to those who in early years preached to us the Gospel of Christ? We could not confer a greater boon upon that interesting portion of our Dominion, the North-West, than by sending these men to lay the foundation of Christian institutions. Some might think we were adding to our financial burdens. He thought it would lessen them, for it would stir up the missionary spirit, and increase the liberality of our people. Mr. Macdonald here referred to several liberal offers which had already been made by friends in different parts of the country. He could not sit down without expressing the gratification he felt in meeting on the platform an honored minister of the parent body. (Applause.) We would go on in our great work trusting in the Lord,

VALEDICTORY SERVICES. 35

"A. W. Lauder, Esq., M.P.P., was then introduced, and received with cheers. He said he was proud to stand among so many honored men, and lift his voice on behalf of the noble brethren who were going out on this mission work. He spoke but the voice of the vast audience when he said that they parted with their pastor (Rev. G. Young) with exceeding regret. He was also proud to welcome among them, in the name of the laity of Toronto, the ablest advocate of missionary work in the world, the Rev. W. M. Punshon. (Applause.)

"The Rev. James Caughey was introduced, and received with repeated cheers. He felt as if he was standing in the sunshine of the congregation. He wished he had a text of some kind to hang a speech upon; but when he looked at the clock, he felt there was scarce time even for what some called 'a nice little speech.' The missionary cause was a good cause; but he did not say that a man should give all he had to it, nor even that he should give a tenth, but he would wish to take a man to the cross, bid him look upon the dying Son of God, and then say to him, 'How much owest thou unto thy Lord?' 'Pay that thou owest.' He would say to the missionaries that there were thousands in Canada who would sustain them by liberal contributions and by earnest prayer.

"The 700th hymn was then sung.

"The Chairman had been largely anticipated in the work he was to perform. The duty he felt to be a privilege, the duty of officially introducing the Rev. W. M. Punshon, M.A. The announcement was received with hearty applause.

"Rev. W. Morley Punshon was introduced in flattering terms by the Chairman, and received with applause. After a few words, expressive of his pleasure in meeting his audience, he compared his position to that of the Irishman who applied for a situation and was asked for his character. He replied that he left it at home, because he thought he would be better without it! He would very much rather have been allowed to make his own way than to have been introduced in such flattering terms by certain of the gentlemen who had preceded him. He had been thinking since entering the meeting of his early experience, his first venture to put his foot on a missionary platform. In the early part of his ministry he attended a meeting at which the speakers successively entertained their audience with a list of the talents with which they thought God had blessed them. They did so mainly as one of those convenient apologies that enable a man to glide easily into a speech. One said that God had not blessed him with a silvery tongue, but he had a talent for singing, and he had cultivated that. Another talent was instructing children in the Sunday School, and it was his special vocation to bring them when young to the fold of Jesus. Another, who happened to be an Irishman, said while his talent had not shown itself he thought that in the original distribution he could not have been left out, that there must surely have been a talent but it was difficult for him to find out what it was. He had, however, found out that his talent was to make apologies; and it so happened that the speaker had the last speech to make, and as all who preceded him had been talented brethren, and as one might as well be out of the world as out of the fashion, he found himself possessed of a talent to be happy at a missionary meeting, and rejoiced now that something of the old feeling came over him. At the ring of the true metal there was the same subtle electric sympathy in Canada as in England. Thinking of this and rejoicing in the catholic and kindly feelings evinced, his contemplations took a higher turn. But he felt somewhat diffident from the nature of the work he had to do. He could make a missionary speech, and even a valedictory address, but could not combine them. In the early days of missionary work there was the excitement of novelty, of opposition, of romance; but we must now try to get it on the broad foundation of Christian principle. There were peculiar difficulties in the way of missionary work. It was difficult to dislodge a previously conceived opinion; but our missionaries went not to war against wrong opinions, but against lusts and sins—not merely to subdue a man, a neighborhood, but a world. The separation of the world into different nations, governments and languages, interposed another difficulty. There were dangers also to be encountered. There was enmity in every human heart. There were also the divisions and heresies of the Church itself; and a spirit of indifference where there should be ardor. Looking at all these things, it was not easy to convert the world. Mr. Punshon then proceeded to speak of the principles on which the work must be based. Mean or selfish motives could not long sustain a man in this work—*principle* alone could do it. If there be nothing but imagination to sustain, the romance will soon be rubbed off. We must have faith, and then imagination will not lose its sense of duty. If those who go forth are sustained by love, then they will be successful indeed. He would remind those who were going forth that they must work in patient hope. We were an impatient people in reference to missionary success; but we must remember sowing and reaping were two different things. One might go forth only with the seed-basket; but a time was coming when both sower and reaper would rejoice together. The sower goes alone, and he needs to encourage himself with the word, 'be patient, therefore, brethren.' God works by means, and He won't do anything we can do. We can't raise Lazarus from the dead, but we can roll away the stone *before*, and unwind the grave-clothes *after* the resurrection. Every member of the Church had a part to do in this work, and he would conjure them by the constraining love of Christ to present their bodies a living sacrifice. We wanted all engaged in this work, the young with their sympathies, men in their prime with their energy, the aged with their wisdom—we want them all. Surely not one would refuse to make the consecration. Mr. Punshon resumed his seat amid loud applause.

"Dr. Taylor then called for the collection, and in his own inimitable way pressed the claims of the work,—humor, pathos, and earnest appeal following each other in rapid succession. The congregation cheerfully responded, sending up a collection of about $180.00. On one of the plates was a piece of paper, which, on being opened, was found to contain a twenty-dollar gold piece, and the following words: 'For the mission to the Blackfeet Indians, from a great debtor to grace. Alleluia!'

"The hymn beginning, 'Joined in one spirit to our Head,' was then sung, the Rev. S. Rose pronounced the benediction, and thus closed one of the most interesting meetings ever held in Toronto."

A FAREWELL BREAKFAST.

From the "Globe":

"This morning the missionaries to Red River and the Saskatchewan were entertained at a farewell breakfast in the basement of the Richmond Street Methodist Church. The attendance was very large, being nearly sufficient to fill the church comfortably. The breakfast was served in the basement and was an excellent repast considering the circumstances under which it was prepared. The six large tables running from one end of the room to the other were not sufficient to accommodate those present all at once, and they were therefore spread a second time. The room was slightly decorated for the occasion. Along the south end were the words "Missionaries to the Red River and Saskatchewan regions," while the north end was decorated with the British flag. The missionaries were seated at a cross table at the south end. After singing a hymn, grace was said, and the good things were then paid particular attention to.

"*The Missionaries.*

"The gentlemen in whose honor the breakfast was given, and who are about starting to the North-West to engage in the missionary enterprise, are four in number. The following are their names: The Rev. Geo. Young, Toronto; Rev. E. R. Young, Hamilton; Rev. Peter Campbell, Rockwood; Rev. George McDougall. The latter has for many years been engaged in Christianizing the savages of the North-West, and came down here recently for the purpose of procuring assistance. He has been successful in inducing those able ministers to return with him. The three gentlemen will take their wives with them. The Rev. George Young will officiate among the whites in the Red River Settlement, while the other three will be engaged among the savages farther west and north. They go by the American route, through the city of St. Paul, and start on Tuesday next. It will take them several weeks to reach their destination. Mr. McDougall and Mr. Campbell will go 1,000 miles beyond Red River, away to the Rocky Mountain region, and will still be in British territory. This shows what a vast territory we have away in the centre of the continent.

"Meeting in the Church.

"After breakfast had been attended to, the congregation assembled in the church, which they comfortably filled. On the platform we noticed the Revs. W. Morley Punshon, M.A., Dr. Wood, Dr. Ryerson, Dr. Jennings, Dr. Willis, Dr. Taylor, Bishop Richardson, Dr. Caldicott, Mr. Reid, F. H. Marling, Dr. Green, Mr. Manly, Mr. Rose, Mr. Wallace, Mr. Blackstock, Mr. Baker, Mr. McDougall, Mr. G. Young, Mr. E. R. Young, Mr. Gregg, Mr. Campbell, Mr. Topp, Mr. Byrne, John Young, John Macdonald, Esq., William Gibbs, Esq., Rev. Wm. Stephenson, Mr. Beatty, M.P., and Revs. Mr. McClure, Dr. Cochran, James Elliott, and others.

"The chair was occupied by Mr. John Macdonald, Treasurer of the Missionary Society. The proceedings were commenced with singing and prayer.

"Rev. Mr. Elliott said that it afforded him much pleasure to introduce Mr. John Macdonald, the Treasurer of the Society, who would now take the chair.

"Mr. Macdonald, on taking the chair, said that on many occasions it had been his privilege to be present at meetings in this church, but he had never more pleasure than on the present occasion. Last night they had met to bid farewell and say 'good-bye' to those who were going to a far distant land. These missionaries were going to Red River, to Norway House, to Woodville, to the wild, warlike and untamable Blackfeet, and in their mission to that country they would complete the chain of missionary enterprise extending from continent to continent, and when the men have gone friends will remember that our missionaries have their Bibles in their hands to preach the Gospel of Christ—to extend the field of missionary enterprise from the Atlantic to the Pacific Ocean. It might be asked, Why do we send them to the Red River, where there were already those missionaries of the Presbyterian and Episcopal churches? Our friends, however, go with a catholic spirit to work and heartily co-operate with their fellow-laborers in the west. The brethren know well from their knowledge of Brother Young that what he is to do he will do well. Then Brother McDougall was at any rate more than half an Indian and was never so happy as when he was among the savage tribes, and stood beside the bedside of the Crees or Ojibeways when he has seen them pass from beds of sickness to beds of eternal glory. As for Brother Campbell, of Rama, he goes warm-hearted to the work. Brother Young has been of much use in Hamilton, which proves a sure guarantee that he will do his work well. Brother McDougall's son, who goes to the Blackfeet, is more than all the others with his life in his hand—that tribe being one of the most savage. The speaker would not detain the meeting, but beg to introduce Rev. Egerton Ryerson.

"Dr. Ryerson, being called on, said that the present opportunity took his thoughts back to the time when forty-two years ago he received orders to go out to the Indians. It was the brightest year of his labor in a comparatively chequered life when he slept in the Indian tents, with only a mat and a blanket between himself and the ground; when in the early morn he took the Indians out four by four and taught them how to plough, or to build fences, prepare their gardens or repair their implements, or when he had to go from house to house teaching the women how to wash their clothes—(laughter)—and sweep their houses, telling that the one who did it best was the one with whom he would dine that day. The speaker was one who had drawn up the first report of the Canadian Missionary Society, and he could assure the audience that it took just as much trouble and labor to raise $500 then as it does to raise $62,000 now. He wished the missionaries God speed, health and strength, and although they might not be with them at the sowing, still they hoped to be with them at the reaping."

Appropriate addresses were also given by the following ministers and laymen: Rev. Drs. Willis, Jennings, Caldicott and Cocker, Rev. Messrs. Manly and Stephenson, and Messrs. Gibbs and Beatty.

"The Rev. W. Morley Punshon was then called on, and stated that he was not accustomed to speak under such difficulties as then surrounded him. To be the centre of a battery of eyes on either side of the platform, and in front of the platform, was a Canadian novelty which he never had the opportunity of becoming acquainted with, and which needed a good deal of nerve to overcome. On this occasion he felt disposed not to speak, but to talk, and those of the audience who knew the force of the synonym would see that there is a difference in what appeared at first sight to be the same. This he apprehended was a social meeting, and one in which they could say anything that suggested itself, and one in which it was not necessary or even preferable to put in the newspapers. Expressing his pleasure at the unanimity displayed in the presence on the platform of ministers of different denominations, he also rejoiced in the familiar character of the meeting. They had, he continued, representatives from he did not know how many denominations, all animated by one spirit and expressing the same hearty good wishes for the success of the cause, and blessings on the men who are to carry the Gospel to the far west. Indeed it was a very encouraging indication of the spirit of Christian principle, and the working of the leaven that marks the increasing efforts for Christian union, and he did not know why it should be otherwise. The Bible enjoins that we are to endeavor to intensely labor to keep the unity of the spirit in the bond of peace. Constituted as human society was, to expect a union of all would be visionary, and with deference to those who were of greater age than himself, he would say it was undesirable. Comparison with others has. sometimes been productive of important results, and the Church that may be leaning back listlessly and lazily will rise from its lethargy when stimulated by more active Christian effort. To illustrate this, he proceeded to define the term 'beauty,' which was an harmonious combination of varieties. There was no beauty in the simple element. The prismatic varieties fascinate and charm. One banner in an army would create but little attention; it·is the host of streamers. Now the Church should be the army of banners—should be the iris illuminating the globe with its beauty. The light should stream from her windows, scattered as the rays, yet one as the sun. The tide of our benevolence should flow onward, distinct as billows yet one as the sea. He was glad, moreover, that this greater unity was brought about by greater effort. There was nothing better calculated to bring Christians together, and it is a well understood axiom that when men are engaged in a great work they have no time for quarreling. Those who are engaged in spreading the work of the Lord have a breadth of ideas which tramples on the more insignificant feelings which are the engendering of strifes among men. At the same time, while he was a believer in the most extensive catholic unity, he liked his own fireside best. He is a churl who cannot warm himself at any other hearthstone but his own, but he is only half a man who does not love his own fireside best. (Cheers.)

The man who is a general lover, without any one particular object, is one that should not be trusted—except Dr. Taylor. (Laughter.) But after all who were they that supported the great charities? Not the men who have no homes, not the loungers at the cafe or club, but the men who have learned from the preciousness of their own family retreats the worth of such blessings, so wherever he saw a man without a spiritual home he thought of him as a spiritual Ishmaelite, his hand against every man and every man's hand against him. He did not think there was anything wrong in denominationalism as long as there was Christian charity at the root. He believed he could work best with the organization that reflected his own spiritual sympathies, and while thinking so he could shake the brethren of other Churches by the hand and bid them God-speed in the great work.

"We can appeciate the excellences of the great Republic, but sing with patriotic ardor 'God save the Queen' notwithstanding. The speaker then proceeded to discuss their missionary work, remarking: Then as to this Methodist Missionary Society, Dr. Newton used to tell that on one occasion a gentleman met him and said he believed he was going to have a great missionary 'do' at his church to-night. He said we have all along had a great missionary 'do,' and while discoursing as he had, the practical should not be forgotten. His figures were not all figures of speech. He was told there was a vast amount of debt on this missionary organization and that there were some awful things in the shape of bank discounts and advances by the Treasurer, so that if they really meant to prosecute this work, something special must be done. There must be a missionary 'do' as well as a missionary 'say.' He would, however, leave this with them while he reminded them of what duty brought them together. Their friend Mr. McDougall did not need much of their sympathies, because he was going home. But they were sending out six missionaries. The speaker, hesitating, said—Yes, six; their wives go with them. If they were Moravian, they would count two; but with us the honored wives claimed the sympathy of all, as well as their husbands. They were really sending out six missionaries, and these had to be maintained. These are women who hazard their lives as well as the men—women who make our manhood cheap, because they are privileged to go forth without a murmur to the sustentation of those whose name they bear; and let us, he said, not forget to pray for the wives, as well as the men, that they, with frailer organizations, though perhaps a well-knit network of nerves—for there is not so much of the robust muscular strength—may be preserved for the trial. They are as brave, as well as firm and fervent, and trust in Christ, and are entirely devoted to the Great Master and His work. Do not, he continued, forget them in your prayers and their wants in connection with the refinements of life. The cheese-paring economy that would abridge one cent of the efforts of the missionary, is a dishonor to the Gospel of Christ. They go out with their lives in their hands and offer up their ease, social status, and all the other comforts of the well-regulated Christian city home; they go out as the heralds. See to it, he added, that their families have power to surround themselves with the things that will give them a memory of your interest in them.

"Their friends, the missionaries, had had condolence and congratulation. They needed both. It struck him that if any of them should feel any misgivings as to their safety, they might, perhaps, get a crumb of comfort from an interpretation of Scripture to which their attention had not before been directed. They remembered that the disciples were in two storms in the Lake of Gennesaret. They were in two storms, the last greater than the first. The first was in the day time, the second in the deep, dark, inhospitable night. In the first, the wind was in their favor and they were near where they wanted to be. In the first storm, above all, Jesus was in the ship. But in the last Jesus was not there. The storm was contrary and driving them on the rocks; but they did not know that He was praying for them on the shore all the while. He saw them toiling against the wind, He came to them, and that angry sea as soon as it felt His footstep subsided like a slumbering child. He got into the ship and took the source of their terror away before He rebuked them, and then said, 'Why do ye fear, O ye of little faith?' Why did He say that? Because they were not entirely alone in the storm. You will see, Mr. Punshon said, that before they got into the boat Jesus said, 'Let us go over to the other side.' And depend upon it, if God says to anybody 'Go over to the other side,' He never lets them sink in the middle. That thought had comforted him very much, and he would like it to comfort them. By His grace keeping them they will more than conquer. Sometimes, he added, they were paid to go over. They remembered the young man who was privileged to wait on the prophet. He said, 'Alas, Master, what shall we do?' The answer was, 'Lord, open his eyes'; and the moment they were opened he saw that round about him were chariots of fire. Some one had remarked the great difference between contributions now and when they first began, and in taking up this point the speaker referred to the death of Mr. Evans, and his meeting with Mr. Rundle, another missionary. He also knew Bishop Anderson, of Rupert's Land, who now occupied a living adjoining the speaker's own charge. He was not so communicative as when in the North-West.

Snake-fences of this country, he said, were somewhat easier to be got over than the briar fence at home, and interchange of courtesies were not now so common. Returning to the missionary operations of the Church, he noticed that the first contribution to the support of a missionary of the body was made in the British Methodist Conference. They taxed themselves, and the collection was £52. Two ministers were despatched to a field of labor by this assistance, but when the Conference sent them away they thought they were altogether done with them. They afterwards went to visit their lay friends in what is now one of the best fields for missionary contributions. After the meeting, the laymen's contribution was ten shillings. Times, he added, had changed. Do not let us, he said in conclusion, be the poor pensioners on the memory of the past—the spendthrifts of the bounty of the present. Labor, and pray, and give—this is the trinity of man's duty—so that this great work may be carried on even to the uttermost parts of the earth.

"The Rev. Dr. Taylor intimated that the collection of last evening amounted to $168.33. Further collections to the amount of $18.00 were made, and the assembly dispersed after singing the doxology."

An interesting item—to me at least—not referred to in these reports, was the presentation to myself and family of a purse well filled with gold, and also two beautiful testimonial addresses, one from the officiary of the church and the other from the young men. As I feel sure that my readers will be much interested in these addresses, I will incorporate them along with the reports already given of the valedictory addresses,

FROM THE QUARTERLY OFFICIAL BOARD.

"*To the Reverend George Young, Wesleyan Methodist Minister, Superintendent of the Toronto City West Circuit:*

"REVEREND AND DEAR SIR,—Prompted by the warm friendship which we entertain for you, we embrace the occasion of your departure from amongst us as a missionary to the North-West as a fitting time to address you in this formal manner, and to give a permanent and tangible expression to feelings prompted by the very high place which you have in our affections as a Christian minister.

"We are not unmindful that your removal to a new field of labor will eventually be looked upon as marking a distinct era in the history of Methodism in British North America; and while we are willing to cheerfully submit to the authorities of the Church, and to recognize the guiding hand of a wise Providence in this missionary movement, we very much regret your departure from the circuit, and we shall cherish with more than ordinary care the remembrance of your kind, zealous and faithful labors.

"You have labored amongst us affectionately and faithfully in the cause of your heavenly Master. We rejoice to know that many have been greatly blessed and built up in the service of God through the instrumentality of your instructions and kind admonitions.

"Many of us, as parents and as the friends of the rising generation, have to thank you most heartily for the affectionate and painstaking manner in which you have labored to bring the young men of our congregations under the blessed influence of the Gospel and the practical relationships of a religious life. The work of God in all its departments has been much benefited by your labor and untiring oversight since your appointment to the position you have held amongst us during the last two years.

"Many Christian friends throughout the length and breadth of the Dominion will join heartily with us in wishing you great happiness and in praying that the great Head of the Church may grant you every needful blessing in the discharge of the onerous duties which must necessarily devolve upon you in the 'Far West.'

"The noble work of preaching the Gospel to the inhabitants of those almost inaccessible and far-off regions, and the organization and perfecting of a more permanent system of missionary operations in the North-West, has been given to you. We shall rejoice at your success, and no doubt many of us will hereafter read with deeper interest the missionary intelligence from Red River and Saskatchewan, seeing that one who was loved as a pastor and esteemed as an affectionate friend, labors and toils there—far away from many of the valued refinements and endearments of Christian society.

"Be assured that you have to accompany you to Red River our warmest friendship, and you shall have our most earnest prayers—supplemented, no doubt, by those of hundreds of as equally sincere friends in other places—that God in His great mercy and goodness would bless abundantly to yourself and family this remarkable period in your personal history.

"We desire, dear sir, through the medium of this address, to communicate to your kind and faithful partner in life our earnest and warmest greetings, and we would especially desire to speak cheering words to her, knowing the self-denial to be exercised on her part, and feeling as we do the certainty that she will have to undergo trials and privations of a kind to which she has hitherto been unaccustomed.

"We hope that you will accept these tokens of our affection and esteem which accompany this address as an indication of the acceptability of your labors in God's cause amongst us, and we trust they may serve to remind you of your Methodist friends in Toronto, when separated from them by hundreds of miles of broad lake and expanding prairie.

"On behalf of the hundreds of friends you leave behind you, we wish you God-speed and pray that your steps may be ever under the direction and guidance of our Omniscient and Infinite Father.

"We remain, honored and dear sir,

"Yours most truly,

"C. A. DREDGE,
HENRY GRAHAM,
JAMES ROONEY,
ADAM MILLER,
A. W. LAUDER,
JAMES B. MARSHALL,
JOSEPH HOWSON, M.D.,
C. S. HAYMAN,
E. S. BARRICK,
D. THURSTON (U. S. Consul),
Members of Committee.

"JNO. C. CHARLESWORTH,
Chairman of Committee.

"HENRY E. CLARK,
Secretary and Treasurer.

"GEORGE COCHRAN,
Associate Minister.

"Toronto, May 8th, 1868."

I cannot repress a feeling of sadness as, in reading over the names attached to the foregoing address, I reflect that only four of these kind friends are now living.

FROM THE YOUNG MEN.

"*To the Rev. George Young:*

"REVEREND AND DEAR SIR,—On behalf of the YOUNG MEN in connection with the congregation of the RICHMOND STREET WESLEYAN CHURCH,

"We take the present as a fitting opportunity of conveying to you an expression of the high appreciation in which we, in common with the rest of the attendants upon your ministry, have held your faithful services as a preacher of the Gospel, and as one who, with untiring zeal and fidelity, and uniform Christian kindness, has exercised the pastoral care pertaining to your office.

"Upon this the occasion of your removal from our midst to another and distant field of labor, we would fail in justice to our own feelings did we not give you an earnest assurance of the heartfelt and sincere regret with which we contemplate your departure. At the same time, permit us to say that we fully appreciate the truly missionary spirit actuating you in the readiness with which you have yielded to the call of duty, and the intimations of Divine Providence in accepting a position with which many of the trials and hardships peculiar to a new country must necessarily be connected.

"In this honorable resolve, involving self-denial of no ordinary character, we are persuaded you will be fully sustained, that the promise, 'Lo, I am with you alway, even unto the end of the world,' yea, and to the ends of the earth, will on your behalf as on that of every true minister of Christ, be fully realized.

"In your capacity as a teacher of the truth we take pleasure in bearing testimony to your zeal and faithfulness. In dividing the Word of Life you have not failed to declare the whole counsel of God. As a man and a Christian you have gained the highest respect of all classes. And as a pastor you have endeared yourself to the hearts of many, through your faithful visitations, and the marked and unvarying kindness that has ever characterized your performance of this important part of the Christian minister's work.

"Although at times you may have gone to the discharge of your duties in such weakness of body and depression of mind and in doubt as to whether or not you were materially contributing to the building up of Christ's cause on the earth, yet we are pleased to know, and to you it may justly be matter of rejoicing, that 'your labor has not been in vain in the Lord'; for from this and many other congregations throughout the length and breadth of this land there will arise souls who, redeemed through your instrumentality from the bondage of sin and death, will in the day of righteous recompense be publicly given to you as the attesting seals to your ministry, and the full and satisfying reward of your zealous efforts in the work of soul-saving. The consideration will prove powerful to your support and comfort—that for the toilers in God's vineyard, for the watchers on the walls of Zion, and for those who have mingled in the vale of strife in closest conflict with the alien forces of evil—for all such there cometh a time of rest and with it the hour of reward.

"We request your acceptance of this testimonial as in some slight degree tangible evidence of the esteem and affection we individually and unitedly entertain for you; and with it the prayer that you may be abundantly successful in your mission work, and that a happy and prosperous future may be granted unto you and to your esteemed family.

> " ROBERT MACDONALD, *Chairman*,
> RICHARD JONES TACKABERRY,
> GEORGE WRIGHT, A.M., M.B.,
> HENRY J. KEIGHLY,
> WM. R. HAMILTON,
> FRED. R. STEWART,
> ROBERT THOMPSON,
> M. L. HUTCHINS,
> *Committee.*

" Toronto, May 8th, 1868."

CHAPTER III.

THE FORTHGOING OF THE MISSIONARY PARTY.

THIS took place on Saturday the 9th of May, when we left Toronto for Hamilton, where we were to spend the Sabbath and attend the opening services of the new Centenary Church, there to enjoy the much-desired privilege of hearing Dr. Punshon's dedicatory sermon, which, I need not say, was a magnificent discourse. On Monday we were all exceedingly busy in completing the preparations for our forward movement. Horses, harness, waggons and some luggage, as well as the entire party, except Mrs. Young and myself, going *via* the Welland Canal and Lake Erie, left for St. Catharines, where they took the steamer for Milwaukee.

As I was charged with the responsibility of bearing, guarding and distributing the funds furnished by the General Treasurer of the Missionary Society to meet the expenses of the journey, and in part as appropriations made as salaries, I remained a day longer with Dr. Taylor and Mr. Sanford to perfect arrangements for the exchange of our Canadian money into United States currency, as "greenbacks" were then considerably below par.

THE FORTHGOING OF THE MISSIONARIES. 55

On the 14th of May we rushed on to Detroit, where we took the steamer at midnight according to appointment. On landing at Milwaukee, we were, as a matter of course, visited by the Customs officials, who, despite the letters and assurances of the United States Consul in Toronto, on which we fully relied as an all-sufficient passport through their country for ourselves and belongings, demanded duty on the entire outfit ere we could be allowed to proceed. This demand occasioned us some perplexity and a full day's delay, with hotel expenses. Assisted by a good friend whom I had known years ago in Belleville, we communicated by telegraph with the authorities in Washington, giving the facts, whereupon the message came forthwith to these officious officials—" Allow the mission party to proceed." We proceeded. I have not troubled the Milwaukeeans since. Thence we travelled by rail to the Mississippi River and thence by steamer to St. Paul, where upon our landing a general reconstruction took place, and waggons and horses and all our effects put in shape in a hurry for another onward movement. The freight and the luggage were sent on by rail to St. Cloud, while we "hitched up" and drove some eighty miles to Clearwater, a small village pleasantly situated in a fine country.

I will now avail myself of a letter written by me at Fort Garry, July 20th, 1868, which will suffice as a description of the tedious journey before us:

"At Clearwater we pitched our tents in the midst of good pasturage for our horses, and where our Canadian animals received their first lessons in 'hobbling,' to their great discomfort and annoyance.

"This hobbling process, which consists in tieing the forelegs of the horse together, or within a few inches of each other—ordinarily by a strap, with us by a piece of cotton, one and a-half yards long and eight inches wide—seems a barbarous practice, and yet a necessary evil on the plains. How else could we keep them from 'stampeding' when assailed by mosquitoes? When thus tied the poor creature can neither run, trot, nor walk,—but barely 'hobble.' For some time they fret considerably; but they become reconciled, and then get up and down and roll over quite readily. Here several of our party went into tent life; others found comfortable board, at reasonable rates, at the Temperance House,—while Brother McDougall and myself, Mrs. Young and Miss McDougall received a hearty welcome to the home of one of the most generous men with whom it has been my privilege to meet—a Mr. Stevens, formerly of Stanstead, Canada. This large-hearted man and his equally kind lady entertained us in the kindest manner during our stay, and gave nearly all their time to the furtherance of our objects. We feel under very high obligations to Mr. and Mrs. Stevens, and pray that they may receive their reward both in this world and in that which is to come. Here the strange appearance of Mr. McDougall's Red River carts amused us all not a little. Since that we have seen so much of them that all power to amuse has been forever lost. A very peculiar kind of thing is the Red River cart. A pair of very large awkward-looking wheels, attached to a frame that serves for shafts, and also as box, and all without iron. The raw hide of a buffalo or ox supplies the lack of iron, both on the wheel and axle. But little grease is ordinarily used on them, and as a consequence they make music not exactly like an organ, and when one hundred of them make up a train they can be heard, as they come groaning and screeching along, for a long distance. Mr. McDougall had a number of these beauties at Clearwater to be repaired and got ready for our journey—and we all required time to buy our provisions, waggon covers, and other comforts and necessaries 'too numerous to mention,' and to get our goods ready for transportation to Fort Garry, and thus we were detained for several days between Clearwater and St. Cloud. Leaving St. Cloud, we left all railroading and telegraphing behind us for a time. How strange it seems that I cannot now travel by steam and communicate by lightning, nor even ride in a stage coach; these things are not here as yet. And then, instead of two or three mails a day, and daily papers from many points, here we get a weekly mail and a weekly paper. From this point, too, we strike out upon our long prairie drive of six hundred miles to Fort Garry—and well-nigh sixteen hundred to Edmonton House for Brothers Campbell and McDougall.

"All along our road to Sauk Centre, seventy miles from St. Cloud, we found settlements where we bought milk, or eggs, or bread, paying quite enough always for the article. The railroad now reaching to St. Cloud will next year, it is hoped, reach Sauk Centre, and so the glory will depart from the former and go westward with 'the star of empire,' even to the latter. Alexandria is a small village to which we were conducted by a most wretched road through eight miles of woods. Leaving it we forded a river with some trouble, and soon found ourselves beyond the settlements—few houses being seen between Alexandria and Fort Abercrombie. And Abercrombie itself, though marked on the map, is vastly more in the imagination of the student of the map than it is a reality before the eye of the traveller. A few log-houses and long stables, and one miserable store with prices high enough to frighten one, and a sort of wooden structure called a 'fort'; these make up the celebrated, and to us long-looked for, Fort Abercrombie. Here we fell in with, and well-nigh *into*, 'Whiskey Creek'—it is not whiskey, though else I fear many would emigrate thither and form a settlement. We found it a miserable mire-hole and unbridged, and so we had to set to work on a fearfully hot day to fill it up with oak bushes and brush, and then dash our tired horses across the abominable place and up a steep bank, as best we could.

"'Honor to whom honor is due,' therefore I wish here to acknowledge our great indebtedness to the experience, energy, courage and presence of mind of our good Brother McDougall. Of course he was commander-in-chief all through, but in these troublesome and dangerous places we all looked to him for guidance and help, and did not look in vain. We certainly did plunge into some of the deepest slough holes, where bottom seemed afar off, and climb up some of the steepest and most slippery banks, and run across some of the most rickety bridges, and rock and roll along over or into some of the worst ruts I have ever seen. These things considered, in connection with the cruelty and neglect of some of these teamsters, it is no marvel that the bones of so many faithful horses and oxen are left annually along this road to whiten on the plains.

"Through mercy our animals got through safely, and, with one or two exceptions, not much poorer than when we left St. Cloud.

"The mosquitoes were not so bad as last year, yet bad enough, certainly. Nor are these prairie mosquitoes dwarfs by any means. A wit once said, 'Many of them would weigh a pound'; I suppose you know how that held good. Our horses were tormented occasionally by a large fly—called 'bulldogs' out here. They are larger than our Canada ox fly, and most cruel in their bite. In fact the 'mosquito,' 'buffalo-gnat,' and 'bull-dog' seemed to have prairie appetites, and every traveller across these plains knows what that means. The fact is, everything here is on a large scale—here is pasturage for a continent, a vast meadow of God's own planting that almost resembles the ocean for extent.

"How appropriate that the appetites of all living things, travellers, mosquitoes, horses and oxen, should correspond! Through the greater part of the road settlers are not to be found. We travelled a week across this 'living green' of high prairie grass and low bushes without passing a human habitation. At

other points we saw them ten and fifteen miles apart
—but little opportunity for tale-bearing in such
cases.

No doubt thousands of families long ere this would
have settled along this line of road and occupied
these fertile and beautiful plains but for the great
Sioux massacre which took place a few years ago.
We felt sad in gazing upon the ruins of many a house
where happy families once lived, whose blood was
shed by these cruel savages. The present scattered
population still have a dread of them, and asked us at
different places, 'Are you not afeard of the Injuns?'
Well, I am happy to say, we were kept from any
fear on that point and did not meet, so far as I know,
a single Sioux Indian. A large number passed close
by one day, and had we been an hour earlier we
should have met; but we did not, nor did we desire
the interview. They are great thieves, and might
have coveted some of our horses. Glad I was that
temptation was not put in their way by us. They
hate the 'Yankees,' as they call the new settlers and
soldiers, and intend to scalp all they can; and there
is no lack of hatred on the other side toward these
'red devils,' as they call them. Up at 'Devil's
Lake'—what a name!—to which we saw many
waggon loads of provisions going for the soldiers
working at the fort, they have recommenced their
cruelties, and several have been scalped. Of course
this must come to an end; the barbarian must succumb before the onward march of civilization. O
that he might be Christianized and saved! But there

are many among these frontier men with whom extermination is the one idea. They have little faith in our efforts to evangelize, and would send the soldier, and repeating rifle, and revolver, instead of the minister, and the Bible, and the school.

"Georgetown is the name of a little village consisting of a store and a few houses, and about half-way to Fort Garry from St. Cloud. Here we ferried the Red River. In high water the steamer comes up from Fort Garry to this place, and with a little expense and with a smaller boat it might go up nearly all the season. When we passed she was going up to Frog Point, about thirty miles, I believe, below Georgetown. The sight of a steamer amid the solitude of these uninhabited plains produced quite a sensation in our camp; and in a neighboring camp of Canadians, who were from near Goderich, a greater excitement was caused, for five or six fine horses broke away and stampeded ten or twelve miles ere they were caught. Pembina is another small place marked on the map, and whose name is often on the tongue of the traveller out here. It is the extreme north-western boundary of Uncle Sam's extensive farm. Of course there is a Customs house and post-office here. A large business is done in the former, and to the latter the United States postage stamp will bring a letter from any part of the States, or one Canadian ten-cent stamp from Canada, but the postage hence to Red River Settlement is one penny sterling on every letter and paper. This can't be prepaid, as the postal arrangements are peculiar. Friends sending papers or letters can put on the proper stamps for Canada and the States, and send on, and we'll do the rest. Just across the lines here the Hudson Bay Company have a comfortable and safe-looking fort. But, perhaps, like some other places out here, ' 'tis distance lends enchantment to the view.'

"After crossing into our good and beloved Victoria's dominions, our party joined heartily in singing the national anthem, after which our loyal brother, E. R. Young, hoisted the Union Jack, a beautiful flag with which he was presented in Canada. This little manifestation of loyalty had a twofold effect. It indicated to the settlers our nationality and home feeling, and then it either frightened or vexed a pair of United States horses connected with our train to that degree that they forthwith ran away. The skedaddlers' were soon overhauled, and with the good old flag leading us we pursued the even tenor of our way.

"Leaving Pembina, nothing special occurred until we arrived within four miles of Fort Garry. On that day we fully expected to see the fort, and pushing on, were not a little disappointed, and perhaps annoyed, that a miserable piece of a road, in a neglected and miry condition, kept us back, and as night was upon us we were compelled to camp within four miles of the fort amid swarms of mosquitoes, and in a place that seemed very uninviting. In this there was a special Providence. About two o'clock the next morning, amid much lightning and thunder, a fearful storm of rain and wind, a sweeping tornado, came suddenly upon us. It was indescribably terrific—a real prairie storm, such as the 'oldest inhabitant' does not remember to have experienced before. Two tents were borne down by the first rush, and their occupants left without shelter under the pelting storm. Our tent was in danger of being run down by our waggon and buggy, which were driven by the wind right against it; but the Lord kept us in safety, and when the storm had raged out its hour we were all thankful to find but little harm done. And now mark the Providence. Had we reached the settlement and tented in the open prairie where the storm was more severe, our waggons and tents must have been destroyed. Near the fort one cart was blown right across the river and many were broken, several houses were demolished, and a new Episcopal church was levelled to the ground and a man killed.

"We felt that the hand of God was upon us for good, and that it became us to bless His holy name for His continued care. On the day following, we crossed the Assiniboine by a ferry, looked into Fort Garry and Winnipeg, and then passed on to an encampment on the prairie six miles out, where the horses could rest and graze during the Sabbath. Thus have we been brought to our destination after a month's journeying from St. Cloud to Fort Garry."

But what a sorry scene was presented by that long-thought-of town of Winnipeg on the day we entered it! What a mass of soft, black, slippery and sticky Red River mud was everywhere spread out before us! Streets with neither sidewalks nor crossings, with now and again a good sized pit of mire for the traveller to avoid or flounder through as best he could; a few small stores with poor goods and high prices; one little tavern where "Dutch George" was "monarch of all his survey"; a few passable dwellings with no "rooms to let," nor space for boarders; neither church nor school in sight or in prospect; population about one hundred instead of one thousand as we expected—such was Winnipeg on July 4th, 1868.

How unlike that fine city at this date, with a population of thirty-five or forty thousand, and its magnificent churches and colleges, fine public schools, Parliament buildings, Court House, City Hall, stores, residences, railroad stations, factories, street railway, parks, hotels and bridges. "The former things have passed away."

"Distance lends enchantment to the view," and so it was that Fort Garry and its environs fell short of our expectations, and enchantment gave place to a feeling of disappointment, with a strong tendency to discouragement. Moreover, a locust plague was on all the land, and fields and whole farms, where growing or ripening grain should have appeared, were swept clean by these detestable devourers, so that great scarcity, and even suffering from want in the near future, seemed inevitable; flour even then was selling for from twenty-five to thirty shillings sterling per hundred pounds, and oats for horse feed two dollars a bushel, with the prospect of advance. The buffalo hunters were despairing of success.

WINNIPEG IN 1863.

After a brief rest in our encampment on the prairies, during which our finances were adjusted and a statement of all expenses up to date prepared for the "Mission Rooms" in Toronto, our party, which had grouped together from Hamilton as a unit, separated and became three parties. Rev. E. R. Young and wife, taking passage in the little Hudson Bay trading and freighting boat, worked by oars or sails, as most convenient, proceeded down the Red River to its entrance into Lake Winnipeg, and thence up that lake to Norway House, a distance of about three hundred miles, to their future field of toil; Revs. George McDougall and daughter, Peter Campbell, Mrs. Campbell and two daughters, and Bro. Snyder, wended their toilsome way to their more distant missions in the great Saskatchewan country, to be reached only by a tiresome journey of about one thousand miles; while the missionary for the "Red River Settlement," wife and son, remained in Winnipeg to "set up our banners" as best they could in the little muddy embryo city and surrounding regions.

CHAPTER IV.

PERPLEXITIES AND ENCOURAGEMENTS INTERBLENDING.

Having parted thus with our fellow missionaries, our first effort was to secure a house to rent as a parsonage, and failing in this, as well as in our efforts to secure a boarding-house, we began to fear lest we should be compelled to "tent out" for a still longer period. This was decidedly perplexing. Just then, however, a kind-hearted couple invited us for a short time to occupy a room in their rented home, into which, with our tent furniture, we gladly moved. There we remained for the next three months, and there, on his invitation, I opened my commission on the following Sabbath by preaching my first sermon in the Red River Settlement, my text being, "I have a message from God unto thee."

The work of

FOUNDATION LAYING,

to which I at once addressed myself, and which thenceforth occupied my thoughts very fully, was entered upon in the different localities which seemed to promise best as centres of missionary operations; a work in which my immediate successors, and in fact all our pioneering brethren who have toiled in these vast prairie regions since that period, have been engaged—ever and everywhere finding it, as I did, a toilsome, tedious, expensive and undemonstrative, as well as an indispensable, work. This early "breaking ground" involved the surmounting of many difficulties, a few of which only shall be indicated just now.

In October, 1868, I closed a letter to the *Christian Guardian* with these words : " Mercies abound, and so do difficulties. Methodism was never yet established in an important field like this without earnest and persevering effort. The devil and bat-like bigots have always opposed its introduction, but as the sun shines in spite of all the owls and bats in creation, so 'Christianity in earnest' will advance if God give His blessing."

Again in December, 1868, I wrote Dr. Wood thus: " I am not a prophet, but I will predict for this mission, whose foundations I am now trying to lay, a glorious future." Whether in that I was really " foretelling," or only " forthtelling," I must leave to some of the highest of the " higher critics " to decide. What has transpired since then within the bounds of the old Red River Mission seems a glorious carrying up of a grand superstructure on the foundations then being laid; and the numerous self-supporting charges, the fine and costly churches and parsonages which have been built, the large congregations and Sabbath-schools which have been gathered, and the converted and influential membership which has been enrolled—and last, but not least, our college work, now being so successfully prosecuted, with prospects so encouraging—all seem to show that I was not prophesying falsely, even though not a professed prophet.

My first sixty-mile trip through the settlements along the Assiniboine River—my son accompanying me—resulted in the securing of permission, from several kindly-disposed strangers, to hold service and preach in their homes to any whom I might persuade to come and worship with us and hear the Word. The journey commenced with three Sabbath appointments—Winnipeg, Sturgeon Creek and Headingly; then came a long, tedious drive on Monday of some thirty-five miles through a very scattered population, except in the "White Horse Plains," which was occupied by French half-breeds, whose language I could not use, and who, I presume, thought they had no use for me, as they were well provided with a church and bell, and priests and sisters of charity. But from "Windmill Point," in the "Poplar Point" country, to Portage la Prairie, through a very inviting region, we found many who accorded us a hearty welcome, and showed us needed hospitalities. True, all were not like-minded. I suppose the exclusive, narrow-minded and narrow-hearted bigot may be found everywhere—at any rate, I discovered as many of his kith and kin in various parts of the country as I desired to meet, for I felt then, as I feel now, that it will be quite soon enough to come into close acquaintanceship with such when we meet, if we ever do, in the "Promised Land."

In the estimation of such I was an intruder, and my coming an impertinence, an invasion of their rights; for they, seemingly, thought that they held a sort of pre-emptive right to execute "the great commission" in that country—a right without any obligation being coupled therewith. At "Windmill Point" I was permitted to open an appointment in the home of a kind man, an English half-breed—Mr. Sandison, the miller—who later on became a useful and much-respected member, and, I think, a class-leader. The Rev. Mr. Robison, who came to my aid in 1869, was made a great blessing to this neighborhood. Blessed revival services were conducted and a little church erected, which, having become dilapidated, is just now being replaced by a better one. A few miles farther on I was permitted to open an appointment which has ever since been known as "Gowler's," from the fact that Mr. William Gowler had kindly and promptly opened his house and home to me on my arrival. Mr. Gowler was and is one of "nature's noblemen," whose nobility of character, as well as his enjoyments in religion and zeal for God's glory, were ere long greatly augmented. His house has been a resting-place for many a weary missionary since he so heartily welcomed me thereto in 1868. Here also a class was formed and a church erected, and blessed revivals experienced a little later on. I was greatly delighted at meeting him at the Conference in Winnipeg, June, 1892, as one of the lay-members of that Conference, and to be reminded of the pleasing fact that, having himself led the way into the "ark of Christ's Church," he was soon followed by "all his house," and many of his relatives and neighbors as well.

It has been said, "Variety is the spice of life," and so just here I will mention a somewhat spicy occurrence which took place in those early days of foundation laying in this locality. A certain fussy little half-fledged, not over-gifted nor unduly popular official regarded the advent of Methodism with much disfavor and evident uneasiness, and thought it his duty to express himself to Mr. Gowler anent the impropriety of which he had been guilty in opening his house for Methodist preaching and in showing hospitality to the wandering preacher who had the audacity to come there to preach; affirming, moreover, that it was very impolitic to do so, as I would soon become discouraged and return to Canada, and then he would find himself awkwardly situated, in view of what he had done; and still further, that I had no right to preach, not having received authority from the bishop. And so passing around the neighborhood ahead of my appointments, using the same arguments, he warned the people against attending those meetings. This expenditure of logic was duly reported to me, and drew forth the following reply: "Say to Mr. ——— that I was preaching the Gospel before he was in the cradle, and should continue doing so during the Lord's pleasure; and, also, that Methodists and Methodist missionaries would be found in that region until the millennium." More than a quarter of a century has elapsed since, and it looks very much just now as if this forthtelling, or foretelling, were likely to be literally fulfilled, for both at Windmill Point and at Gowler's the work of erecting new and greatly improved churches is being pushed forward to completion by a people who are grateful for the introduction of Methodism and its prevalence, despite the puny opposition or cold-shouldering it met with in 1868; and who, with help from above, will continue faithful to the truth and loyal to Christ and His Church until permitted to see either the millennium or the New Jerusalem.

My next appointment was opened at the "High Bluff," in the home of Mr. and Mrs. Angus Smith, who kindly invited us to use a portion of their house wherein to lodge and also to conduct services. Here we organized the first class in the settlement—Mr. and Mrs. Smith, Mr. and Mrs. Inkster, Mr. and Mrs. Norquay, Mr. and Mrs. Dillworth, Mr. Murray, and several others becoming members thereof, with Mr. Dillworth as their first leader. I shall never forget the blessed influence experienced on that occasion, as I addressed the people from "Fear not, little flock, for it is your Father's good pleasure to give you the kingdom," and as we held our first communion after organizing the class. No wonder we went on our way rejoicing after such a gracious uplift. Proceeding thence seven or eight miles to Portage la Prairie, we were favored by very kind Presbyterian friends, Mr. and Mrs. McBean and their young people, in whose home we found a comfortable resting-place, and a room in which to conduct worship and preach the

PERPLEXITIES AND ENCOURAGEMENTS. 73

Word. As this was practically the westerly limit of the Red River Settlement at that date, I retraced my steps to Winnipeg, to enter upon my next Sabbath's duties.

As the weeks passed by, while we were occupying the "one room" already referred to, we were ever on the lookout for a house to rent wherein we might winter and hold services. Failing in this, I arranged for a building then in course of erection on the corner of Portage Avenue and Main Streets at a monthly rental of $26.00, the place to be ready for occupancy within six weeks. But at the end of that term the building was far from completion, while the owner's funds were exhausted. As there seemed but one way out, I deemed it advisable, under the circumstances, to advance him three months' rent to enable him to complete the work; and after all we were compelled to wait for many weeks more while we took board at "Dutch George's" tavern. To expedite matters I employed a plasterer, and turned in myself to prepare and serve him with mortar, until the place was roughly plastered. The intense cold soon froze the plaster, which left the walls in a condition to render our moving in for some time extremely hazardous. However, we were tired of living in a tavern, and so by keeping up fires in the rooms we succeeded in "thawing out" and partially drying the walls so as to make our entrance warrantable, despite the steam and dampness that prevailed. On Saturday, the 13th of December, we took possession of the building, and on the next day opened the lower flat as our first

"Wesley Hall." I preached at 10 a.m., and Mrs. Young commenced Sabbath-school work at 3 p.m., while I took my other two services in the country. Our congregations, which had become small in the little uncomfortable court-room at the fort, now increased very considerably, and an evening service and class-meeting during the week were commenced forthwith. Thus we struggled on, with our high rent and heavy outlay for fuel and provisions, etc., during the severe winter of 1868-69.

My experiences during my first winter in the "Red River Settlement" were decidedly unique, tending to acclimatize on the one hand, and to test my faith and hope and to tax and develop my sympathies on the other. The season, to strangers in the country, was a severe one: intense cold, blizzard gales and deep snow-drifts combined to suggest for one's safety buffalo-skin coats, fur mitts, and moccasins with heavy feet wraps, with grizzly bear-skin or buffalo robes for the cutter in day travelling, and for a bed of warmth in the night season. The fuel brought by the natives to our Winnipeg market was generally of the poplar-pole sort, often green, and at best but a poor substitute for the harder woods of Ontario and Quebec, and yet equalling the best as to the price! But these experiences, with the long and tiresome drives up and down the rivers and across the wild prairies to the scattered settlements, were less trying to the physical, than was the scarcity of life's necessaries, which was but too apparent in many a home.

PERPLEXITIES AND ENCOURAGEMENTS. 75

THE FAMINE SEASON.

The winter of 1868-69 in the country now known as Manitoba will be remembered by multitudes as a season of famine, with urgent appeals from the needy to those possessing abundance for speedy assistance to prevent suffering and possible starvation. The reason of this scarcity is easily given. To some extent the cause was a two-fold failure—an utter and universal failure of the crops on the one hand, and failure of the buffalo hunt on the other. The locust plague was upon the land, hence the failure of crops. It is well-nigh impossible to give an adequate idea to those who have never witnessed the coming, in air-filling clouds, of myriads of these detestable devourers, and of the widespread devastation which is speedily effected by them. In some respects such a scene is better read of than witnessed. Pity the agriculturists who are compelled to witness it! In the autumn of 1867 the Province was invaded from the north-westerly and less paradisaical portions of Uncle Sam's domains, by a strong force of these "abominations" that cause desolation. Their arrival was too late to cause much mischief in 1867, as the crops had been already secured, but they speedily set to work to do the next worst thing for the settlement, viz., to deposit their eggs, myriads upon myriads of them, in the soil of gardens, fields and prairies, and along the hard-travelled road tracks, to render certain in the early spring an upspringing of a great army of infant destroyers, simultaneously with an upspringing of vegetation to feed and fatten on, to the prevention of the harvest that men had hoped and toiled for.

The heavy frosts of the winter did not seem to interfere with the aims of these parent locusts, for with the coming of the warmth of spring came also the hatching-out process, until it seemed as if every blade of grass and every sprout of grain were pre-empted by a score or more of these vigorous and now naturalized hoppers. The tender plant was quickly eaten off, and even quite down into the roots, and this repeated until all vitality was gone and the eater alone survived. Ere June ended, this work of destruction had been about completed, and without waiting for their wings, they took up their line of march in a southerly direction, hopping along in triumph until a further development should come, when, fully equipped, they should ascend to the region of the clouds, and taking advantage of fair winds, should more easily and rapidly proceed in quest of pastures fresh and more abundant. Our party of missionaries, passing out of Dakota into Assiniboia, met these hordes of evil-doers about July 1, 1868. It was as if the "prince of the power of the air" had marshalled this powerful detachment of destroyers to indicate his might, and discourage those from entering the country whose mission was one of salvation; in the meanwhile soliloquizing thus: "If I can't prevent your entering in, I will at least either starve you out or make you very miserable after you get in."

There seems as little of the haphazard and as

much of order in the movements of an army of locusts as is manifest in those of a swarm of bees. That there is leadership in both cases one can hardly doubt, but the whereabouts or *personnel*—so to speak—thereof is perhaps not so apparent in the former as in the latter case. They appear much averse to any effort to get around a difficulty or obstacle, but greatly prefer surmounting or climbing over it. The stone walls of old Fort Garry did not tumble at their approach, and so carrying out their principles and acting out "final perseverance," they continued hopping against the rocky barrier until they fell, rather ingloriously it must be admitted, as many poor obstinate human fools have done, in attempting the impossible. So great was the number of these stupid suicides that, for sanitary reasons and to get rid of an intolerable nuisance, the Hudson Bay Company's officials sent a gang of men with wheelbarrows to trundle these defunct devourers over the bank and into the current of the Assiniboine River, that they might be swept down stream to Lake Winnipeg for the benefit, possibly, of the jackfish and catfish and sturgeons of that great lake.

Soon after our arrival it became apparent to us, as to many others, that there was not a sufficient supply of food in the country to tide the population over the coming non-producing seasons of winter and spring. Many were very slow to take in the situation, and having a sufficiency for themselves and families from what they had kept over from the harvest of 1867, they hesitated not to declaim against any agitation of the question of the country's peril as unnecessary and injurious to general interests. My first missionary journey of one hundred and twenty miles through the best grain raising portions of the settlement satisfied me that, however safe a few might be from scarcity of food, the many must be brought into great straits and even peril if left entirely to their own resources; and this conviction deepened and strengthened as the days went by and my knowledge of the existing state of things extended. In a few weeks, and mainly through the representations of our only newspaper, *The Norwester*, many were brought to see the need of concerted and immediate action in order to ward off threatening calamity; and as a result a co-operative relief association was organized and a large committee was appointed, consisting of the bishops and ministers of the churches and several prominent and influential citizens, whose duty would be to make appeals to the outside world for aid, to take in charge all contributions that might be sent, and to inquire closely and thoroughly into the circumstances of the families seeking aid, as well as to distribute through sub-committees the supplies required.

The result of our investigation was sufficiently alarming to warrant solicitude and urgent efforts to save large numbers from suffering, as the following statement, made up as early as November, 1868, will show: The schedules carefully filled up and sent in from various parts of the country showed that there were of the Protestant section, 216 families, representing 951 persons, in need of immediate aid; and in the Roman Catholic portion, 207 families, representing 1,391 persons, in similar need, making a total of 423 families and 2,342 persons even then requiring help if "the wolf was to be kept from the door." Twenty barrels of flour per week, with a large quantity of meat, were distributed as early as the date above given. A little later on, the number of cases needing help increased to over 3,000, and the quantities of food given out proportionately increased. Great difficulty was experienced in getting the supplies forwarded in time to prevent suffering, inasmuch as long stretches of unoccupied prairie intervened between the terminus of the railroad—at that time—and their destination; and, winter having set in, the freighting of these supplies across those untracked regions, for three or four hundred miles, became both tedious and hazardous as well as expensive. Many of our hardy Red River freighters, however, undertook the task for the consideration of one-half their loads on delivery—they having no share in the gratuitous distribution. As the weary winter months passed along, some were able to supplement the aid received with game they were fortunate enough to shoot or trap, or fish secured from the lakes and rivers. In one of my missionary visits to White Mud River, some eighty miles from Winnipeg, I found the people of the settlement subsisting mainly on a scanty supply of rabbits snared in the bush, and jack-fish taken from under the ice in the river. The unsuccessful buffalo hunters had very "hard luck" also, for, after their long journeys to the distant plains, where they had been wont to fall in with vast herds of buffalo, they utterly failed to find the over-hunted animals, and were compelled to kill for food some of their ponies to prevent starvation on the homeward journey.

From these statements it will be seen that our first winter in the Red River Settlement involved a good deal that taxed heavily our sympathies, our faith and hope, and also our slight income. Provisions of all kinds went up to a high price. I paid in one instance thirty-six shillings sterling a hundred for flour, and for many months two dollars a bushel for oats for my horse, a supply of which, by the way, I always took with me on my journeys, for it was more prudent for me to miss a meal than that my hard-driven horse should go without grain. But the "good hand of God was upon us for good," and we were brought through it all in safety and in His good time. With the opening of spring came in, by flat boats and steamer, additional supplies of food for the needy, and large quantities of seed grain and potatoes for those who were pledged to plant and not consume them. The summer, when it came, brought us once more an abundant harvest, for which we brought our offering of thanksgiving.

During the winter I received from many kind friends, through the late Rev. Dr. Rose and others, collections and contributions from various parts of our work, to be distributed by me among the more

PERPLEXITIES AND ENCOURAGEMENTS.

needy of my flock apart from the general distribution. This was a great kindness and help. We had not as yet any poor fund, and yet we had needy ones whom we greatly desired to assist.

Together with this duty of caring for the needy, my attention was given during the winter to the necessary preparations for building both a parsonage

JAMES H. ASHDOWN, ESQ.

and a church in Winnipeg. Accordingly I made arrangements with two of the members of our little class at High Bluff, Messrs. Norquay and Smith, for the getting out of such timber—oak and poplar—as would be required for parsonage and church, they to raft it down and deliver it on the bank of the river at Fort Garry in the spring of 1869. These brethren did their work faithfully and well, and these requisites were on hand when needed. My kind friend, Mr. Ashdown—then about the most industrious and courageous of all the new comers, and now one of the most prosperous and wealthy of all the hardware merchants in Manitoba and the North-West—aided me greatly with additional timber, and also in lathing, painting, glazing, etc., in the completing of our parsonage. Many a hard day's work we put in together on those premises. Mr. Ashdown is now, and has been for years, an active member of the Trust Board of Grace Church and the management of Wesley College, and a liberal supporter of these interests. May he long be spared to his kind family and to the Church.

My application to Governor McTavish—who was ever a true friend of mine—for a site on which to erect a mission-house and a church, was presented by him, with his recommendation, to the Governor-in-Council of the Hudson Bay Company in London. Owing to his influence, I presume—and may I not add, in answer to our earnest and importunate prayers?—the company granted an acre of their land for that purpose, leaving the locating thereof to the Governor himself. In his absence there came about a little hitch between the official in charge and myself anent the location. I wanted it where he did not wish to give it, and where he wished to give it I did not want it. We finally struck this compromise: I agreed, with his consent, to draw the timber then on the river bank, with other building material, to the spot I had chosen, and then on the Governor's arrival —which was looked for daily—if he refused me that site, to remove it as he should direct. The material was drawn, the contract for putting up the mission-house was let, and the carpenters engaged to commence work in two or three days, and yet no arrival. As aforetime, we went to the great Helper for help, and help came. The Governor arrived in time, and at once, and heartily, he gave me the site I had chosen, to the great surprise of not a few. After much hard work in hauling timber, stones, and carrying lumber, etc., we succeeded in getting our new mission-house and stable ready for occupancy, and took possession of it as a family and held a class-meeting in it on the same day (August 17th, 1869), reserving the lower flat for our services. I preached my first sermon there on August 22nd from the text, "Hitherto the Lord hath helped us." In this room, as our "Wesley Hall" No. 2, we continued to hold service until our new church was completed in September, 1871. The reason of this delay in the erection of the church I may give later on.

The following report of a specimen trip in February, 1869, given in a letter to Mr. John Macdonald, may not be deemed inappropriate in this connection.

"My mission now extends from this point, where the Assiniboine River flows into the Red River, up along the banks of the former eighty miles; and as I occasionally visit the lower fort, which is twenty miles below this, on the Red River, I have a field of one hundred miles in length. I shall give you the best idea of my work, by placing before you, in diary form, the work of a 'trip,' as we call it out here:

"January 31st, Sabbath—Conducted Sabbath-school

in 'Wesley Hall,' town of Winnipeg, at 9.25 a.m. A very fair attendance and the best of attention. A good number of verses were recited, and the catechism lessons were well prepared. At the close of the school a good congregation assembled, and service commenced at 10.30; the subject of meditation was 1 Peter iv. 7. I trust 'the seed fell into good ground.' A drive of six miles brought me to Sturgeon Creek, where I conducted service on Sabbath at 2 p.m., in a dwelling-house kindly opened for the purpose, the parish deacon's protest to the contrary notwithstanding. Here an exceedingly attentive little company listened closely to a conversational style of discourse on the beautiful text, Rev. xii. 11, 'The blood of the Lamb.' What a theme!—and then, victory over Satan '·by,' or an account of, or through the amazingly efficacious blood of Christ.

> "'Dear dying Lamb, thy precious blood
> Shall never lose its power.'

Another drive of four miles and the Gowler farm was reached, where at 4.30 p.m., I superintended a small Sabbath-school, and then at 5.30 held service, and warned all 'neglecters' of salvation from the good old text, Hebrews ii. 3. In this neighborhood my congregations have greatly increased of late, and a nucleus of a society has been formed by four persons whose hearts God hath touched, and who have, in consequence, banded themselves together as those 'desiring to flee from the wrath to come.' After sermon I met them as a class; and so, after conducting two Sabbath-schools, preaching three sermons, travelling ten miles, and holding a little class and prayer-meeting, I closed a blessed Sabbath day with conversation and worship with this kind family, and wrapping myself in my two buffalo robes, with some good, sweet, soft hay in the corner of a room, as my bed, I slept sweetly, and dreamed of some of my kind friends in Canada.

"Monday morning, rose at five o'clock, and got off as soon as practicable on my long day's drive. The cold was as severe as I have felt it here, but in this high latitude we can bear it far better than a less degree in a damp region. Travelled forty miles in all, and preached to a full congregation gathered on two hours' notice, and felt it good to be there. In all my travels I have not seen a congregation who seemed to drink in the word as those do who compose this one. Surely the Lord will shortly pour upon them the spirit of His grace!

"Tuesday, drove eight miles, and preached to another very solemn and attentive company of worshippers at the High Bluff. Here, by God's blessing, despite all misrepresentations, a class was formed in October, and continues to meet each Sabbath, with encouraging prospects. The neighborhood had been greatly neglected until my arrival. Since that, although I may not have 'provoked to love,' I certainly have to 'good works,'—at least of a certain kind. Never was so much clerical attention experienced here before. In a fellowship meeting which I had held here, one of the newly gathered spake to this effect: 'In our neglected condition I have often prayed that some one might be sent to preach the Gospel plainly to us, that we might understand it and feel its power, and now I thank God He has heard my prayer, and sent that blessed Gospel into our very houses.' Some of these 'babes in Christ' were, a short time ago, actively engaged in rebelling against the Divine throne and Government. One who was in danger of descending to a drunkard's hell, but has been quickened into newness of life, has written me a letter, which I have just received, in which he says, 'I am happy to say that we are encouraged every Sabbath, more and more, by God's help in our meetings for worship. We thank God that He has sent you among us, as an instrument in His hand, to put it in our hearts to meet and pray together. We never lived so happy as we do at present. Trusting in God, we find that we get through the world much easier than we did before. May God bless us and give us strength to endure to the end.'

"On Wednesday morning the parties who came from the White Mud River—twenty-seven miles from the Bluff—met me according to appointment, and we drove that distance without resting. We passed the twenty miles across the prairies without seeing a house until we reached the little settlement. As we passed along I was surprised to see the tall prairie grass in some places standing erect, and reaching above the snow some three and even four feet. Bands of horses were wintering on it, and looked well. At 6 p.m. I preached to a little neglected company in the presence of a poor sufferer, from John v. 6. After visiting from house to house these poor families, who subsisted chiefly on fish, and preaching next morning at nine o'clock, and giving the Sacrament of the Lord's Supper to a few aged people, and baptizing a babe, I returned to the High Bluff, twenty-seven miles, on Thursday evening.

Friday morning it was my privilege to minister to the comfort of an aged woman, who is said to be fully one hundred years of age, and is the great-great grandmother of the babe I baptized the day before, and the mother of a Church of England missionary. I need not state to you that I felt a peculiar pleasure in communing with this 'agéd disciple.' My guide for this two miles' walk and back through the woods, and who accompanied me to White Mud River, is an aged man, whose case is a very interesting one. He was brought up among the Indians, and, until he was eighteen or twenty years of age, knew not that there was such a being as a God. Subsequently he came among the whites, but says that he understood very little of the *read* sermons to which he listened from Sabbath to Sabbath, and often wished the ministers would come and explain the Scriptures to him. I have tried to render him the aid required, and the poor man has followed me up from place to place on this trip, travelling over sixty miles, and hearing me preach five sermons. May he be saved! Another poor man said to me, at the White Mud River, 'We are thankful to you for coming among us, as we can *understand you well*, and if I had money enough I would never let you go away.' On Friday night I preached in a neighborhood near the Bluff in a new appointment, and on Saturday night lectured on temperance, when over twenty signed the pledge. This land is rum-cursed, and I feel it my duty to preach and lecture temperance everywhere.

"Sabbath, the 7th February.—Met class at nine; preached at 10 a.m.; drove eight miles, and preached at one o'clock, and then pushed on rapidly fifteen miles, visiting a sick woman along the road, and preached again at five to a crowd. After receiving three members on trial as the nucleus of another class, and driving a mile after eight o'clock, I felt that 'the sleep of a laboring man is sweet.' This day I travelled twenty-five miles.

"Monday morning, rose at half-past four, and set out on my return journey of a forty miles' drive, as soon as practicable; and after resting for the night at Headingly, I reached home Tuesday about noon, thankful indeed to find all well, and for the strength thus to preach the blessed Gospel in the 'regions beyond.' Oh, how delightful it is, my dear brother, to preach 'Jesus and the resurrection,' to these hungry and thirsty souls. But I can't bear the thought of seeing so many desiring instruction, and yet feel, as I do, that I can't supply all the lack. Let the patrons of your—*our*—noble Missionary Society but know the case, and I am sure the fault will not be theirs if an assistant be not sent out in May next. Many are waiting to see if I will get help before they cast in their lot with us, for they say that I can't keep up this field alone, but getting tired or worn out will give them up, and then they will have to go back where they were.

"'Pray for us, and choose me out a good man, full of faith and of the Holy Ghost,' and send him forward to help reap 'the fields already white unto harvest.'"

CHAPTER V.

THE ARRIVAL OF AN EFFICIENT HELPER.

On July 14th, 1869, I was reinforced—not very numerously, it is true, and yet very efficiently—by the arrival of Rev. Matthew Robison as my assistant. I had been pleading very importunately with the Mission Rooms, Toronto, for a helper, urging, however, that none but an earnest, devout, adaptive and consecrated young man—one who would be willing to face difficulties and hardships and much hard work—should be sent to fill that position. The selection was wisely made, and Mr. Robison, from the first, filled the bill as well, probably, as any other would have done whom they could have chosen. After a tedious journey across the plains from St. Paul, Minnesota, in company with some Red River freighters, he reached Winnipeg at 11 p.m., on Wednesday, July 14th, and reported himself at once at our little mission home as ready for service at any point I might indicate. On Thursday he accompanied me to one of my week-day appointments a few miles up the Assiniboine River, and opened his commission by preaching his first sermon in the settlement. His text was, "The Lord is my portion." Possibly he

THE ARRIVAL OF AN EFFICIENT HELPER.

may have concluded already from our surroundings that he would hereafter have special need of a "portion" such as earth cannot afford; be that as it may, he preached a plain, practical, earnest and comforting sermon. The privilege of hearing a sermon from some one else than myself was a rare one, and much enjoyed, while the prospect of having the counsel and co-operation of a missionary of our own Church tended to relieve that feeling of isolation and even loneliness which I had experienced during the year past, as well as to strengthen my hands in the great and good work. His arrival afforded much comfort to the mission family, as well as to myself, inasmuch as it would render unnecessary those long trips and absences from home, and from my work in Winnipeg, which had been too frequent in the past for the good of the cause.

After securing for him the needful outfit of horse, harness and buckboard, I accompanied him on his first trip through the country, and introduced him to the people, with whom he soon became well acquainted, and to whom his ministrations were greatly blessed. Henceforth the old "Red River" mission of magnificent distances became two missions, Brother R. taking High Bluff as his centre of operations, and undertaking to sustain the appointments I had opened in the neighborhoods adjacent, Windmill Point, Gowler's, the Bluff, Portage la Prairie, White Mud River, etc., and to open new ones as soon as opportunities might be afforded; while I undertook to supply as best I could the appointments I had commenced at Headingly, Sturgeon Creek, Woodlands, Rockwood, Lower Fort Garry, Springfield, Prairie Grove and Winnipeg. Each mission was still rather too large for the comfort of the missionary.

The people of the High Bluff mission soon found in their new pastor one whom they unanimously regarded as "the right man in the right place." Nor could it well be otherwise, for his Christian simplicity in spirit and manner, his ardent desire, manifest in his preaching and pastoral visits, to do them good in the highest sense of the term; his readiness to sacrifice ease and even to devote his scanty supply of funds in order to the extension and consolidation of the good work, commended him to them as a true minister of Christ. His preaching and exhortations had the genuine old Methodist ring in their definiteness, incisiveness, and faithfulness; while his personal testimony for Christ was given in tenderness, without any seeming self-exaltation, and his prayers in family or congregational worship were as free from cold formality and stiltedness on the one hand, as from a rhapsodical verbosity on the other. His free use of the gift of song was a help and no hindrance to his ministry.

At first all our services were of necessity held in the homes of those who kindly gave us the privilege solicited; but Mr. Robison, as soon as practicable, summoned his hearers to co-operation in the work of erecting two or more small churches for their better accommodation. His method—as mine had been,

THE ARRIVAL OF AN EFFICIENT HELPER. 93

and later on as that of Revs. M. Fawcett and J. M. Harrison of those early days, and as has been of those who have succeeded us and have succeeded in their work—was not to say go, but *come*, and the people generally showed a readiness to come. What it cost him in hard work and weariness for months together to get out timber and build and fit up those little churches cannot be imagined by those now occupying that field. Matthew Robison was no loiterer, standing idle in the market-place and " waiting for something to turn up." Pioneer missionaries who are too dignified or dilatory to assist, or even lead on, in such a work, or to care for their own horse in journeying, or to assist, now and again, when they have time and strength to do so, the brother whose hospitality they have shared, are not sufficiently Pauline to make much headway among the people. I am sorry to say that I think I have known a few such. To themselves their want of success seemed a great mystery, while it was not so regarded by the toil-worn ones to whom they had been sent as laborers in the Master's vineyard, and whose prejudices they had so unnecessarily turned against themselves. I have no patience with, and not over much expectation from, a Methodist preacher, whether on missions or self-supporting circuits, who is manifestly guilty of neglect or cruelty towards the poor animal whose misfortune it has become to be compelled to carry or draw him through mud and storm in heat and cold, and to and fro in the performance of his duty; and I am persuaded that the right thinking of his hearers will think and feel as I do. In all my journeyings, through all the years of my itinerancy during which I required a horse, I am glad to be able to say that the people with whom I lodged, if they still survive, will bear me witness that I never relegated to others the work of feeding, grooming or harnessing the horse I used. Those who pursue an opposite course from the love of ease, and especially among new settlers, or those who are pressed with their own work, oftentimes bring upon themselves, unwittingly, reflections that would be very unpleasant for them to hear.

In 1869 and 1870 Brother Robison, as well as myself, had much to meet with that was trying to patience and faith and hope. There were two setbacks to the work which occurred during those years, to which I will refer but briefly just here, and more lengthily later on. First there was the locust plague, the embarrassing results of which were still apparent when he came. Such a pre-occupancy of thought *re* the necessaries of life could not but prove very influential for ill in preventing the Word preached from having "free course" in the minds of its hearers. The fact that "the bread that perisheth" was so scarce with many, drew away their thoughts frequently from the "Bread of Life" offered so freely in the Gospel. This operated as a hindrance to the good work. And then, secondly, and much worse than the former, came that inexcusable agitation which certain restless spirits caused by their misrepresentations of the arrangements made for the aforetime asked-for transfer of the vast territory of the

THE ARRIVAL OF AN EFFICIENT HELPER.

Hudson Bay Company to Canada, and the unreasoning uprising of the French half-breed portion of the country's population, with the unprincipled Riel at their head, to prevent the establishment of the Government decided on at Ottawa.

Notwithstanding these set-backs to our work, Mr. Robison prosecuted his labors in visiting outposts; in keeping up his appointments; in working with his people in erecting the churches already referred to, and in visiting the sick and dying, especially in and about Winnipeg, during a season when a distressing and often fatal fever was sweeping away many who had but recently arrived in the country. His special evangelistic services in the two newly-built churches were signally owned and blessed of God. Many were "brought from darkness into a marvellous light," and added to the Church of Christ. In the midst of this great activity and usefulness, to my great regret he was led, I know not by what means, to decide on retiring from the work in Manitoba, in order to pursue a course of study in Victoria University at Cobourg. Knowing, as I did, his attachment to the people of his charge, and their strong regard for him, and the grief his severance from them must occasion, his decision came to me both as a surprise and a cause of much anxiety. I urged a reconsideration of the question, and in view of all the facts—especially as we had no one in the country at that date fully competent to fill his place—earnestly entreated him to remain at least a year or two longer with those he had gathered into the fold of the Good

Shepherd. Just at this crisis he was summoned by his mother, then rapidly declining in health, to hasten to her home that she might see him once more ere she departed. This decided him to act promptly, and in a few days he started upon his long and hazardous journey across the prairies in a season of severe cold and fierce storms. Could the dear ones at home have known what exposure that journey would involve, they would have hesitated to urge him to undertake it. The long prairie trail from Winnipeg to Moorhead was traversed by miserable stages, and but irregularly, because of the deep snowdrifts, and the railroads thence to St. Paul just then were badly blocked, so that it was extremely difficult for him to accomplish the journey. But, what was saddest of all, the ending of the journey only brought to him sore disappointment and grief—his mother had passed away days before his arrival. This to our brother was a severe blow, and one that called forth great sympathy on his behalf. After several weeks in Ontario, and due consultation with the Mission authorities, he returned to Manitoba in time to attend the Missionary Conference which was held there in July, 1872. His decision remained unchanged, and contrary to the entreaty of the friends on his mission, and the advice of Drs. Punshon and Wood and Mr. Fawcett and myself, he still pressed his claim to take a course of study in college.

In all this Brother Robison had the courage of his convictions, and was thoroughly honest, I doubt not, and yet I am compelled to think to-day, as in the

THE ARRIVAL OF AN EFFICIENT HELPER.

past, that in this persistence he unwittingly diverged from his providential course, and realized, as many who have erred in the same direction have done, disappointment and ultimate failure. Under the pressure he put upon himself in hard study and close confinement at college, his health ere long gave way, and after struggling along for a while, supplying the work at a few points in Ontario, and battling heroically with diseased throat and lungs, he was compelled to accept the inevitable. In the autumn of 1878, when much enfeebled by disease, he decided to visit Manitoba again, hoping that the invigorating air of the higher altitude might prove helpful, and that meeting again with those converts to Christ who loved him as their spiritual father, he might possibly afford comfort and help to them as well. Alas! it was too late. He stayed a night with us in Toronto, on his way west, when it was painfully apparent that his strength was unequal to the undertaking. His rapid decline after reaching Manitoba led to a speedy return home, where, after the wearisome journey, he arrived at length in great debility of body, but joyful through hope, to await his Master's call. On December 17th, 1878, the summons came, and my former co-laborer in the West, and the faithful servant of Christ, passed away from the loved ones of earth and went to see "the King in His beauty." Summoned to attend the funeral solemnities, I preached a memorial sermon from, "Well done, good and faithful servant," etc. "Blessed are the dead which die in the Lord."

A PECULIAR CORRESPONDENCE.

My correspondence was considerably increased by letters asking for information, of which I will give two specimens. A stranger asked me to furnish an anxious enquirer with the names of all the tribes of Indians living in British North America, the language and dialects spoken by the same, the religious denominations to which they belonged, the number of souls in each tribe, the number speaking each language, the numbers of each tribe belonging to each Christian denomination, the number of pagans, and the names of the districts inhabited by each tribe. All these questions were also asked separately regarding the Esquimaux; and all this asked for simply, as alleged in the letter, to gratify a desire to acquire statistical information! I also received the following letter, which is given *verb. et lit.*:

"Sir,—I depend upon you as a friend to give me a correct statement of the Red river country and all the parts you have travel through

And in particular the kind of Gaim let me know iff the buffalo is as plenty as they formerly was

There is a lot of familyes would imigrate there in the spring iff they could have the particulars of the country and in particular about the crops

plese state whether there is any deer or bear or wolves and all kinds of wild animals and all kinds of fish and state the climate and soil an what kinds of crops there is this year and the markets and the mode of living the people has and the best rout for going there and what it would cost a young single man to go there Mention all kinds of fowl in particular it has been a cold wet frosty summer here i would like to know how much snow you had there last winter there is a good many would like to know if there is any rattle snakes there mention all kinds of snakes sir if there is any thing not asked as we are inquiring about the particulars of that country i trust you will mention it Sir i trust you as a friend will answer this letter direct to Ethell pos office ——— ontario."

CHAPTER VI.

TROUBLOUS TIMES.

OUR efforts to prepare the foundations which I had been trying to place in position for an enduring superstructure, met with a very serious reverse in the troublous times of 1869 and 1870. There were some in the country at that date, as possibly there are now, of the milk and water class, whose principles (?) would not allow of their using the term *rebellion* in this connection, and so they could only write or speak of the "troubles" through which the Red River Settlement was passing. Yet to many of us these troubles were even more than troublesome, and the troublers themselves none other than organized rebels, who, having in a treacherous way possessed themselves of power, were now using that power in terrorizing, plundering and cruelly imprisoning many of Her Majesty's loyal subjects, whose misfortune it was, for the time, to be their fellow-citizens.

I should state here, preparatory to my remarks on the insurrection, that the Government of the Province of Assiniboia, of which the Red River Settlement was a part, consisted of an elective Council, presided over by the Governor of the Hudson Bay Territory, and was recognized by both the Imperial and the Canadian Governments. As I have already intimated, Governor McTavish was at this time at the head of the Council.

The beginning of the insurrectionary movements, which so soon culminated in this miserable rebellion, were seemingly too insignificant to be a reason for alarm. Early in 1869 we were warned by our only newspaper, the *Norwester*, that an agitation was then going on and gaining headway among a certain portion of the people of the country (the French half-breeds) on account of the proposed transfer of "The Hudson Bay Territory," including the Province of Assiniboia, to the Dominion of Canada, and the establishment, at an early day, of a Government by the authorities at Ottawa. This seemed at first all the more incredible, inasmuch as a numerously signed petition had been forwarded by the people to the Canadian Parliament, as far back as 1857, asking that the necessary preliminaries be arranged, as soon as possible, for the bringing about of such a transfer; and, also, inasmuch as the supplies of food and seed grain, which had been so generously sent forward by Canada to prevent suffering and even starvation during the famine season, and which had been participated in very largely and eagerly by these people, were not yet exhausted. That they could cherish and manifest so much ill-will toward the source of so much of their greatly-needed relief did seem to many in the country both incredible and ungracious. Nevertheless it soon became only too apparent that mischievous agitators were at work circulating reports that were as false as damaging, and that many of the people, uninformed and unsuspecting, were receiving these misrepresentations as true, and were becoming greatly excited in view of the alleged wrongs which, they were told, the Imperial Government, the Hudson Bay Company and the Government of Canada were conspiring to inflict upon their country.

Emboldened by the countenance given him by some, from whom better things might well have been expected, and encouraged by the manifest influence he was exercising over those among whom he was operating, the leading spirit in this movement (so far as was apparent; I cannot vouch for what was going on behind the scenes) openly summoned his fellow-countrymen and co-religionists to meet from time to time at their church doors at the close of the Sabbath service and elsewhere, to listen to his exciting eloquence, as he harangued them anent the peril in which their possessions and homes and altars and liberties were becoming involved, urging the necessity for concerted and prompt action on their part, that they might be able to avert these threatening dangers. Those who have listened to Riel when speaking on this hobby of his, and when at his best, as he was in 1869, will readily admit that as a speaker in his own language, addressing his own people, he was possessed of marvellous power to excite and dominate according to his pleasure.

The result of these public efforts, which probably

TROUBLOUS TIMES. 103

he was aided in planning and executing by older and wiser heads, very soon appeared in the organization, in military form, of well officered companies, composed well-nigh exclusively of French half-breeds, and exclusively of his co-religionists, who were kept well in hand by means of these frequent gatherings and stirring appeals. When it became known that a Government for these Territories had been outlined at Ottawa, and a Lieutenant-Governor (the Hon. Wm. Macdougall) appointed, neither of which was according to their liking, and that said Governor-elect, with a party of officials, were on their way to establish that Government, they speedily ranged their forces in positions the most favorable to resist and repel these audacious invaders.

Their first step in open rebellion against the Government and laws of the Province of Assiniboia was taken on October 21st, 1869—a few days after Mr. Howe's mysterious visit had terminated—when a large detachment of armed men, with their officers, took possession of the highway of traffic, and at a narrow pass near Stinking River erected a large cross, and proceeded to barricade that highway and to stop all travellers and all trains of freighting carts with their loads, subjecting them to a close examination and allowing none to pass except those having permits from their head officials. In some cases these loads of freight were allowed to pass on to Winnipeg, but in others the property was declared confiscated and appropriated to their own use. The incoming supplies and furniture, with some small arms and ammunition, for the use of the Lieutenant-Governor and his party were thus eagerly expropriated and appropriated. On October 25th, the Governor and Council of Assiniboia met and urged the leaders in this insurrection to cease their opposition to the incoming of Mr. Macdougall, but to no avail. A few days later, having become aware of his arrival at Pembina, they despatched an officer with a document, which was duly handed him, forbidding him to enter the Territory on any account except by their permission. This prohibitory enactment of theirs did not actually prohibit, for the party crossed the boundary line and entered the Territory not many hours later on, but having camped at the Hudson Bay Company's trading post, were soon after waited on in a threatening manner by a company of armed and mounted guards, led by Lepine, who warned them to leave the country by nine o'clock next morning or take the consequences.

About eight o'clock next day the rebel party returned, and with still more threatening demonstrations declared that if they did not leave by nine they would not answer for their lives, and proceeding to arrest Mr. Hallett, who went with a message to them, they tied him to a cart, forbidding him to speak to any of the Governor's party. Finding himself in the midst of such unreasoning and determined foes and utterly defenceless, Mr. Macdougall wisely decided to retrace his steps across the boundary, and await further developments at Pembina.

In thus refusing the right of the highway of travel

to the party, and expelling them from the country without giving any opportunity for such explanations as the Governor might wish to make to the people, these French half-breeds acted entirely on their own responsibility, and as though they were the sole occupants and owners of the country, or at least as though they alone had the right or competency to decide whether or not the residue of "the people of the North-West" should have an opportunity of receiving any explanations whatever from Canada through its appointed representative. They never conferred, up to that date and prior to that outrage, with the other and larger and more intelligent and influential portions of the people in relation to this matter; but treating the entire Protestant population of English, Scotch and Irish half-breeds and Canadians and Americans as if they were nonentities, took it upon themselves to rush into rebellion for the twofold purpose of preventing the establishment of a Government such as the majority of the people would have voted for if asked, and in order to secure the establishment of a government of their own with their "head centre" as governor. It is true that subsequently to this expulsion of the Lieutenant-Governor elect from the country, Riel did consent to a conference between a few representatives of the English-speaking Protestant population with himself and an equal number of his confederates, in which it was supposed the advisable would be freely discussed; but as soon as these anti-insurrectionists expressed a desire that Mr. Macdougall should be brought into the country, that the intentions of Canada might be explained to the people, he excitedly and indignantly protested, affirming that "he could only come in over their dead bodies," thus terminating very abruptly a conference which he never intended for free discussion of the situation and free action subsequently. On November 17th the Governor and Council of Assiniboia met again and issued a proclamation, duly signed, urging the insurrectionists to lay down their arms and submit to the Queen's authority; but these masters of the situation gave no heed to the proclamation.

THE REBELS SEIZE FORT GARRY.

The seizure took place on November 3rd, 1869. After having turned back the incoming Lieutenant-Governor, Riel lost no time in making his position, and that of his confederates, as secure and comfortable as possible, by taking possession of the fort, with the enormous stores it contained, as the principal receiving and distributing depot of the Hudson Bay Company. This he accomplished without resistance as he marched through the gate of the fort at the head of one hundred and twenty-five armed half-breeds, who forthwith took possession. And now they were really masters of the situation so far as the fort, and even the surrounding country, was concerned; for, being thus organized throughout their settlements in companies embracing a totality of five hundred or six hundred men, a hundred and more of whom were within the walls of Fort

Garry, and well equipped and supplied, as they had never been before, with comfortable quarters, and clothing and food, what could the unorganized and unequipped loyalists, who were widely scattered, reasonably hope to accomplish by any attempt they might make in this wintry season of the year, to dispossess them?

Their first step when within the walls was to get the cannon and rifles and ammunition now entirely at their service—they had thirteen six-pounders and four hundred Enfield rifles—into such positions in the bastions and about the gateways as seemed to promise the greatest availability and effectiveness in repelling any attack that might be made. When the Chief Factor in charge of the post asked Riel, "Why have you brought all these men into the fort, and closed the gates?" he received the unsatisfactory reply, "To protect the fort." "From what?" was asked. "From all danger," was the only answer vouchsafed. This rather unique seizure was accomplished so quietly, and with such precautions, that the people of the village knew nothing of what was occurring until one of the clerks in the Hudson Bay Company's store (a young Canadian), having taken in the situation, made a dash for the outside, spiking one of the guns on his way, and leaping from the walls, soon reported the fact, to the amazement of those who were not in sympathy with the rebels. From this date the tyranny of this well-fortified and well-provisioned upstart tyrant was seen and felt, both within and without the fort, for ten long months, until Colonel Wolseley and his expeditionary force put in an appearance, on the morning of August 24th, 1870. Just prior to this capture of Fort Garry by Riel and his following, a number of loyalists had advised its occupancy and defence by themselves, but for want of unanimity nothing was then attempted.

A COUNTER MOVEMENT

in the interests of peace and good order had its inception at this date, and on this wise: Mr. Macdougall, still at Pembina, having been assured, on what seemed most reliable authority, that the "transfer" would take place on the 1st of December, proceeded on that day to issue his celebrated "Queen's Proclamation," and also to commission Colonel Dennis as his "Lieutenant and Conservator of the Peace for the North-West Territories," authorizing him to appoint officers and organize into companies, and equip and drill for service, those loyalists who might volunteer for the suppression of rebellion and the re-establishment of peace. For a brief season this enrolling of names went on briskly until some four hundred men, mostly of the lower settlements and Winnipeg, had joined in with the movement; but a feeling of discouragement became manifest as soon as it was realized that no sufficient supply of the munitions of war for this hastily extemporized force was forthcoming, and, what was well-nigh as serious a matter, that they were without that steady-handed and able generalship which was essential to success in such a critical time. As a consequence, there was, ere long, a considerable falling away, until the number of those who were willing and ready to do and to dare became ominously small. The "Conservator of the Peace," however, had about fifty volunteers in quarters at the lower fort, to guard it and its surroundings from rebel invasion. This, I take it, was a wise precaution. But his next step was not equally wise, for with an unaccountable short-sightedness he placed about fifty or sixty poorly-equipped and insufficiently-officered volunteers in an unprotectable position, to guard some Government provisions, then in store in Dr. Schultz's buildings, with the hope, no doubt, of imposing a check thereby on the ambitious controller of affairs in Upper Fort Garry. This movement, though well-intentioned, was most impolitic and hazardous, and soon proved very disastrous. These buildings were quite within range of the fort guns, and easily surrounded, and so, cut off from all possible supplies of wood and water, a circumstance quickly perceived by the opposing force and utilized in order to a victory. Colonel Dennis, still at the lower fort, feeling himself unable to afford relief, ordered them, we were told, to "fall back" to a place of greater safety; but whether the order fell into the enemy's hands, or was received and disobeyed, I know not, but this I was compelled to know, that after being surrounded and besieged for three days, they had no alternative save one. To attempt to fight their way against such odds would have been sheer madness, and so these brave, loyal, but badly handled men were compelled to listen to the propositions of those who were seeking to negotiate a surrender. In view of the preparations being made at the fort for an assault upon the buildings thus occupied, I decided, on the morning of the 7th of December, to try to dissuade Riel from an act which would certainly result in much bloodshed, and also to secure, if possible, the release of our son, who was one of the volunteers. In my desperation, I presume I put the case before him pretty urgently, receiving in return such browbeating and insulting language as was decidedly trying to patience and self-respect, until, seeing an opportunity as we neared the buildings, I beckoned my son, and, unhindered by the surrounding guards, we both made our way to our mission home close by. Immediately I returned, and urged that others whose families were in need of their help should be allowed to leave at once, when he very indignantly dismissed me with, " You are going'too far; this is my business," etc. Thus repelled, I stood aside to witness one of the saddest scenes I ever witnessed. At this juncture, Riel was approached by Mr. Bannatyne, one of the merchants of Winnipeg, and others, for the avowed purpose of negotiating a cessation of hostilities, on terms that might be agreed upon, and which, after considerable delay, were made known and acceded to. These terms, we were informed, were that the surrendering parties should "leave their guns, ammunition, etc., in the buildings, and be marched to the fort, and then allowed to go where they pleased."

Some doubted the sincerity of the promise, but on being assured, as we have been told, by Mr. Bannatyne that the agreement would be faithfully kept and that he would personally guarantee all private property, they surrendered. Pursuant to this agreement, some fifty disarmed and anxious loyalists, with three ladies—Mrs. (Dr.) Schultz, Mrs. (Dr.) O'Donnell and Mrs. Mair, who accompanied their husbands—were ordered into line and, surrounded by Riel's guards, wended their way into the fort, the gates of which were closed upon them as soon as they entered, revealing to them very quickly the painful fact that they had been cruelly betrayed, and that now a very uncertain fate awaited them. Undeniably the promise made by Mr. Bannatyne induced the surrender, and as undeniably that promise was basely violated; but the question arises, Who in this instance was the betrayer? Was Mr. Bannatyne authorized by Riel to make it? If so, then he was grossly imposed upon; and if not so authorized, then his course was highly censurable. Certainly there was treachery somewhere, and cruel disappointment and great and prolonged suffering followed in due course.

A GLOOMY OUTLOOK.

After the surrender there came to these betrayed loyalists such indignities, privations and sufferings as far exceeded all that the most timid among them had feared before they passed within the walls of the now rebel-ruled fort.

The *personnel* of these prisoners stood about as

follows: Several were married, with families either in Ontario or the settlement, while others, perhaps the majority, were bachelors; but all alike had come to the country intending to pursue their respective professions or callings. Physicians, druggists, clerks, mechanics and farmers were all represented, as was proven after the days of their captivity ended, when many of them sprang quickly to the front in social and business circles—some taking up and holding important positions in the community as medical practitioners, merchants, magistrates, and others as legislators. One, for whom Riel had nothing less than death in store, became Lieutenant-Governor of Manitoba; while others distinguished themselves by the ability and enterprise they have manifested in matters commercial, political, educational and religious. Such, in brief, were the loyal men who were kept for months caged up in the prisons of Fort Garry, as if too vicious and dangerous to be allowed their liberty. In regard to ecclesiastical preferences, they were divided principally among the Episcopalian, Presbyterian and Methodist Churches, with two or three Roman Catholics; a majority of them, however, had attended our services either at Winnipeg or at some out-appointment.

On the morning following the surrender I went at an earlier hour, as seemed advisable, waiting for the subsidence of the night-long pow-wow, in which these over-stimulated captors had indulged, to seek from Riel permission to hold service with them on Sabbath in such place as he might order. My application was promptly and emphatically negatived: "No, you cannot meet them altogether, nor speak to them, but you may go and pray with them only, for they much need to be prayed for." I was thankful for even that much in the way of permission. Their condition in their places of confinement, as I found to my sorrow on that day, was indeed a most pitiable one; no description that I can give will convey an adequate idea thereof to those whose good fortune it was to neither experience nor witness it.

The prisoners were all at first located in the upper flat of a two-storey building, ordinarily occupied by the Hudson Bay Company's staff of accountants and clerks; the lower flat being used as offices, while the five or six small rooms in the upper storey were their sleeping apartments, which opened severally into a central corridor, reachable only by an outside stairway. This roomy corridor came into use as a "guard room," while the five or six stoveless, bedless and chairless rooms were packed with prisoners; so crowded in fact as to necessitate the breaking of a pane of glass in each room to prevent suffocation, in consequence of which the piercing winds and stinging frosts came in upon them to their great discomfort, and the imperilling of health and even life. No marvel that some became very ill as the result of such overcrowding and exposure, and that several contracted ailments from which they never fully recovered. The crowded state of these rooms was relieved somewhat by the removal of a number to the little jail outside the walls, in which there was a court-room and several small cells, which were found, as described by Mr. McVicar, to be "very filthy and crawling with vermin." The court-room was required, of course, by the gentlemen "guards" who might be on duty from time to time, and who frequently became very uproarious through a free use of "Hudson Bay rum," greatly to the annoyance of the prisoners in the cells. The food supplied to them was mainly pemmican of poorest quality, and tea; which, however, was soon supplemented somewhat by the kindness of certain loyal ladies in Winnipeg, who prepared and sent baskets of bread, biscuits, cooked potatoes, etc., which not only relieved hunger but probably warded off disease. These much-needed supplies were generally carried to the prisons by Mr. Crowson, a deeply afflicted loyalist friend of the prisoners, who was often annoyed and grieved beyond measure at seeing much that he had with such difficulty brought to their doors, snatched from his baskets by these already well-fed bandits. As he reported back these acts of unutterable meanness, we all felt with him that these things were hard to bear, and yet these true "sisters of charity," aided by this "Christian brother" of the right stamp, continued thus to minister to their imprisoned friends, while there were such to be ministered to. Will not such ministrations be remembered in two worlds?

I availed myself of Riel's permission to visit the prison and pray with the prisoners, generally twice during the week, and once each Sabbath morning, always, however, under strict surveillance—an armed guard attending and standing by me during my brief services in the different rooms. To be thus closely watched while seeking to worship God was to me a new and most unwelcome experience, and yet I had to submit to it, not only in these prison exercises, but also when visiting a sick lady—wife of a prisoner—in her own home; for even there, and notwithstanding her severe illness, a rough fellow as a "guard" invariably entered her room when I did, and seating himself on the side of the sufferer's bed, watched me while I besought the God of mercy for "mercy and grace to help in that time of need." As I recall these experiences to-day, I fear I was not always as free from unkindly feelings toward these men, nor as hopeful of doing them good, as I might have been. Be that as it may, I will just here narrate an incident reported to me years after by a surveyor, who was just in from a remote settlement, which may seem to have some bearing on this matter. I give it as he gave it to me, without either vouching for or questioning its correctness. He said: "I feel, Mr. Young, that you should be told a fact that came to my knowledge not long ago. It is this: The half-breed guard who used to stand guard over you during your services in the prisons in 1869 and 1870, and who has recently died, when urged in his last illness to have the priest brought, said to his friends, 'If you can bring Mr. Young, I should like him to come and pray for me as I used to hear him pray with the prisoners in Fort Garry.'" I was not sent for, I am sorry to say, but I shall hope that this poor man, who had but little light, was mercifully remembered by the "Sufferer of Calvary," and so received into Paradise when dismissed out of this life. I should like to meet him in "the house of many mansions."

These short services of Scripture reading and prayer, in these five or six different prison rooms, were followed on each Sabbath by my three regular preaching services in this order, viz.: Our mission hall, Winnipeg, 10.30 a.m.; then a drive of six miles and a service at 2.30 p.m.; and then a drive of about six miles more, and a service at 6 p.m., after which I generally returned to Winnipeg, making a round trip during the day of twenty-five miles, which was frequently done in deep snow and in severely cold and stormy weather.

CHAPTER VII.

ESCAPING FOR LIFE.

From the 7th of December, 1869, to the 9th of January, 1870, our suffering fellow-loyalists languished in close confinement without indicating any intention of attempting an escape; but on the night of the 9th a surprise was given their over-confident oppressors. In the morning of that day, as on previous Sabbaths, I conducted a short service with those in the outer prison, and, going beyond Riel's permission, left with them a Bible and some tracts for their perusal. During that night, which was severely cold and stormy, ten of their number "broke jail," and struck out into the darkness, to make their way, if possible, over deep snowdrifts and across trackless prairies in quest of liberty and safety. As may be supposed, they were unsuitably clad for such an exposure, and in consequence suffered much as they tramped their weary way during that terrible night. One of them —a Mr. H——, from London, Ont.,—was so badly frozen as to be compelled to seek refuge in a house, where he was recaptured and forced back into the prison from which he had so recently escaped, while the nine succeeded in reaching places of refuge in either the lower or upper settlements. At a late hour of night, one of the escaping men called on me to get the money he had deposited with me for safe-keeping at the time of the surrender, after which he heroically started for distant Canada, an undertaking which seemed, under the circumstances, most preposterous; and yet he and many others preferred to brave the hardships and perils that would be involved therein rather than hazard liberty and life in a prolonged imprisonment such as they had been enduring. How this man accomplished that journey I know not; but he did accomplish it, and after the reign of terror was ended, returned with his family and became a settler.

A coincidence, which was to me for a time the occasion of some uneasiness, occurred on the night of Sabbath, 23rd of January, 1870, when a more notable escape was effected from one of the inner prisons. After visiting the other prison-rooms in the morning of that day, I had a short season of prayer with Dr. Schultz, who, for reasons unknown to me, was then in solitary confinement, and who asked me to favor him with a Bible. As I had a few minutes before designedly left one on the floor where I knelt in another room, I requested the guard in attendance to bring it and hand it to the doctor, which he did, relieving me thereby of any responsibility in the matter. The coincidence referred to came in just here and in this wise: The escape of the ten men from the jail outside followed my leaving them a Bible, and now two weeks later the giving of another Bible to another prisoner was followed that same night by his escape also. When told of this sudden departure without any leave-taking, it occurred to me that Riel's suspicions might be aroused, and that he might order me into the room so unceremoniously vacated by my friend. My fears, however, were not realized. When the prison was found empty in the morning, and the prisoner actually unfindable, there was no small stir among the rebel rulers of the fort, and no little wonderment and gladness among the loyalists both within and without. At first it was supposed that some of the guards had "taken the shilling" and looked the other way, and that some friend in the secret had been in readiness outside the walls with horse and sleigh to expedite the escape; but, as I afterwards learned, all this guessing was at fault, and that notwithstanding the many and great difficulties in his way—*e.g.*, the presence of the guard at his door, the distance of the ground from his window, the height of the fort wall, and the absence of such appliances as would seem indispensable to his escape, as well as the severity of the night and the distance to a place of safety—yet he did most certainly, and without human aid, make well his escape. Nor do I know how to account for it, unless that the means at his command, which seemed so utterly insufficient (consisting barely of a small gimlet, pocket-knife and buffalo-robe), were made effectual to his deliverance by a Presence and a Power unseen by mortal eye. With less nerve and determination he would have abandoned all hope of escape after the severe injury he received in falling heavily to the ground, from the failure of either the gimlet or the buffalo-line to bear his weight, and which resulted in much suffering and long-continued lameness. But "liberty is sweet," and life still more so, and hence his persistent efforts, despite his sufferings, to reach a place of safety. Nor was his marvellous escape premature. I doubt not but that the same "council of war" which subsequently, and with inhuman cruelty and for no just cause, sent poor Thomas Scott to his sudden death would, under similar pressure, have voted the same sentence for Dr. Schultz had he been still in their power; for, after his escape, Riel said to me, "The guards are out looking for him, and they have orders to shoot him on sight."

His escape was not fully assured, however, until after he, with his faithful friend and helper, Monckman, had completed their adventurous and toilsome tramp of five hundred or six hundred miles through the wilds then intervening between the Red River of the North and Fort William. Snowshoeing their way, and drawing along a little sled loaded with scanty supplies of food and blankets, resting over night occasionally in a friendly Indian's hut, and sometimes by their camp-fire in the thicket, they toiled on, crossing the ice-bound lakes and rivers, as well as the vast uninhabited wilderness regions that were in their way until, after twenty-four days of hard struggling, despite their scant fare and the doctor's lameness, they once more crossed the bounds of civilization. I still hold a letter which Dr. Schultz wrote me from Fort Alexander, while making that wonderful journey, in which the true source of the guidance and help and the unceasing protection he so much needed, was duly recognized and prayerful remembrance earnestly solicited. As I now recall the perils which were thus escaped twenty-seven years ago, and then note the position he reached and the work he was enabled to do for his country in subsequent years, I think I see some at least of many reasons why the hand of God was manifestly in this history of deliverances.

A wonderful history was that of my friend Dr. Schultz. Our first meeting was on the wild prairies, somewhere between Georgetown and Fort Abercrombie, in 1868, he journeying toward St. Paul and I moving slowly toward Fort Garry. During my early toils in Winnipeg I ever found him ready to oblige me when he could do so. His loyalty to Canada in the midst of the disloyal and in times of peril needs no mention from me—his record through the years that followed, as well as the positions to which he was elevated by his country and Government, his occupancy of the Lieutenant-Governorship of Manitoba for so long a term, as well as the richly-merited honor of knighthood conferred upon him, all testify thereunto. His was for many years a life of suffering. I doubt if much of it was not the result of the injury he received while escaping from Fort Garry, and the strain and exposure associated with his wonderful journey through the wilderness. It was not long after he had been relieved from the responsibilities of the Governorship, and while in quest of relief from feebleness and disease in a foreign country, that he received his dismissal from the life that now is, and entered, as I firmly trust, into a state of being where the "wicked cease from troubling and the weary are forever at rest."

A second and more disastrous counter-movement than the one already recorded was inaugurated for the relief of the prisoners who, despite all the promises given by Riel for their release, were still held in close confinement. The result was that further humiliation and suffering were endured by those participating therein. Some of the loyal people of the western parishes, such as Portage la Prairie, High Bluff, Poplar Point and Headingly, in conjunction with those of the "lower settlements," unable longer to endure the painful suspense in which they had been kept waiting, moved simultaneously for a grand rally at some central point, that should serve both as a demonstration and an opportunity for consultation and concerted action along the line of persuasive measures for the relief of their friends. Some seventy or more true and brave loyalists volunteered their services, and proceeded, under command of Major Boulton, toward the point of general rendezvous. As their line of march led through the White Horse Plains neighborhood, where disloyalty predominated and from whence Riel had drawn a large number of his "guards," their movements were at once observed, and quickly reported to their leaders in Fort Garry, who forthwith called in all available reinforcements, so that by the time Boulton and his poorly-equipped little force passed by for Kildonan, a force of five hundred or six hundred well-armed men was in readiness to defend their stronghold and repel its assailants. These western loyalists were joined at Kildonan on February 15th by a much larger number of Canadians and natives, who had also volunteered for active service. And now the question, "What persuasive measure shall we resort to in order to secure the result at which we are aiming?" I suppose, came under anxious consideration. But while they were thus deliberating and resolving and re-resolving, a most deplorable occurrence took place in the neighborhood of the camp, involving the slaying of an estimable and promising youth, connected with one of the principal families of the parish. The attendant circumstances, as reported, were as follows: A half-breed, thought to be a spy sent by Riel, was arrested and brought into camp, who, watching his opportunity, made a dash for liberty, snatching a loaded gun as he ran. Just as his fleet pursuers were overhauling him, most unfortunately he was met by young Sutherland, who was riding toward the camp, but not in any way participating in the movement; whereupon, supposing that he was going to aid in his capture, or else hoping to expedite his escape by securing the horse, the half-breed fired on him, inflicting wounds that proved fatal in a short time. This was one of the saddest outcomes of this most unfortunate counter-movement. Taking place, however, just when it did, it may have had some bearing on the decision soon after reached, to pursue the more pacific course of sending a message to Riel, instead of making an immediate attack on the fort. Be that as it may, a message was soon sent demanding the release at once of all the prisoners, which was followed by several interchanges, until an arrangement was entered into securing the release demanded, and also involving the disbanding and peaceable return to their homes of the volunteers on the following day.

In the early morning of February 17th, 1870, these western men, as a part of the force thus disbanded, "struck camp," tied up their few belongings (blankets, buffalo robes and food for the journey), and, supposing that they were "homeward bound," joyously faced the west, hoping soon to meet their released friends and return to their own pleasant and peaceful firesides. But a great disappointment was before them, and ere it was noonday it was realized by them. That they might not on their return pass offensively near the fort, they had agreed (it was said by Riel's request) to diverge from the travelled road, just north of Winnipeg, and strike across the untracked prairies, to the Portage la Prairie trail, making a detour of about two miles. It was doubtless well known to Riel that there were ravines then completely filled with snowdrifts, which it would be difficult to cross. The sequel seemed to indicate his object in making the request, and that those who complied therewith were treacherously and humiliatingly outwitted. While I was watching their slow and toilsome movements, as men and horses were struggling through these snow-filled ravines, I was greatly surprised and distressed by the rushing from the fort of a large number of armed guards, mostly mounted, who, with their usual accompaniment, the terrifying war-whoop, struck for a point where they could head off and surround the returning party. Some, it was said, were disposed to resist, but this seemed useless, as many of them where without arms, and besides, they were told by those in command of their assailants that Riel simply desired them to call at the fort and see him before their return home. After reluctantly complying and entering the fort, the gates were closed upon them, as was the case in the surrender of December 7th, and they were forthwith declared prisoners, and their horses, sleighs and property seized and confiscated, while they were hustled into the very prisons from which their friends had been liberated only a day or two before. What a complete reversal of circumstances! These men, at risk of liberty and life, came for the deliverance of others, and succeeded, and now they were themselves in need of deliverance. But whence, and how, and when that deliverance should come was a problem none of us could solve. My duties within the fort, which I had hoped were ended, were now considerably augmented, and that, too, for a very uncertain period—duties, as ere long appeared, involving greater trials of patience and faith and fortitude than I had faced aforetime. A reign of terror, including tyranny and cruelty far exceeding what had been already endured, was now seemingly established, and what the end would be no one could predict.

It soon became evident, however, that Riel was not disposed to regard all these prisoners with equal disfavor, and that while all were at the outset subjected to harsher treatment than were their predecessors, some were predestined by him to much severer punishment than others. Of these, Boulton, Scott, Powers, McLeod and Parker occupied foremost positions, and Major Boulton was the first to receive special attention. The "council of war," it was said, met at once, and decided that he was guilty of treason and should be shot, whereupon Riel sentenced him to be shot at noon the next day. Archdeacon McLean was sent for to minister to the now condemned man, and his intercessions were so far regarded that the execution was postponed until midnight, Riel declaring that he would yield no further unless Dr. Schultz should be recaptured in the meantime, in which case he would be shot instead. It was also reported that up to 10 p.m. of the 19th of February no consent for the sparing of his life was obtained, and then only by the importunities of Commissioner Smith (now Sir Donald) and the Archdeacon, and their promise to proceed, even at that midnight hour, to the lower settlements and persuade, if possible, the people to fall into line and elect representatives to the "Assembly" that Riel was intent upon having established; then, and not till then, did he so far yield as to suspend that terrible sentence, awaiting results, declaring, at the same time, that "On your success depends the lives of the Canadians in the country." The efforts of their intercessors proved successful, and for that reason only, so far as I know or believe, Major (now Senator) Boulton escaped the bullets which Riel's guards, on the word of command, would have sent through his heart on their mission of death.

And yet a more horrible tragedy, that we could not avert, has to be recorded.

As a connecting link, the following letter of mine to the *Guardian* will not be deemed out of place:

"WINNIPEG, RED RIVER, Jan. 22nd, 1870.

"MY DEAR MR. EDITOR,—Events of considerable importance have transpired in connection with the revolutionary movements in this country, since the date of my last communication. A gentleman who landed here a few weeks ago, and reported himself at Riel's headquarters, to which he was conducted, as Mr. Smith, an official of the Hudson Bay Company, despite the watching and guarding to which he has been subjected,—(and he has had two or more guards charged with that duty, and has not been outside of the fort since his arrival)—has become developed into a real (and, if you will) 'live' commissioner, duly appointed and fully accredited by His Excellency the Governor-General of Canada. On the arrival of Mr. Smith and Mr. Hardisty, another official of the Hudson Bay Company, and his travelling companion and guide, they were both taken into the office of 'President' Riel, where they were closely catechized as to their business here and any papers in their possession; whereupon Mr. Smith assured the catechizer that he had not in his possession, at that time, any documents except such as he would show him; and suiting the action to the word, he opened his desk for his inspection. Of course nothing contraband was found. After remaining quiet for some two weeks he seems to have deemed it time to be 'up and doing,' and accordingly it is said he intimated to Mr. Riel that he was *now* under instructions to inform him that when he should have permission to do so, he had certain things to say to him from the Governor of Canada, and also certain documents at Pembina which he would like to present. This information, I doubt not, took our little Napoleon by surprise; but as he keeps his wits generally about him, Riel directed, I understand, a guard to accompany Hardisty and bring in the papers. In the meantime some of the most influential and intelligent and brave of Riel's counsellors and army had become 'enlightened' ('tis not necessary to say how), and a goodly number of this class, we are told, set out to meet the party returning with the papers, and having met them, forthwith demanded the prized documents, and took the guard and all under their charge. Proceeding towards Fort Garry they met Riel, who, not going about his business as they thought he should, it is said one of his French fellow-religionists placed his revolver to his presidential head, and hinted that he must be careful how he acted or he would send him where he would not care to go. Arriving at the fort, some thirty or forty of the loyal French, with some others, were there to receive and guard the papers, and to insist that the commission of Mr. Smith should be made public, and these messages or proclamations, whatever they were, should be read and made known. After a good deal of parleying, and some sharp hints from the 'seceders,' Riel, I am told, consented, though reluctantly, that a 'mass meeting' should be called, when Mr. Smith should explain his mission and read his papers. On Tuesday last, at noon, a large number of both parties assembled in the fort, in the open air, and although the thermometer was 20° below zero, yet there they stood, till 5 o'clock, trying to learn all about a matter in which they felt a deep interest. It is doubtful if a gentleman so perfectly gentlemanly as is Mr. Smith, and representing a Government of so much importance, and having the best and kindliest of aims for the country visited, was ever so cross-questioned and badgered as he patiently and good-humoredly submitted to be on that occasion, for the sake of peace and this country's good. He was treated all through the early part of the meeting as if suspected of being a mere pretender with the worst of intention.

"When he read a letter of instruction from Sir John Young, signed simply 'John Young,' he was roughly asked 'Who is John Young?' 'Why does he not sign his name as Governor, then?' As the day was ending and the business of the meeting not completed, it was decided to adjourn until the day following,—whereupon a Mr. Burke called the attention of the meeting to the state of the prisoners, who for nearly two months had been kept in close confinement, and urged their release that evening. His language was earnest, and I presume by a portion of the French guard understood, for directly the abominable Indian war-whoop was heard, and off they rushed to their guns and bayonets. With a few threats and a good deal of noise the excitement passed off. The next day a larger number of people came, and a greater number of guards were under arms, but the meeting was quiet. Mr. Smith had fewer interruptions and received kindlier treatment. The documents were read and well received by the people. The liberal policy, declared to be that which the Government intended to have adopted, took all by surprise, and made some, I judge, regret that anything had been done by them to keep such a Government from being established. The meeting ended with this immediate result—each class, that is of English and French people, to appoint *twenty* delegates to meet next Tuesday to deliberate on the matters brought under their notice by Mr. Smith. When this council shall have done its work I hope to write you again. I send you herewith a copy of our new 'annexation' paper, which contains a report of the meeting referred to, and also the different communications from England and Canada which it was our privilege to have had read to us by Mr. Smith; in regard to whom I may here state, that throughout he has managed this very delicate business with great prudence and tact, and yet in a very straightforward and honorable manner. The scheme of annexation to the United States, which this paper has undertaken to 'write up,' *does not meet* with approval even among the French people. It is stated that even Riel must 'cold-shoulder' that scheme, or be cold-shouldered by his former friends, and furthermore it is rumored that the paper in question will be very apt to *back down* a little on that scheme ere long. But rumors here are the veriest uncertainties, and especially now. The prisoners, poor fellows, are still held in their close quarters, constantly expecting to be allowed to go about their business, and yet daily doomed to sore disappointment. Dr. Schultz's property, it is said, is wasting away, and not very slowly either, especially certain casks of what has been called 'distilled damnation,' which some of those who have been represented as having sworn not to touch the intoxicating cup are now using freely for other than 'medicinal purposes.' Business matters are as stagnant as ever, and many intend to emigrate in spring if there is not a speedy and satisfactory settlement of these 'vexed questions.' The winter is more severe than the last was, though the snow is only about a foot deep."

CHAPTER VIII.

THE CLIMAX OF CRIME AND CRUELTY.

THE criminality and cruelty of Riel and his "council of war" reached a most deplorable and never-to-be-forgotten climax in that bloody tragedy which they enacted on March 4th, 1870. After disposing of Major Boulton to his satisfaction, and making all the capital possible out of the case, Riel proceeded forthwith to give special attention to another of those he had recently captured, toward whom, for reasons never clearly defined, he was harboring feelings of intense hatred and cherishing purposes of the utmost barbarity. I refer to that brave and loyal young Irishman—the unfortunate Thomas Scott. In a former chapter I stated that he was one of the ten who escaped from the outer prison on the night of December 9th, 1869, and also referred to his volunteering in association with Boulton's Portage Company, forty-eight of whom were so treacherously entrapped and thrust into prison on February 17th, 1870. Thus he was twice a prisoner, and yet in neither instance taken under arms. When first arrested he was bearing a request to Riel that the ladies then resident in Dr. Schultz's besieged buildings should be permitted to retire therefrom, as they were suffering from prolonged excitement and alarm. The request was refused and he was forthwith shut up in prison. His second arrest was, if possible, still more treacherously effected, inasmuch as he, with the forty-eight already referred to, had disbanded and were returning peaceably to their homes pursuant to an agreement with Riel, and in full confidence of being unmolested, when they were suddenly surprised in their helplessness, and then decoyed into the fort, when the trap was sprung and their imprisonment entered upon. I am the more desirous of emphasizing this fact, inasmuch as false and damaging representations have been widely circulated, designed to excuse the severity of his punishment. It has been stated, *e.g.*, that in order to secure his release from prison he took what amounted to an oath of allegiance to Riel, violating which he rendered himself liable to the punishment that followed. Unhesitatingly I pronounce this a malicious misrepresentation and vilification. He was never released from prison except by self-help, and never took an oath of any description of Riel's proposing.

On Sabbath, February 27th, while visiting the various prisons, I was pained to learn that Scott had been sent into solitary confinement, and going at once to his room, found him in a most pitiable condition—a dirty and fireless room, a single blanket to rest on or wrap himself in, and with manacles on both wrists and ankles. No marvel that he shivered and suffered under such circumstances. On my asking if he knew the reason of this increased severity, he assured me

THE CLIMAX OF CRIME AND CRUELTY. 133

that he did not, and readily promised to carefully avoid, in action and utterance, whatever might be offensive to the guards. After our season of worship, with much anxiety concerning his fate, I passed on to meet others who were awaiting a pastoral call. On the evening of March 3rd, just after returning home from an appointment in the country, I was surprised by a call from one of the guards, who requested me to accompany him to the fort, as I was wanted there, and when asked for what, replied that Riel had sent for me as a man named Scott was to be shot at noon on the morrow, and that he wished to see me at once. Promptly obeying this startling summons, I was soon by the side of the condemned man, who, as we conversed freely *re* probabilities, said, "I believe they are bad enough to shoot me, but I can hardly think that they dare do it;" to which I replied that "the only safe course for us both would be to act on the assumption that the sentence would be carried out," to which he readily assented. In his so-called trial, before the seven members of the council of war, Riel acted as prosecutor, witness and judge, and when Scott objected that he did not know what he was accused of, as he did not understand the language used by them, he was simply told that he was "a very bad man and must die." Learning these facts from the prisoner, and wishing to ascertain if possible Riel's intentions, as well as to remonstrate as best I could, I proceeded to his headquarters in the fort, but failing to obtain an interview returned immediately to the prisoner to render such help as might be possible by counselling, encouraging and praying with him as he groped his way toward the light and faith and hope now so absolutely essential as a preparation for the sudden termination of his probationary life. It was wickedly stated in communications which appeared in certain partisan political Quebec papers, sent evidently by Riel or some of his accomplices, that I found him indifferent, and that my exhortations and prayers were unheeded until "Riel and some two hundred of his guards, moved with pious solicitude, knelt in prayer that God would give him repentance, after which, as was soon known, he became contrite."

I cannot affirm that no such prayer-meeting was held by this devout (?) "president" and his guards, many of whom were in a state of semi-intoxication at that hour; but I do affirm that Mr. Scott was from the first most attentive to my ministrations, and, so far as appeared, contrite in spirit and earnest in prayers for the needed mercy and grace which, I trust, was granted him. At a late hour he suggested that I should retire and seek rest and return early in the morning, and that he would write to his mother and brother in the meantime. To this I consented, offering, however, to stay with him to the last if he preferred me to do so.

Quite early in the morning I went in quest of co-operation from several persons who seemed friendly to Riel, hoping to bring such pressure to bear as would lead him to spare Scott, as he had Boulton, but this effort availed nothing. They one and all regarded it as a "scare" only, and did not interfere. I then waited on Mr. Commissioner Smith, who consented at once to go to Riel and remonstrate and plead, suggesting, however, that I should go first, and if I failed, send a message and he would do his utmost in behalf of the prisoner. Gaining the hearing desired, I was informed by Riel that the sentence would be executed, whereupon I urged, in effect, as follows: "He is now powerless as your prisoner. His life spared can endanger no one; and what has he done to render it proper for you to take away his life?" His reply was quite emphatic and to this effect: "He is a very bad man, and has insulted my guards, and has hindered some from making peace; so I must make an example to impress others and lead them to respect my government, and will take him first, and then, if necessary, others will follow." I then urged for delay, at least for a day more, that I might have more time with him, saying, "It is dreadful to send a soul so suddenly into eternity." But finding this of no avail, I sent a messenger to Mr. Smith, as arranged for, while I returned to my sad duty in the prison. Riel was urged by him with pressing importunity to spare his life, even "for the sake of One who died for us all." But Riel continued unmoved, notwithstanding the touching allusion.

The eleventh hour had now come, and as we were engaged in spiritual exercises, Scott inquiring and I answering, and both pleading with God for the mercy and grace so much needed, we were interrupted and startled by the entrance of several guards, who were sent to bind and blindfold the prisoner and to lead him out to the place appointed for his execution. All hopes for deliverance vanished at once. At my request the guards withdrew for a few minutes to allow us another opportunity for prayer, but this delay gave annoyance to Riel, who came to the door vociferating his reproofs and orders as if intent on hurrying up the execution or *murder* about to be perpetrated. The only request made by Mr. Scott was to be permitted to bid his fellow-prisoners "good-bye," which being granted, and as I led him to their rooms and opened the doors, he with wonderful calmness and tenderness said, "Good-bye, boys," after which we were conducted down the outside stairway and through the east gate of the fort to the spot where the sentence was to be carried out. As we were moving slowly forward, the following words were uttered by him, which I can never forget, and have often repeated since that sad hour, "This is horrible! This is cold-blooded murder. Be sure to make a true statement." Twenty-seven years have elapsed, and on many a platform and frequently through the press I have tried to obey, as I am now obeying, that solemn injunction. At my request we were again allowed a brief season of prayer, and kneeling in the snow we unitedly lifted our hearts to God for help in this time of special need. "Can you now trust in Christ for salvation?" I asked. To my great comfort he replied, "I think I can." And after advising him to remain kneeling, and by his request placing the blindfolding cotton more directly

FIRING PARTY.   O'LONE, KENNEDY, O'DONOGHUE.   RIEL.   REV. G. YOUNG.   ALFRED SCOTT.
THE COFFIN.   THE VICTIM.

THE DEATH OF THOMAS SCOTT.

THE CLIMAX OF CRIME AND CRUELTY.

over his eyes, we bade each other a solemn "goodbye." Immediately after, I spoke to the captain commanding the firing party, urging him to spare his life at least a day longer. I was told promptly, "His time is come and he must die," and then speaking to O'Donohue I said, "I know you have the power to stay the execution for a day longer. Will you not do so? It is dreadful to send a soul into eternity with so little time for preparation." He admitted that it was, but simply said, "It is very far gone," and did not interfere. The poor, brave loyalist was then placed in such a position as they desired, a few yards east of the present track of the street railway, when he again knelt in the snow, and then, at the signal given, several rebel bullets were sent on their mission of death, into and completely through his breast, causing the snow to be stained and saturated with his heart's blood, while his spirit quickly passed from the presence of his murderers to the presence of God. Immediately after the firing I approached the prostrate body, then quivering in death, and saw a half-drunken guard fire a revolver at his head, as he held it quite near, after which all seemed to be over. Thus it was, in brief, that those who were responsible for this tragedy reached a terrible climax in crime and cruelty.

A rumor was circulated in a day or two that Scott was not dead when the body was placed in the box called a coffin, and was living five hours later, when he was put to death by Riel and one of his guards in the bastion to which he had been removed. This intimation was made to me on the evening of the murder by the editor of the *New Nation*, a paper that was started in the interests of the rebels, and designed by many of its supporters, I have ever believed, to favor annexation to the United States. It was decidedly anti-Canadian in its spirit and influence. At the time I disbelieved the rumor utterly, in view of what I had witnessed at the shooting, and also because of the large quantity of blood which saturated the snow where he fell and struggled. However, long after the *New Nation* ceased to exist, its former editor, Major Robinson, made a statement in the St. Paul *Press*, to the effect that Scott was not only shot by order of Riel, but that, after his body had been pierced by the balls of the firing party, he was fastened up, still living, in his coffin. I quote from the article referred to as follows:

"Major Robinson stated that he could not credit that the deed of blood had been actually perpetrated, and expressed his incredulity. Seeing this, President Riel asked him to come with him, and led the way into the court and to one of the sheds which lined the interior of the walls, where there was a sentry. Riel and his companion approached, and the former threw open the door, exposing the fatal box, from which the blood dripped into the snow. Hardly had he realized this grim fact, when Major Robinson was horrified to hear a voice, proceeding from the box, or coffin, in anguished but distinct tones exclaim: 'Oh, let me out of this! My God! How I suffer!' With blood curdling in his veins, he retreated from the spot. Riel called the sentry, and the two entered the shed and closed the door. A moment later there was the sound of a shot within, and the murdered man was probably released from his torture. Riel returned with the major to the fort, where he dismissed him with a significant warning to secrecy. To comprehend the full horror of this tragedy it must be remembered that this last incident of Scott's life occurred five hours after he had been shot and coffined, and with the thermometer many degrees below zero."

On March 5th, the day following the tragedy, I wrote Scott's brother in Toronto, and, as it may be noted, very cautiously, for the outgoing and incoming mails were tampered with by this unprincipled tyrant, who, I knew, would not hesitate to put me along with those in prison if I gave the least ground of offence.

"*To Hugh W. Scott, Esq.:*

"MY DEAR SIR,—It is my very painful task to convey to you intelligence of the most heart-rending description. I promised your late brother, Thomas, in his last hours, to write you, and give you a true statement of all that he was charged with, and his trial and end. It will be proper for me to delay giving that statement for a little, as it might not be allowed to pass out with the mail, and might also involve me in unpleasantness.

"Let me then express my deep sympathy for you and your bereaved family in this sore trouble. As you know, probably, already, your brother was taken prisoner by Mr. Riel in December last, and made his escape after many weeks' imprisonment. But, joining another company of volunteers, he was again captured with forty-seven others. The day before yesterday he was singled out and tried for these offences, as well as for 'insulting Mr. Riel and the guards by something he said'—which he positively denied—and was sentenced to be shot at noon next day. I was sent for as a minister who had visited the prisoners regularly, and was known by him. During the evening I stayed with him, giving instructions and exhortations, and engaging frequently in prayer. He was deeply penitent and earnestly prayerful before God. Next morning I went again and begged personally of Mr. Riel, and got Commissioner Smith to do the same. We urged one day more to be given him to prepare. But alas! all in vain. I was with him to the end. He prayed fervently—said 'it was dreadful to put him to death'—but expressed a hope of salvation. He was led out a few feet from the walls of Fort Garry, where again he knelt in the snow and prayed—remaining on his knees until the fatal shots were given. Poor Thomas! many tears were shed for thee, but in vain.

"I have begged the body which Riel intended to bury in the fort, and I think, through others helping, we shall get it, when we intend burying it at the Presbyterian churchyard, five miles below this. . . . If we should get the body interred in time for the mail, I will write again and enclose with this. May God sustain and comfort you. I do believe Thomas is saved.   "G. YOUNG.
"Winnipeg, March 5th, 1870."

Mr. Hugh Scott replied to my letter of the 5th of March on the 8th of April as follows:

"TORONTO, April 8th, 1870.

"REV. AND DEAR SIR,—Your esteemed favor of 5th ult. I duly received, and although containing news of

THE CLIMAX OF CRIME AND CRUELTY. 141

the most painful description—yet news which filled my soul with gladness—I cannot convey to you in words my heartfelt thanks for the kind and Christian interest which you manifested towards my late brother. May God reward you for it.

"Sad indeed to me was the fate of my poor brother, but that was forgotten in the joy at the hopes of his soul's salvation. Your kindness shall live in my memory while life shall last. I am satisfied that you did your duty as a Christian friend and minister. What consolation it will be to his aged father and mother when they read your letter.

"I hope and trust that you are safe from the attacks of these ruffians and murderers, and that no hurt will befall yourself or family.

"I shall be very glad to hear from you when you find it convenient to write. Just enclose a note as you did before. Thomas had some photographs which I should like to get if possible, but I suppose all was taken from him. I may mention that his cruel murder has aroused the feeling of all the loyal people in the Dominion, and all are anxious of having the opportunity of avenging it. I also shall not make my letter any longer, as Mr. Clark has kindly consented to enclose it with his, but hoping to hear from you soon and again asking you to accept my best thanks for your kindness and love,

"I remain,
"Your faithful and esteemed friend,
"HUGH SCOTT."

Mr. Hugh Scott, whose letter I have given, lost his reason after the death of his brother. I visited him when in the asylum, but, poor fellow, his mind was so wrecked as to forget that he had ever had a brother called Thomas, and ere long he passed away, and, I trust, entered upon a life where the mind will never become unbalanced.

MRS. SCOTT'S REQUEST.

Before his death his aged mother in Ireland wrote her daughter-in-law, wife of the afflicted man, the following very touching letter:

"DEAR DAUGHTER,—I am very glad to hear of the Rev. Mr. Young calling to see my poor son. I would desire that Mr. Young should attend his funeral if it is the Lord's will to take him; and if I may not be permitted to meet him on earth, as it seems I never shall, may we all meet around the throne in heaven, where parting is no more; and I shall ever feel grateful to Mr. Young for his kind services to my poor son Thomas in Red River. I have thanked God many times that there was a minister in that place to attend to my poor son before his death; and I shall ever bear a fond remembrance of Mr. Young on my heart while I live. Poor Thomas! There was no father, mother, brother or sister with him in his dying hour, but there was the all-seeing eye of Him who is ever near to those who put their trust in Him. May God be with us all and enable us to submit to His will."

A short while before the death of her son at the Asylum in Toronto, Mrs. Scott was called to lay aside her heart-breaking sorrow and enter into rest.

A FEW "IN MEMORIAM" REFERENCES.

These must be very brief, because of my scanty store of needful facts. I am glad, however, that I have enough of these to show that Scott was not thus

THE CLIMAX OF CRIME AND CRUELTY. 143

treated by Riel for any justifiable cause. Among his papers which I forwarded to his brother, Hugh Scott, of Toronto, were many commendatory letters of introduction, with certificates of good character, from Sabbath-school teachers and the Presbyterian minister with whose church he had been connected in Ireland, as well as from employers whom he had served faithfully. I quote one entry which appeared in his journal, made on Queen's Birthday, 1869, which is peculiarly admonitory: "Brother and I were out rowing on the Bay (Belleville). I wonder where we shall both be ten years from to-day?" Alas, poor fellow, before ten months had passed away his lifeless body, in its shroud of chains, was resting on the bottom of the Red River of the North!

Captain Rowe, of Madoc, Ont., to whose company he had belonged, thus described him in his report to Colonel Brown, in command of the regiment: "I have to inform you that the unfortunate man, Scott, who has been murdered by that scoundrel, Riel, was for a time a member of my company, and did duty with the battalion at Sterling in 1868. He was a splendid fellow, whom you may possibly remember as the right-hand man of No. 4, and I have no hesitation in saying, the finest-looking man in the battalion. He was about six feet two inches in height, and twenty-five years of age. He was an Orangeman, loyal to the backbone, and a well-bred, gentlemanly Irishman."

It is a significant fact, which makes his murder wear a blacker aspect, that all who knew Scott were favorably impressed by his manliness and courtesy.

Mr. Charles Mair, who frequently shared his blanket with him, speaks of him in terms of the warmest admiration. Mr. S. H. Harvard, who spent several months at Red River in 1869, in a private letter to a friend in this city, says:

"On my outward trip last summer, I reached St. Cloud, where the railway then terminated. On getting into the coach next day, I found just one other passenger—a fine, tall, muscular youth of some twenty-four years of age. One glance showed he was a Canadian, and in a land of strangers and foreigners. I felt drawn towards him. He was a stranger to me. I knew nothing of him; but he behaved properly, and I was singularly struck with his inoffensive bearing towards those with whom we came in contact. The day before we reached Abercrombie, we stopped for the night at a lonely roadside inn, and beds being scarce, we shared one together. I found from him that he was going to Cariboo, to the gold mines; that he had been working at Madoc. This man was Thomas Scott, who has lately been murdered in cold blood."

It cannot be deemed inappropriate that we inquire respecting the impression that was made on the public mind by this most cruel criminality. The report given in the *Guardian* of a large meeting held in Toronto is as follows:

INDIGNATION AND SYMPATHY.

"It is a long time since Toronto has seen such an immense and enthusiastic meeting as that held last Wednesday evening, to welcome the deputation of escaped prisoners from Red River, to express indignation at the murder of Scott, and to urge upon the Government the importance of prompt action for the relief of the loyal Canadians suffering from the tyranny of Riel. An attempt was made to hold the meeting in the St. Lawrence Hall; but it was found that no building could be found large enough to hold the people, and the meeting adjourned to the square in front of the City Hall. The crowd was immense, and the expressions of sympathy were unmistakably enthusiastic. After the Mayor and Mr. M. C. Cameron had spoken, Mr. Setter, Mr. Mair, Dr. Lynch and Dr. Schultz successively addressed the meeting. At different points in their speeches they were greeted with vociferous cheers. The spirit of the vast concourse showed that the people of Ontario are not disposed to temporize with Riel and his disloyal clique in Red River. While Mr. Cameron was speaking, the Queen's Own, headed by their band, playing military airs, marched past, and were saluted by loud cheers from the crowd. The remarks of the speakers added little to our previous knowledge; but it was rousing to hear the thrilling story of suffering from the lips of men who had been imprisoned by Riel and escaped from bondage. Dr. Schultz alluded to the unfounded boast of Riel, that he would turn the Indian tribes against the Canadians; and said that the reason he came there from Fort Garry to Fort William was to ascertain the feeling of the Indians in that section, through which our troops must pass, and that he had slept in the wigwams all along the route, and found them unflinching in their loyalty to our Government. Whatever faults of judgment Dr. Schultz may have shown, it is impossible not to admire the pluck and endurance of a man who baffled the vigilance of his enemies, and leaving his family behind unprotected, came at such an inclement season all the way from Fort Garry to Fort William, on snowshoes. It beats Xenophon's retreat of the ten thousand Greeks.

"Another immense gathering was held on Front Street, on Saturday night, to express indignation at the murder of Scott, and to press upon the Government the necessity of immediate and decisive action to suppress the insurrection in Red River, and annex the country to Canada. The chair was taken by Ald. Metcalf, and stirring speeches were made by Mr. Thomas Nixon, Ald. Dickey, Mr. Boulton, Mr. Hugh Scott, Mr. Fleming, Mr. Robin, and Mr. Cunningham of the *Globe*. The resolutions, which were enthusiastically adopted, gave no uncertain sound on the question of the hour."

But are we warranted in regarding the death of Thomas Scott as *murder* and those who sentenced and put him to death as *murderers*? Consider the following utterances of those high in authority, and then judge:

LORD DUFFERIN.—"The killing of Scott was not an exercise of jurisdiction known to any form of law, but an *inhuman slaughter of an innocent man, aggravated by circumstances of extraordinary brutality*."

He also states, "The utmost alleged against Scott is that he used violent language in the prison, and that he had alluded to an intention of capturing Riel and retaining him as a hostage for the release of the prisoners; but even these allegations *were not proved*, nor, had they been ten times over, could they have rendered him liable to serious punishment."

And, further, "All the special pleading in the world will not prove the killing of Scott to be anything else than a cruel, wicked and unnecessary crime."

THE CLIMAX OF CRIME AND CRUELTY.

Lord Carnarvon in his despatches designated it as a "*brutal and actrocious crime,*" and spoke of it as a "murder" no less than five times in the course of his remarks, and concluded by saying that "such a murder as that of Scott cannot be allowed to go unpunished."

The Hon. Edward Blake, then member for South Bruce, in an exceedingly able address on this subject, remarked as follows: "The murder of Scott was perpetrated on the ground of pure personal revenge, and . . . it was a most *unprovoked and damnable* murder."

The Chief Justice of Manitoba, in passing sentence upon Lepine, said to the prisoner: "You robbed Her Majesty's loyal subjects of their property and plundered whenever you could do so, with impunity. And, lastly, you crowned the catalogue of your crimes with the slaughter of Thomas Scott for no other offence than loyalty to the Queen."

The late Sir George E. Cartier, in a private communication to Lord Lisgar, says, "The killing of Scott was an excessive abuse of power and cruel barbarity."

CHAPTER IX.

POST-MORTEM INDIGNITIES, ETC.

THE name of Thomas Scott will never perish from the earth so long as the Canadian histories relating to that period shall continue to be read. Neither tomb, tablet, nor monument shall be needed to perpetuate his memory. The cruelties attending his death were narrated in my last chapter, and now two questions may with propriety be considered.

First: Why was he put to death?

It was not, certainly, because he was such a desperado as to render his continuance in life a menace to the liberties and lives of others. Nor was it because he was guilty of any offence punishable by death according to the laws of the British Empire, of which he was a subject and within which he suffered. True, he was twice a prisoner, but was never taken "under arms," as I have already shown. It has been charged that he brought this punishment upon himself by his violent and insulting conduct while a prisoner. But what authority had Riel and his confederates in rebellion to inflict capital punishment, even for conduct ever so violent and insulting? Besides, I was assured by his fellow-prisoners that his conduct in prison was not in any way exceptionally violent, and that the offence cited against him by his enemies, as giving special annoyance, really occurred on this wise : He was suffering from an ailment which compelled him to ask permission to retire frequently to premises in the rear. On this occasion he was cruelly and insultingly refused by the guards, and as he urged his request, O'Donohue entered the corridor and reproved him sharply for the disturbance he was causing, reminding him that he was now in prison; to which he replied that they should be treated decently, even though they were in prison. This was pronounced an insult to an officer, and the offender was ordered to be put in irons and in close confinement, from whence he was taken a few days later to receive his death sentence. That this was the reason for his being thus sentenced was the merest, shallowest and meanest pretence imaginable, as the following facts clearly show. Two ex-insurrectionists, Bruce and Dumas, testified in the witness-box at Lepine's trial, —the former that Lepine, the "adjutant-general," told him about twenty days before Scott's death that "the prisoners would be let out soon, but that one or two would be shot first;" while the other swore that "for about a week before, it was talked about among the guards that Scott would be shot." The offence which some have declared brought on the death punishment had not been committed on either of those dates, and the secret of this great cruelty was not so much in what Scott had done, as in what Riel expected to be able to do by means thereof. It was probably in his mind, and in the minds of some who were secretly co-operating with him, that this stroke of policy would lead the loyalists of the western settlements to elect representatives to his Assembly, and thereby, seemingly at least, support his government and secure the passing and sending to Ottawa of the "bill of rights," which in that case would be regarded as expressing the views, wishes and demands of a united people! Thus this young life was sacrificed, I fully believe, to strengthen and intensify the terrorism he was exercising; in a word, as a masterstroke of policy.

Secondly: What was done with the body?

A rough box had been brought to the place appointed, before Scott and I arrived; but before the body was placed therein, I requested permission of Riel to remove it to my home, and take it thence to Kildonan for Christian burial. To this he consented at first, but quickly withdrew his consent. In the morning I was informed, by one whose aid I had asked for, that Riel had consented that if I would come, together with the Bishop of Rupert's Land, and guarantee that the burial should take place quietly, "without any demonstration," he would allow us to remove the body; but when we applied, as advised, he promptly refused us, on the ground that the adjutant-general insisted that it must be buried in the fort, telling us that a grave was then being dug sufficiently large to contain it and any others that might have to follow. But was it so disposed of? Undoubtedly it was placed in the box, and the box and body placed in one of the bastions of the fort; but, as undoubtedly, only the box and rope used in binding the arms were placed in the long, trench-like grave. After the arrival of Colonel Wolseley and his troops, and the dispersion of this abominable confederacy, we were allowed to open the grave and search for his body. The following account of our proceedings and the results appeared in a Winnipeg paper of that date:

"THE LATE THOMAS SCOTT—UNSUCCESSFUL SEARCH FOR HIS REMAINS.

"On Thursday forenoon the inside of the quadrangle of Fort Garry presented a scene somewhat singular. A few paces in front of the north end of the store, some half dozen men were seen, by turns, busily at work digging out what looked to be, and what was thought to be, a grave. They were searching for the remains of Thomas Scott.

"There was a large crowd around, amongst whom we noticed His Excellency the Lieutenant-Governor, Rev. Messrs. Black, Fletcher and Young, Drs. Codd, Schultz and Lynch, Mr. J. McTavish and Messrs. Cunningham and St. John of the Toronto press, etc.

"The excavation was carried on under the direction of the Rev. Mr. Young, and was proceeded with with great vigor. As the hole deepened, the excitement became the more intense, and when, after digging some six feet, the spade struck on a board, and when the earth was removed and disclosed a deal board shaped like a coffin, everyone held his breath. But the excitement was turned into something like disappointed rage when one of the diggers thrust his arm into the box and pronounced it empty! It was empty, excepting only the rope with which Scott's arms had been pinioned."

Now, more frequently than ever, the question was asked, "Whatever have they done with poor Scott's body?" After months had elapsed, one of the ex-guards gave me the following information, which I have ever since regarded as a satisfactory answer to the question. He stated that before the box was buried, the body, now stiff in death, was taken therefrom, and after it was weighted heavily with chains, placed about it like a network, it was plunged through a hole in the ice, and thus made to sink quickly to the depths of the river, where, being thus anchored, it will probably remain for long ages. Thus, having pursued the poor young loyalist to his death, and denied Christian burial to his mutilated body, they rested not until they had chased it down to the deepest depths of their deep, muddy river.

CERTAIN UNDERRATED CRUELTIES.

In the previous chapter the "climax of crime and cruelty" was represented as reached when, by order of Riel and his "council of war," Thomas Scott was barbarously put to death on March 4th, 1870.

I am very glad and thankful that it may be truthfully stated to have remained without a parallel during the entire course of the rebellion, but am sorry to have to add that some speakers, and even authors, in making much of that fact, representing it as "Riel's one dark crime," have used language seemingly intended to imply that but for its commission all his

POST-MORTEM INDIGNITIES.   153

other wrong-doings would have been regarded as mere trivialities, which were either justifiable or condonable. This disposition to minify his lesser cruelties, I take it, is attributable either to ignorance of both their nature and number, or to the desire to mislead others. If those who have taken such lenient views of the case had been compelled to experience, or even witness, these cruelties, they would not have so erred in underrating them. The "foot hills" near the Rockies are not regarded as mere mole-hills because small in comparison with Mount Sir Donald or Mount Lord Stephen. Having already referred to the treatment accorded to Dr. Schultz, Major Boulton and Thomas Scott, I shall now specify certain other cases of severe suffering which have been generally overlooked. Even prior to Scott's murder, Messrs. Hallett and Gaddy, worthy natives of the country and respected members of the community, had the misfortune to come into special disfavor with Riel. They were both, I think, employed by Colonel Dennis, before the outbreak, as guides and helpers, and on the arrival of Governor Macdougall at Pembina, Hallett was sent to pilot him and his party into the settlement, and with them, after being roughly handled, he was ejected by the French half-breeds. Returning to his home near Winnipeg, he came into notice soon after in association with Scott on an errand of mercy to Riel, which resulted in the imprisonment of both. After enduring close confinement and hard fare with his fellow prisoners for many weary weeks, and while Riel was in a most unamiable mood on account of the fortunate escape of Dr. Schultz, he seemed moved to pay special unkind attention to Hallett, and to make his prison life a severer punishment than hitherto. As testified to by an ex-prisoner at the Lepine trial, the beginning of greater severity was on this wise: While the poor man, well on in the sixties, was, by permission of the guards, seeking a little warmth by the stove in the corridor, Riel entered and indignantly demanded of the guards, " Why are these dogs allowed out here?" Hallett, replying simply, " We should not be treated worse than dogs," was ordered to be handcuffed and sent into solitary confinement. The little room from which Dr. Schultz had recently escaped, with the broken window as the fleeing doctor had left it, became his prison, and as the cold outside was thirty below zero, it is simply wonderful that he did not perish then and there. In this cold, wretched place he was kept for several weeks. Is there any marvel that the sufferings caused thereby did not terminate with his imprisonment? From that date, it was stated, his health was completely and irretrievably broken, and, what was vastly worse, his mind, through physical ailments and sufferings, became so unbalanced as to lead to his seeking relief in suicide! Doubtless in this he was entirely irresponsible; but not for a world would I have resting on me the responsibility of having tormented him into insanity and irresponsibility.

The other case, that of Mr. Gaddy, was likewise one of prolonged suffering. He was accused with acting as a spy for Colonel Dennis, and condemned to death: but for some reason, instead of being shot, he was placed in one of the rough stone bastions, and there kept in a most pitiable condition for weeks, until he made good his escape. During his imprisonment the report was circulated—I suppose for the terrorizing of his friends — that he had been put to death; a report which he was enabled to contradict himself by his unlooked-for arrival at home. Whence, in such instances as these, and after such sort, came "man's inhumanity to man," this de-humanizing of the human? I know not, unless it resulted from the coalescing and co-working of the two well-nigh ubiquitous spirits, the spirit of rum and the spirit of the nethermost regions. As Riel had stated to me that after the terrible example he had made of Scott, should the result contemplated not follow, and especially if the prisoners were not more careful, others would certainly follow in the same way, beginning with certain persons whose names he mentioned, I proposed, with his permission, to see the prisoners and dissuade them, if possible, from giving offence in any way to the guards and their officers. To this he at once consented, and I went forth on the errand I had suggested. Intimating to them that I viewed their situation as most critical, I advised them to studiously avoid all, in word or deed, that might give offence, and also to do whatever might be required, so long as it did not involve sin, which they one and all without hesitation promised. The names he gave me as standing first on his black list were, Powers, McLeod and Parker, a trio of loyal, respectable and brave men. Sergeant Powers, who prior to his arrest resided on his farm west of Winnipeg, had served many years in the army, and at this date was one of Her Majesty's pensioners. He was soldierly in appearance and manners, and highly esteemed, where best known, as an intelligent, honorable, peace-loving member of the community. After the suppression of the rebellion his worth was recognized in his appointment by the Government as Warden of the prison in Winnipeg, where it became his duty to turn the keys upon several of his former oppressors, notably the notorious adjutant-general referred to—a turn in the wheel, certainly, on account of which many rejoiced. But Riel hated him, as he did Hallett and Parker and McLeod, with no ordinary hatred, as the sequel will show. The promise I have referred to as given me by the prisoners, was soon subjected to a test much more severe and disgusting than we had thought possible; but it stood the strain and was fulfilled to the letter. I witnessed with sorrow and indignation the testing a few days later, when I saw these men, each walking between two armed half-breeds, with wheelbarrow in hand, and engaged as directed, in scavenging of the most offensive description, in clearing away and wheeling to the river the accumulations from the rear premises of the fort. That such brave and worthy subjects of our Gracious Queen should be compelled to do such vile work at the bidding of these contemptible rebel masters, was greatly in excess of our forebodings. Nevertheless, they kept their promise, and thereby, I shall ever believe, escaped what was planned as a second "stroke of policy" for the hastening of the desired consummation. Remembering these facts as I do, I must be excused from regarding these underrated cruelties as mere uncensurable trivialities.

BRIGHTENING PROSPECTS.

Soon after the period referred to in the closing sentences of my last chapter, the dark clouds, which for so long seemed to be lowering just above our heads, began to brighten somewhat, through a few rifts which had been caused to appear here and there betokening the approach of a brighter day for our disturbed and terrorized country. "Let honor be given to whom honor is due;" but the question arises, to whom is the honor really due of causing those rifts and of bringing about such a brightening of our prospects? In order to avoid being misapprehended by any, I will try to be very explicit, and may be deemed, by some, rather personal in my statements. Ever keeping in view that "the heavens do rule," and that while "man proposes God disposes," we may nevertheless gratefully acknowledge indebtedness for help and deliverance to those whose efforts became the means of bringing that help and deliverance. The mission of Mr. Commissioner Smith (now Sir Donald) to "the people of the North-West," at that particular juncture, was confessedly one of great importance, and his eminent and exceptional fitness for so responsible a position was, I presume, considered with much care ere he received his "special" commission, nor have I seen reason to doubt that the bearings of his patient, gentlemanly and prudent, as well as loyal, conduct under Riel's brow-beating and insults during his semi-imprisonment in Fort Garry (for although a duly certified commissioner, he was nevertheless treated rather as a prisoner, and not allowed to pass out of the fort unless attended by two armed guards), and his earnest efforts in behalf of the liberty and lives of imperilled loyalists, were very influential in bringing about the changes at which I have hinted. I am aware that there were those both within and without the prisons who, worn out with weary waiting for their own release, or the release of their friends, through his influence became impatient and complaining on account of what they regarded, through not knowing the circumstances, as sheer tardiness, indicative of a censurable want of either sympathy or courage. Such, however, were not my views. Had I been circumstanced as they were, possibly I should have felt as they did, but knowing what I knew from personal observation and contact with all parties, I felt then, as I feel now, that it was far wiser, safer and likelier to lead to success that he should "make haste slowly." The task he undertook was no easy one, as he saw clearly on his arrival at Fort Garry, but he so prosecuted it as to accomplish vastly more in the way of weakening Riel's influence, and preparing the way for his final overthrow, than has been generally understood. Very true, he was unsuccessful in his efforts to secure the immediate release of the prisoners, and to save the life of poor Thomas Scott, but he was successful in the case of Major Boulton, and in his efforts to gain such knowledge of the views and feelings and wishes of different classes for incorporation in his report to the Government as were most valuable, and also in his subsequent efforts to aid in restoration of order, and in the adjusting of manifold and conflicting interests; so that in these and many other ways, as I view it, Sir Donald has placed the Dominion under obligation for services rendered in the North-West.

The late Consul Taylor, in a carefully prepared paper read before the Historical Society, Winnipeg, bore this testimony: "I believe the time will come when the services of Sir Donald A. Smith to the people of Canada and of Manitoba, in the conferences he held with the people in 1869 and 1870, will be regarded as of the highest value and as constituting the most eventful incidents of his life."

Nor can his worthy example as a philanthropist, as seen in his munificent donations for the establishing, or extending, or supporting of some of the worthiest institutions of our country, fail to do great good by suggesting to other men of wealth that there is "a more excellent way" than that of accumulating and hoarding, and by stimulating them to a similar use of what they are but holding in trust for a brief period, which will be followed by their accounting in full to the one great Proprietor.

I have pleasure here in mentioning the name of

another whose friendship I enjoyed for many years in that country. I refer to the Archbishop of St. Boniface (now deceased). After long absence from his diocese, while attending the Ecumenical Council at Rome, the bishop returned a few days only after the death of Scott. Alas! that he did not return a few weeks earlier; then I am fully persuaded that atrocity had not been perpetrated,—aye, and here let me add, what I fully believe, that his presence at St. Boniface during the autumn and winter preceding would have rendered such a rebellion utterly impossible. He was too wise a man, and too good a Christian, to do else than oppose such a movement, and with Bishop Tache at home, and in opposition, Riel's following would have been most insignificant and feeble; a single official wave of his hand would have proved more potent than all the plausibilities and exciting harangues of that mischievous agitator. It has ever seemed to me very unfortunate, also, that the authority with which he entrusted one of his leading ecclesiastics, to exercise during his absence, was not so exercised as to discountenance and suppress the spreading evil. This he might have done very effectually, I judge, at the outset, but failing to do so he assumed a tremendous responsibility.

Commissioner Smith, who, after the murder of Scott, had no further communication with Riel save in seeking permission to return to Canada, was now, though with seeming reluctance on Riel's part, allowed to leave; and what was still more indicative of a power above the tyrant's presidential throne, which he dared not resist, the bishop's request for the release of the prisoners was so far granted that about half their number were liberated, and a promise given that the remainder would be released very shortly. Those then liberated were required, however, to leave the country at once on penalty of being re-imprisoned. Not very long after this partial gaol delivery another slight " rift in the clouds " appeared, which was reported to have been caused by a peculiar flag manœuvre, which seemed at first as difficult of interpretation as was the " handwriting on the wall " in ancient Babylon. The grand old flag that has so long " braved the battle and the breeze," and which had not been permitted to wave in Fort Garry for many months, was suddenly run up in the place of another—a kind of nondescript, a thing of mongrel type, a sort of Franco-Fenian emblem—which rather appropriately represented the double-headed Riel-O'Donohue rule, with their respective proclivities. How was this? Report, not always reliable, but probably correct in this instance, stated that it was owing to the bishop's influence with Riel, and that a very sharp altercation took place between Riel and O'Donohue *re* the displacing of their mongrel flag, which represented disloyalty, by one that should stand for loyalty, whereupon a compromise was thought of and agreed to, that came like oil on the troubled waters. It was on this wise: An additional flag-pole was erected, and so quite near each other the two flags were permitted to float as if in perfect harmony. Some, I presume, will feel like saying, what a pity that compromise was thought of; far better had it been for the country if these two madcaps had fought it out like "Kilkenny cats" to their mutual and complete extermination.

An instance of sudden conversion in the history of the press took place at nearly the same date. *The New Nation*—Riel's organ—suddenly vaulted over from utter disloyalty and the advocacy of annexation to the United States, to the opposite extreme. This also was deemed significant, and regarded as an encouraging "sign of the times," in which, also, it was thought that the hand of one mightier than Riel could be easily traced.

So much for the brightening of our prospects. "Honor to whom honor is due."

CHAPTER X.

AN ENFORCED EXODUS.

I HAVE referred to the fact that Riel's release of one-half of the prisoners was conditioned on their promising to leave the country forthwith. Such an enforced exodus at that inclement season, of those who had been so weakened and made tender by their prison life, and with such exposures and toil as would inevitably be theirs in tramping their way across the prairies for hundreds of miles, was a further manifestation of the tyrant's cruelty. But they deemed the exposure and toil and hardships of the way preferable to continued imprisonment, and accordingly bravely set themselves to face all in order to regain their liberty. Arrangements were made with a half-breed freighter for ponies and sleds and men to care for them, for the conveying of their luggage, such as clothing, blankets and food, and to assist them in a general way in reaching Fort Abercrombie, where they hoped to connect with a line of stages for St. Cloud, the railway terminus.

At a prior date I had written to Dr. Wood: " As to the direction in which we are drifting, I give no opinion. My trust is in God. 'I know whom I have believed,' etc., but with a sick wife, my present surroundings, and the forebodings of many ever ringing in my ears, it will be no marvel to you if I say I have some rather dark hours. But rest assured *I shall not flee—I stay, even if Mrs. Young's failing health renders it a matter of humanity, and so of duty, for me to get her away for medical treatment in the early spring.*"

And now, owing to two facts, a still further breakdown in the health of my wife, and the opinion of her medical adviser that no improvement might be expected unless she could be removed, and that ere long, from these exciting scenes, and also the peril of our son, who had incurred Riel's displeasure by joining the volunteers—we decided, after much prayerful deliberation, on their making an attempt to accompany the released prisoners on their long journey to Toronto. Accordingly, we arranged with the half-breed referred to for two ponies and sleds, which he was to care for on the journey—one sled to be covered in and supplied with buffalo-robes for the exclusive use of Mrs. Young, and the other for my son's use, and for the luggage and food. One hundred dollars for the service was the sum demanded and paid, though the entire outfit was scarcely worth that amount, and before starting we found that barely the ponies and sleds were forthcoming, and that we had to supplement the sum agreed upon by considerable outlays for a cover to the sleigh, and for buffalo-robes and blankets, which he failed to provide. But this was no time for parleying. The journey to Abercrombie, and even to St. Cloud, proved both tedious and severe, owing to the heavy snowfalls and strong winds at first, which were followed by heavy thaws, causing the ice of the rivers and smaller streams to be covered to a considerable depth with water and slush, through which my son and others were compelled to wade, after many a hard day's walking, in order to secure wood for cooking and warming purposes. It was, I doubt not, because of special Divine protection and blessing that they escaped with their lives, and emphatically so, that Mrs. Young, in her enfeebled condition, and notwithstanding that for many nights she had to sleep out in the open without any shelter, and dependent solely for warmth on their camp fire, was enabled to reach her destination in improved health.

Instructions came from the fort on Saturday evening that the party must leave the next morning without fail. This was to us decidedly embarrassing, as we had not completed our preparations; but the inevitable had to be accepted, and so early Sunday morning we set forth, sadly indeed, from our mission home, to journey together a few miles and then to part, we knew not for how long. I accompanied the party some ten or twelve miles to the place of the "barricade," to assist in getting the required "permits" to leave the country, and then a little further on, and out on the prairies we bade each other adieu with feelings not imaginable, my wife and son undertaking a journey that might end disastrously, and I to return to my mission work and now lonely home, not knowing what might await me there.

Thenceforth for a time our mission premises were occupied by a trio, one belonging to the *genus homo* and the other two, I suppose I must believe, belonging elsewhere. When at home my merriest and most chatty companion was "Poll," the parrot, but when journeying to and from my distant appointments "Polly," my trusty roadster, who served me and the Church for eight years, was esteemed of greater value. "Poll parrot" was an inmate of our home for fourteen years, and evidently felt herself quite at home. During the season of my loneliness she was sometimes very amusing, but occasionally she would express what was too much of a felt reality to amuse me just then—as, for example, when associating herself with me, she would repeat in a most lugubrious tone the words "Poor critters," leading me half involuntarily to respond, "Aye, Poll, we are indeed poor critters."

My duties during the next four months, in addition to ordinary mission work, included journeys to Pembina, U.S., each involving a round trip of over 150 miles, where I conducted services in the village and also in the fort, preaching to the officers and men of the United States army—then, and for years, without a chaplain or public religious services. Besides these outpost duties, there were certain miscellaneous activities requiring attention, such as the collecting of timber, lumber, shingles, sand and other essential prerequisites for the "Grace Church" that was then in my mind, but nowhere else. My work of foundation-laying during those times, when faith and patience and fortitude were being tested, was greatly

AN ENFORCED EXODUS. 167

and annoyingly retarded. A quotation from my Journal on May 24th, 1870, will be excused, I trust: "Hired a half-breed to help me in quarrying stone; drove out six miles; hot day, mosquitoes very troublesome; tired from heavy lifting; a fine lot ready for being drawn. Shall I ever regret these tiresome efforts for a church? I cannot think it." And up to date, 1897, I have not.

Soon after the opening of navigation, my friend Governor McTavish, then much weakened and wasted by sickness and worry, and descending rapidly into the valley of shadows, bade Fort Garry a final adieu, hoping to make the voyage across the Atlantic ere his life voyage should terminate; but the two voyages ended well-nigh simultaneously. It was a sad ending of his official life in the country which owed him much, and whose interests he had grieved to see so ruthlessly trampled on during the weeks and months in which he had striven hard, but unsuccessfully, to brace himself against discouragement and a wasting disease.

A change for the better in my circumstances occurred when my wife and son arrived from Toronto on July 13th, 1870. Through the kindness of the late Mr. Hardisty, of the Hudson Bay Company, and Mrs. Hardisty, they were invited to return with them in their comfortable waggons from St. Cloud to Winnipeg. Thus their return journey proved a great improvement on the outgoing journey; and yet it is noteworthy that while the severer trip was without a death, the homeward trip was attended by the death of one of the party.

A young lady from the Saskatchewan District, who had been at the Ladies' College, Hamilton, quietly breathed her last in their waggon as they were moving slowly toward a suitable resting-place. After a brief halt the body, with appropriate funeral solemnities, was laid away to rest in the little cemetery at Sauk Centre. Their arrival at Winnipeg came as a surprise to Rev. George McDougall and myself, just as we were about to retire for the night. They had not written us of their intended coming, fearing that Riel would get possession of the letters and send his guards to prevent their entering the country. It seemed providential that Brother McDougall had remained with me longer than he had intended, as he was now able to accompany his friends to their home, still one thousand miles distant.

On their arrival at the ferry near Fort Garry, my son was ordered by Riel into the fort, which caused us not a little anxiety. However, after a brief catechization he was permitted to join us in our home, and thus we became a reunited family. What a wonderful turn of the wheel that was which brought Riel a prisoner, after his defeat at Batoche, in 1885, under the charge of my son (then acting Brigade-Major), to whom General Middleton gave command of a strong guard, with orders to hold Riel at all hazards, and to take him with as little delay as possible by river and prairie and rail to Regina, where, after a speedy and safe trip, they handed him over to the Mounted Police for safe keeping. In due course this man, who had caused so

AN ENFORCED EXODUS.   169

much suffering in 1869 and 1870, and now again in 1885, was tried before an able judge, and though defended by the ablest advocates his sympathizers could send up from the Province of Quebec, was convicted and condemned to death; and though appeal after appeal to the utmost limit possible was made and investigated, yet all were negatived, and "the law allowed to take its course." Thus ended a life that might have proved a benediction to multitudes, but, ignobly failing therein, proved the very opposite.

In explanation of the military appearance of the accompanying picture, I take the liberty of making brief extracts from a well-written article in the March number of *Massey's Magazine*, by Mr. W. L. Marschamps, on the Winnipeg Field Battery and my son's relation thereto.

"Captain G. H. Young, whose name figures prominently in the battery history, was the first sergeant-major and was subsequently appointed lieutenant. He had been prominent on the side of the loyal party during the Riel troubles of 1869-70, and in 1878 left the battery to organize the 'Winnipeg Troop of Cavalry'—which was deemed necessary on account of disturbances threatened by the western bands of Indians—but rejoined the battery again temporarily for the campaign of 1885. Of these events Captain Young preserves as interesting relics, the rope Thomas Scott was bound with when led to his death by order of Riel in 1870, and the handcuffs he used himself upon Louis Riel fifteen years later when in command of the escort that took him to prison at Regina—both gruesome mementoes framed together upon the same shield. . . . Sir Frederick

Middleton, in his official report upon the campaign, gave special thanks to Major Jarvis and the battery for excellent service, and praised Captain Young for his zeal and ability, as well as for the efficient manner in which he performed his staff duties while acting as Brigade Major, and afterwards when attached for special duty in the conveyance of Riel to Regina upon his capture at Guardupuis Landing."

It may not be uninteresting to many to state that the prisoner, while on board the steamer which conveyed him and his guard from Batoche to Saskatoon, amused himself by composing a sort of historic poem of several verses, from which I select the following:

" Middleton, you are so generous ;
   I owe you for food and good rest ;
 I have found you magnanimous,
   For your treatment is of the best.

" CHORUS.—Honor to the guards who guard me ;
   The North-West sighs to be free.

" Middleton gave me his own coat ;
   And has he not chosen nobly,
 To take care of me on the boat,
   The courteous Captain Young truly.—*Cho.*

" My fate, as a prisoner of war,
   May lead soon to death and the tomb ;
 Oh, mother earth ! is the time far
   When I shall take rest in your womb?"—*Cho.*

The journey across the prairies from Saskatoon to Moose Jaw was made in waggons in very quick time; and thence to Regina by the C.P.R. As is generally

CAPT. G. H. YOUNG.

(By permission of "Masson's Magazine")

known, Riel was guarded in his prison by the Mounted Police until in due time he was tried, condemned and executed.

The following statements of several who had escaped Riel's cruelties may not be deemed inappropriate. I reproduce here a reference which appeared in the *Christian Guardian* of April 13th, 1870:

"THE REV. GEORGE YOUNG.

" Mr. Charles Mair and some others are very free in blaming the Protestant ministers of Red River for preventing, by their peaceful counsels, the warlike purposes of a portion of the settlers who were disposed to march on Fort Garry. But it is probable that they by this act prevented scenes of blood and suffering. We know what the result of the peace policy is. We cannot say what the result of a war policy would have been. We are gratified to know that our missionary, the Rev. George Young, has acquitted himself like a man and a true Christian in the trying ordeal through which he has passed. The *Daily Telegraph* reports a conversation with a reliable gentleman just arrived from Red River—an eyewitness of recent events—in which Mr. Young's name is mentioned with much admiration. The following is the conversation as given by the *Telegraph:*

"' Reporter—We are particularly desirous of having information as to the Rev. Mr. Young. What is he doing, and how is he treated ?

"' Mr. A. Mr. Young told me the night before I left that he was determined to stay at Red River. He has acted as a man throughout the trying times of Red River. When the prisoners were first taken at Schultz's he visited them and won their confidence, and so impressed was Riel with the man's goodness of heart and upright character, that many favors were granted the prisoners through his intervention.

"'Reporter—He was present when Scott was murdered?

"'Mr. A.—Yes. He was sent for at ten o'clock on the night previous to the execution, and remained with Scott till an early hour the next day. Mr. Young was, up to that hour, under the impression that Scott's life would be saved.

"'Reporter—Has he a large congregation?

"'Mr. A.—Not now, since the Canadians left. He has a comfortable two-storey log house near the fort, neatly furnished, and a large room, intended eventually for a drawing-room, is at present used as a place of worship till a church is built. For his building fund he has received subscriptions from people of all denominations in the settlement. He has shown more courage and pluck than any other clergyman of any denomination at Red River.'

"FROM PERSONAL EXPERIENCE.

"The Editor of the Selkirk, Man., *Record*, who was one of Riel's prisoners in 1870, copies the Rev. Dr. Young's graphic letter on the murder of Thomas Scott, and vouches for its exact truthfulness. He adds further:

"'We remember full well when we were surrounded by Riel's treachery and made prisoners, how Mr. Riel addressed his ragged crew in a bombastic speech, and, pointing at us, said, "*Vous ayez les chiens la; traitez les comme les chiens*"—"You have dogs there; treat them like dogs." And right well his rebel banditti carried out his behests. Twenty-six persons were thrown into a room ten feet by twelve, where we were forced to break some of the window panes to prevent suffocation, and there we were for three months, without fire, and snow often lying thick upon us in the morning, blown in through the broken windows; fed upon rotten pemmican or such garbage as the filthy crowd of robbers saw fit to give us. After undergoing such an ordeal it cannot be supposed that we at least can, for a moment, feel an atom of sympathy for the fate of Riel. The account of the fortitude he displayed on the gallows, the full relation of his last words, the gushing admiration of his beauty when laid in his coffin, the ceremonies attendant upon his remains when consigned to the grave, and the crowd who witnessed his interment, go with us for nothing. We do not have one sentiment of admiration or awe for the whole concern; our views of the whole matter are in unison with those of the Rev. Mr. Silcox—or rather of the prophet Jeremiah. The letter of Dr. Young at the present time is opportune. When men's minds through the Dominion are so divided with regard to the justice or injustice of the sentence carried out upon Riel, this letter will go far to show the worthlessness of the creature that people are so agitated about, as we can truly say that it gives a faithful description of Riel, and a true account of the circumstances connected with the murder of Thomas Scott.'"

CHAPTER XI.

A NOTABLE MILITARY EXPEDITION.

THE reference is to the "Red River Expedition" of 1870, necessitated by the rebellion of a portion of the French half-breeds of the Red River Settlement, and decided on by the Governments of England and Canada, in order to the suppression of that revolt, and to secure the transfer of the great North-West Territory to our Dominion. The totality of thought, consultation and correspondence which led up to that decision, and continued throughout the times of preparation and, in fact, until the successful ending of the expedition itself and the establishment of a Canadian Government in that country, was far in excess of what most people have imagined or ever can imagine. For many months prior to the organization of the "expeditionary force," it was the subject of anxious inquiries and the burden of earnest prayers with tens of thousands of others than politicians and statesmen, and those who became ultimately instrumental in its accomplishment. After the loyal people of the North-West became convinced that both Governments had really determined that the transfer, pursuant to the agreement entered into by them with the Hudson Bay Company, should not be prevented by that unjustifiable rebellion which had been so inexcusably encouraged by certain mischievous non-resident agitators, the quieting feeling quickly prevailed that its suppression and the restoration of right rule in their country would surely be brought about in the near future. But while all were quite aware that great difficulties would, in that case, have to be faced and overcome, only a few were competent to form a correct estimate either of their magnitude or their manifoldness. However, after they had been surmounted, and the "consummation devoutly wished for" reached, and the official reports of the costly preparations made by the two Governments had been published, and especially after the exceedingly interesting "official journal" of Colonel Wolseley had been printed and made accessible, all felt that success had been achieved under circumstances extraordinarily embarrassing, and despite the existence of obstacles seemingly well-nigh insurmountable.

To indicate a few of the many preparations needful in order to the collecting and proper equipment and support and transport of such a force, I quote briefly from a communication of General Lindsay, the chief in command, to the Governor-General, bearing date April, 1870: "The expedition is one of considerable difficulty and magnitude, owing to the number of men composing the force, to the character of the country through which they will have to pass, and to the time occupied by the constant changes caused by alternate navigation of lakes and rivers with numerous portages and dangerous rapids and, above all, the distance of Fort Garry from the base of operations." In view of the facts thus summarized, every probable and almost every possible contingency had to be carefully considered and prepared for.

Colonel Wolseley (now General Lord Wolseley), having been appointed to the command under General Lindsay, suggested at the outset that the force should number not less than 1,200 fighting men. These were to consist of seven companies of the First Battalion of the 60th Rifles, 350 strong, besides twenty men of the Royal Artillery with four seven-pounder mountain guns, and twenty men of the Royal Engineers, and a proportionate number as army hospital corps and army service corps, making in all over four hundred regular soldiers, to be associated with a militia force to be taken from the drilled militia regiments of Ontario and Quebec, and enlisted for a two-years' service, if required, making up two battalions of 350 each of non-commissioned officers and men. Detachments were to be left at different points for the protection of reserve stores: One company of the Quebec battalion at Port Arthur, with two of the seven-pounders and a small number of artillerymen in charge of them; also one company of the Ontario battalion at Fort Frances, for a similar purpose, awaiting the return of the regulars from Fort Garry, when they should proceed to their destination; so that the full force was never massed at any one point after leaving Toronto in May. When the expedition

A NOTABLE MILITARY EXPEDITION. 177

passed into Lake Shebandowan, about the middle of July, moving westward, it numbered, all told, 1,431, of whom 92 were officers, 1,051 non-commissioned officers and men, 274 voyageurs and 14 guides. Many of these voyageurs, having been found inefficient, were dropped out and their places filled by Indians and half-breeds, who were more familiar with the route and the work before them.

The distance of their destination from Toronto *via* the route they took was, in round numbers, 1,280 miles, Thunder Bay being about midway. At the start it was supposed that their luggage would be transported without any detention from Collingwood to Port Arthur by the steamers chartered for that service. But a disappointment came in at Sault Ste. Marie, where the men were given a taste of hard work in unloading, storehouse building, road constructing, and portaging their freight for a distance of three miles around the rapids on the Canadian side. This occasioned an annoying delay, which was all the more annoying because it was occasioned by the unneighborly conduct of our Fenian-influenced neighbors of the United States. The steamers did not offend by attempting to pass the canal with soldiers on board, or their arms and other "contraband of war." These were first landed on the Canadian side, after which they steamed over with their freight to the mouth of the canal, but were peremptorily refused entrance, inasmuch as they had brought up a portion of the force, and might, when once through the canal, take them on board again for Port Arthur. And this act was all the more unneighborly and annoying because of its being well known that we had no boat at that moment on Lake Superior by which the troops could be conveyed to Prince Arthur's Landing. Consequently the Canadian Government was compelled to charter, at an exorbitant price, an American steamer. This arrangement was made, I believe, through the intervention of John M. Hamilton, Esq., subsequently judge at Port Arthur.

By the earnest remonstrance of Mr. Thornton, Her Majesty's Minister, the Washington Government was induced to withdraw the obnoxious restriction. Moreover, the Fenian and rowdy element then abounding on the United States side of the river threatened to raid the stores then waiting to be sent forward, necessitating the keeping up of a strong guard for their protection. Had that been attempted by these worthies, it would have proved to many, if not all of them, their last raid. They also reported their purpose of attacking the vessels while passing through Lake Superior, again necessitating the presence of a strong guard on each. But as these contemptible agitators have always shown themselves more ready to solicit funds and utter threats than to assail a force prepared to meet them, no attack was made. By the 21st of June, the whole of the force, with all the stores, had arrived at Port Arthur. Once landed there, the colonel in command had forthwith to face the greatest difficulties and discouragements of the entire route, and to bring into requisition both the "land transport service" and the "boat transport service" which had been provided by the Government, in order to reach Lake Shebandowan, fifty miles distant from Prince Arthur's Landing.

A large number of teams, waggons, teamsters and laborers, to work at road-making or transporting luggage, had been sent forward, and were either organizing for or engaging in their difficult work. The country intervening was one of the very worst through which to construct a passable road. A succession of steep hills of light sand, reaching some eighteen miles, then a nine-mile stretch of a peculiar kind of clay that became miry after rain; then thickly wooded lands, partially burnt over, and then swampy, muskegy portions, which seemed almost bottomless and required to be corduroyed. Miry creeks and rapid rivers, too, had to be bridged that teams and loads might pass over. Within a distance of about forty-four miles were three good-sized rivers, at distances of twenty-two, twenty-seven and thirty-nine miles from Lake Superior. The Kaministiquia required a strong bridge 320 feet long and 18 feet wide; the Matawan, a bridge 216 feet long and 18 feet wide; and the Oskondagee, a bridge 75 feet long, besides several smaller streams. The "boat transport service" consisted of nearly two hundred boats, each capable of carrying two or three tons of freight, besides ten or twelve men. The voyageurs, a large number of whom accompanied the force, were to manage the boats, as well as aid in loading and unloading and portaging, while the soldiers worked with them in rowing, poling, tracking and dragging the boats up the steep inclines of the many portages they had to cross in avoiding the rapids and falls of the different rivers. On the lakes, when the wind was favorable, sails were brought into use; but more frequently oars, four pairs to each boat, were the means of propulsion. The portages were about fifty in all, making a totality of over eight miles of rough and steep points to be traversed, the boats and their loads of arms and ammunition and supplies of all kinds being carried up and over. Officers, men and voyageurs worked together early and late, in rain and shine, despite the incessant and annoying attacks of swarms of mosquitoes, black-flies, sand-flies and deer-flies. The frequent changes of the heavy luggage from boats to waggons and from waggons to boats, which was unavoidable while passing from Lake Superior to Lake Shebandowan, proved very wearing, not alone on clothing, but on men and boats and luggage as well, and caused great delay. For a length of time the entire force was scattered all along the line, from lake to lake, working at making or repairing roads, or pushing forward the boats and luggage as rapidly as possible.

Lake Shebandowan was left by a portion of the expeditionary force on the evening of July 16th, when three brigades of boats, seventeen in all, with two companies of the 60th Rifles, and detachments of the Royal Artillery and the Royal Engineers, each boat carrying two voyageurs and eight or ten officers and soldiers, with provisions for sixty days, besides much miscellaneous luggage, all moved forward toward their destination. From this point the entire force was divided into twenty-one brigades, each consisting of six boats, with their proportion of men and freight. By August 1st all the troops *en route* for Fort Garry had embarked for Fort Frances, distant nearly two hundred miles, and the Lake Shebandowan post was for a time deserted. Fort Frances—so called in honor of the deceased wife of Sir George Simpson, then Governor of the Hudson Bay Company—is but a trading post of that company, and is situated on the Rainy River, three miles below Rainy Lake, its source. It is 242 miles from Lake Superior, 150 from Rat Portage and 410 *via* Lake Winnipeg from Fort Garry. Rainy Lake is about fifty miles long and about thirty or forty wide, connecting with Rainy River, which is eighty miles long, forming, for that distance, the boundary between the United States and Canada, and connecting with the Lake of the Woods.

At Fort Frances a military store for reserve supplies and a hospital were established, and one company of the 1st Battalion of Ontario Rifles left in charge until the return of the regulars, when they were to move on to Fort Garry. Colonel Wolseley and staff, after seeing the regular troops and two battalions of the militia pass on their way to Rat Portage, left on August 10th for the same point. The Lake of the Woods is a body of water seventy-two miles long, and in certain parts nearly as broad, and forms an important link in this chain of magnificent water-stretches: it is divided by three promontories into what really seem three good-sized lakes, the lower part of the last one, for good reason, being fitly described as a "mass of islands." The most westerly point of this lake is known as "The North-west Angle," which, by a direct line across the country, is within 115 miles of Fort Garry; but as no road had been completed across the swampy, muskegy portion thereof, the expedition was compelled to make the long and difficult, and somewhat perilous, detour *via* Rat Portage, Winnipeg River, Lake Winnipeg and Red River, thereby increasing the distance fully 150 miles, and adding greatly to the toil of the already toil-worn men.

Rat Portage, now a prosperous town on the C. P. R., is situated at the point where the waters of the lakes and rivers, through which they had already passed since leaving the head of Lake Shebandowan, plunge over three large and distinct falls into the rapid Winnipeg River, which, after running 163 miles, and making a descent of 350 feet as it dashes over cataracts and sweeps through cascades and rapids and eddies, pours its waters into Lake Winnipeg. In that distance are twenty-five portages, some of which are long and steep and rough. These the force had to cross, dragging their boats and portaging their loads as best they could. Verily these men were not "playing at soldiering." Fort Alexander, which is an important trading post of the Hudson Bay Company, very pleasantly situated on the banks of the Winnipeg River, two miles from its mouth, was reached by Colonel Wolseley and staff in four days and a half from Rat Portage, 161 miles distant. Here they were joined by the Governor of the Hudson Bay Company, now Sir Donald A. Smith, to whom the force was much indebted for guidance and aid, in a variety of ways, until they reached their destination.

I may here pause to remark, that on this expedition no intoxicating liquor was allowed to officers or men. The good results of this practical application of prohibition may be gathered from the following extract from Colonel Wolseley's report: "From first to last there was a total absence of crime, and I may add, of sickness also. Never has any body of men on active service been more cheerful or more healthy. This has been one of the few military expeditions where spirits have formed no part of the daily ration, and where no intoxicating liquor was obtainable. I consider that the above-mentioned happy results are in a great measure to be attributed to this fact—a large ration of tea was issued instead—and I found that the men worked better than I had ever seen soldiers do upon any previous occasion where rum formed part of their daily allowance." I will also add a brief quotation from General Lindsay to the Secretary of State for War: "I join with Colonel Wolseley in laying great stress upon the advantages to health and discipline resulting from the non-issue of a spirit-ration, and I trust that its days are numbered in the British army."

There can be no doubt—and the fact is now well recognized—that total abstinence from intoxicants by men of all professions, and under whatever pressure by fatigue and exposure, will ever be found the best policy.

On August 21st the little army, consisting of the regulars of the 60th Rifles, and the accompanying detachments of Royal Artillery and Royal Engineers, left Fort Alexander in fifty boats for Fort Garry. Lake Winnipeg, the upper part of which they crossed in order to enter the mouth of the Red River, is a larger body of water by far than most people imagine, it being one and a half times larger than our magnificent Lake Ontario, having an area of nine thousand square miles, and a length of two hundred and sixty-four miles, with an average width of thirty-five miles. The mouth of the Red River is forty-five or fifty miles distant from Upper Fort Garry, the "Lower Stone Fort" being about midway. Arriving at this Lower Fort Garry on August 23rd, the force proceeded very cautiously up the river, an advance guard of scouts preceding them on each bank and keeping up communication with those in the boats, thus feeling their way through the rapids, and St. Andrew's parish and Kildonan, until they reached their camping-ground in the evening in the neighborhood of St. John's College and the English cathedral. The intention of Colonel Wolseley was to push on by day-break to Fort Garry, about four miles distant, and so give its occupants a "surprise party." But the night was fearfully stormy, and the morning not less so, the heavy rainfall filling the creeks and sloughs with water, and rendering the roads well-nigh impassable to both man and beast, so that instead of this early march to Fort Garry direct, he deemed it advisable for the main force to keep to their boats and work their way up the river to Point Douglas, while the scouts continued to keep a very close lookout as they moved along the roadside or riverside toward that point. Landing from the boats in the early forenoon, the storm not abating in the least, they were quickly ordered into readiness for marching, through two miles of the stickiest, slipperiest mud they ever saw—to say nothing of its depth—towards the fort, where they were hoping for an opportunity of testing the courage and generalship of Riel, O'Donohue and Lepine and their guards, of whom they had heard so much. Without a single exception, I judge, officers and men were eager for the fray as they neared the fort, and looked for the first time on its walls and bastion and mounted cannon, and called to mind what many loyal subjects of Her Majesty had suffered within those gates. But they were doomed to be disappointed; the fort and guns and ammunition and stores were there, but the vaunting braves were not there—they had vanished.

CHAPTER XII.

THE TRIUMPHAL ENTRY, AND WHAT CAME OF IT.

OUR long longed-for deliverance came, as already intimated, on Wednesday morning, August 24th, 1870. That was to many of us a day never to be forgotten. Up to eight or nine o'clock of that unpleasantly wet morning, Riel, O'Donohue, Lepine, *et al.*, reigned and ruled and terrorized, and feasted and dissipated to their hearts' content, as they had been wont to do for the ten months last past; but at that time, or thereabouts, their revelry received a check by something more tangible than the mystic handwriting on the wall of Belshazzar's palace.

In the early morning a rumor was said to be afloat to the effect that Wolseley and his soldiers were coming up the river with all possible haste; whereupon a few loyal young men, my son among them, unable longer to restrain themselves, set out on horseback to see if it were really so, and, if so, to greet and welcome them as our country's long-looked-for deliverers. On meeting the advance guard, they were instructed to "fall in," and not precede, but accompany them to their destination. An hour or so before the arrival of the troops, a prominent Kildonian, whom I recognized, galloped quickly through the village and on to the fort, and then, after a brief halt, galloped back as if under the pressure of some excitement. His errand, I suppose, was to warn Riel that Wolseley had come, and to advise him and his confederates to make all possible haste in making sure of their escape. Very soon after his disappearance, O'Donohue galloped past, in evident haste, to Dr. Schultz's buildings, where some of the guards had been quartered, and who were then despoiling the stores of their counters and doors and other movables; and then, with equal haste, returned to the fort, followed by those whom he had warned of coming danger, whereupon a general stampede took place of men, mounted and unmounted, all anxious now to leave the fort which they had been so eager to enter ten months before.

The welcome word that the troops had landed, and were marching at that moment through the village toward Fort Garry, was brought me by the late Mr. Benson, of Peterboro', of the department of the voyageurs and boatmen. In a very short time after his decidedly energetic knock at my door, I accomplished the pleasing task of nailing to our bell-tower a strip of white cotton, prepared aforetime, on which appeared in very large letters the word "Welcome," and then the bell, sent us by my friend Mr. Gibbs, of Oshawa, by my aid rang out our doxology with all the vim and emphasis I could command. Very frequently did I ring that bell, both before and after that hour, but never so joyously as then. The bell-ringing over, I proceeded to the fort to welcome in person these new arrivals, making better time in my walk thither, despite the rain and mud, than I ever did before or since.

In attempting a description of the approach of the troops to the fort, and their entrance, I cannot do better than to quote from a telegraphic despatch which Colonel Wolseley forwarded that evening to General Lindsay, the chief in command:

"FORT GARRY, 24th Aug., 1870.

"It rained heavily last night. Landed early this forenoon at Point Douglas, and marched about two miles to this place. Upon reaching the village the inhabitants said Riel was still in the fort and intended resistance. Could see guns mounted on the bastions and gateway; advanced with due precaution, and found that Riel and his *banditti* had just left. Some of his counsellors while escaping were arrested by our skirmishers, and have since been released. Large stores of ammunition, numerous loaded muskets and several field-pieces found. Have been welcomed by the inhabitants as their deliverer from the oppression and plunder to which they have been subjected for months past."

This triumphal entry was not attended by such "pomp and circumstance" as have attended many events recorded in history. The rain fell too fast; our native mud, so celebrated for its adhesiveness and slipperyness, was too abounding, and the loyal people, who were aware of what was about to take place, were too few and too widely scattered for that; but never was a military entry effected, on however large a scale, that was more heartily welcomed than was this, and all the more so as it was not attended by the slaying of any of the brave men who had come so far to secure our country's deliverance.

Wolseley's description of the Fort Garry of 1870 may not be uninteresting, and especially as it, like many a much stronger hold, has vanished from the face of the earth. "The Upper Fort Garry proper is a rectangular building about two hundred yards by eighty-five in extent. The original fort was built in 1840, and enlarged to its present size about 1850. It has a stone wall about ten feet high, with circular bastions pierced for guns. It stands at the angle formed by the junction of the Assiniboine and Red Rivers; the site is pretty, and commands a beautiful view of the prairie on all sides." All that remains of the fort to-day is the high arched gateway, on the top of which cannon were formerly placed. His description of the little village of Winnipeg of 1870, which is to-day a city of over 30,000 inhabitants, may not be out of place: "I should say there are about fifty houses in all; there are a few stores, but grog-shops are the principal feature of the place, and for the last two nights (August 24th and 25th) these saloons have reaped a rich harvest. Voyageurs, half-breeds and Indians, in all stages of drunkenness and quarrelling, made the place a very pandemonium. But few soldiers were drinking to any extent after the first night, and a strong picket, to patrol the village, was kept up every night till everything was quiet." This is indeed a dark picture, and yet not overdrawn in the least, as I sorrowfully observed. It was most distressing for me to see, on that first night especially, so many of these men—soldiers, voyageurs and Indians—who had abstained from all intoxicants so advantageously to themselves and the entire force, now so crazed with the vile stuff they were buying at very high rates from these abominable rum-shops, as to be actually rolling and fighting in the miry mud holes of Winnipeg.

This dreadful revelry, and worse than beastly conduct, was soon, I am happy to say, checked by the exercise of the authority of Colonel Wolseley in command of the troops, and of the Governor of the Hudson Bay Company, Mr. Donald A. Smith, who acted as magistrate by authority of the Government of Assiniboia, which was not yet superseded by the establishment of our Canadian Government. Such scenes contrasted very unfavorably and suggestively with those described by Colonel Wolseley in his official correspondence, in which he comments most favorably on the conduct of the entire force during their journeyings to Fort Garry. In his official reports to the Military Secretary, he says: "The objects of the expedition having been successfully accomplished without loss of life, I take the liberty of again bringing to your notice the conduct of the troops engaged in it. I have no hesitation in saying that the excessive labor so cheerfully endured and so equally shared in by all ranks has never been surpassed in any previous military expedition. The regular troops and militia vied with one another in their enthusiastic anxiety to push forward, each being mutually determined that neither should outdo the other. This praiseworthy rivalry enabled them to make the entire distance of over six hundred miles in about thirteen weeks, carrying with them their provisions for sixty days, two seven-pounder guns with their equipment, a large amount of ammunition and hospital and other stores, all of which had to be carried on their backs over forty-seven portages, making a total distance of about eight miles. When officers set such an example in carrying heavy loads, their men, as might be expected, imitated them unhesitatingly."

Moreover, during those weeks which elapsed between the disembarkation at Prince Arthur's Landing and their marching into Fort Garry it rained on forty-five days, and often for days together their clothing was wet through. But a brief period was given to the "regulars" after their arrival, as a breathing spell; for having marched into Fort Garry on August 24th, the first detachment marched out again to return by the way they came on the 29th; while by September 3rd the entire force of the regular troops had left *en route* for the east, one company only, as an experiment, going *via* the "North-West Angle" of the Lake of the Woods, the others returning *via* the rivers, lakes and portages with which they had already become so familiar. Wolseley left Fort Garry on his return on September 10th, and reached Prince Arthur's Landing on September 22nd. On August 27th, two days before the departure of the 60th Rifles, the brigades of the militia force began to arrive, and ere long we rejoiced in witnessing the safe arrival of so many of our friends from Ontario and Quebec who had loyally, at their country's call, volunteered for this service.

Those who have followed me in this sketch of the expedition must have felt that the expenditure necessarily amounted to an enormous sum; and so it did, and so have all the military expeditions of any size that have continued for any considerable time. The Abyssinian expedition, for example, which resulted in the rescuing of some half-a-dozen British subjects from the tyranny of a barbarous chieftain, and which commanded the sympathy and flattered the vanity of all classes of Englishmen, cost the nation the immense sum of £9,000,000 sterling; while our Red River expedition, organized and prosecuted for the purpose of rescuing thousands of Her Majesty's loyal subjects from an abominable system of terrorism, and the breaking up of a miserable confederacy which at one time threatened us as a Dominion and Empire with the loss of a magnificent stretch of territory, the incalculable importance of which to us is becoming more and more manifest as the years go by, involved the expenditure, we have been told, of about £400,000 sterling, of which England paid the one-fourth.

Some of the many resultant benefits of the incoming of our troops and the deliverance effected thereby, soon appeared in the revival of business in the country and the incoming of a desirable class of settlers. To me, certainly, there came an inspiriting uplift in my work of "foundation laying," which was so greatly retarded during the rebellion.

READJUSTMENTS.

Immediately after the arrival of the troops, and the suppression of the miserable rebellion which had resulted in the scattering and, in many cases, imprisonment of numbers who had attended our ministry, we found ourselves able to push forward our work more vigorously and expeditiously than was practicable during that exciting period. A speedy restoration of good order and of a spirit of hopefulness in the community followed, as also the disposition as well as the opportunity, on the part of many of the scattered ones, to return to our religious services. This, in connection with the arrival of a strong reinforcement of Methodistically-inclined soldiers, resulted in a speedy augmentation of our congregations and membership and of efficient helpers, together with a complete readjustment of our much deranged church appliances. Among the officers, non-commissioned officers and privates of the Ontario battalion especially, were many who came, not merely with kindly greetings and good wishes, but with willing and generous hearts and helping hands to co-operate with me in the work and services of the church. A considerable number of these had been in membership in Ontario, and desired to retain that membership in military as well as in civil life. This sudden influx of earnest workers afforded ground for encouragement and special rejoicing to the small band who had been toiling under great discouragements, ever trying to avoid the "despising of the day of small things," and to look confidently forward to the arrival of great things. Our week-evening as well as our Sabbath services were very soon encouragingly attended, and our Sabbath-school, which had been suspended for a time, owing to the scattering of the

COLONEL KENNEDY.

families during the reign of terror, was reorganized; and by the aid of those who had been teachers in Ontario, and the attendance of a goodly number of men, advanced classes were formed, and thus the school started out forthwith with unwonted vigor upon a career of prosperity which has gone on increasingly ever since; until now Methodism in Winnipeg rejoices over several large and efficient schools, where we were unable for a time to sustain even one.

Among those of the military who rendered special assistance in this good work I mention with peculiar pleasure the names of Messrs. Kennedy, Mulvey and Gardiner. Lieutenant (afterwards Major) Mulvey, was an Episcopalian, but in the largeness of his heart and catholicity of his Christianity he came at once to our aid and rendered valuable service as a teacher of a large Bible-class and assistant superintendent of the school. Captain (afterwards Colonel) Kennedy taught a large class and sought in every way practicable to promote the prosperity of the school and the church. In after years he became registrar, and for several years mayor of the city; continuing, whatever his position, to show a cheerful and unfailing readiness to assist the pastors of the churches in hospital, educational and ecclesiastical matters. The sudden ending of his mortal life in London, England, from that terrible disease, small-pox, after he had passed through the fatigues and perils of the "Soudan campaign," as a staff officer with Sir Garnet Wolseley, brought to me, as to many others, a feeling of personal bereavement. It seemed mysterious to us that ere mid-life had been passed, and while the regiment he had organized in Winnipeg, and of which he was yet the colonel, was fighting bravely the miscreant Riel and his half-breed and Indian following at Batoche, he should have been languishing and dying in a London hospital. But I trust that grace, mercy and peace were made to abound unto him in those dreary hours of suffering, and that when all was over, a merciful and gracious Saviour received his redeemed spirit into rest eternal. The Imperial authorities duly honored him with their wonted consideration in the burial solemnities, and kindly provided by pension for his stricken family. The constancy, wise counsels and liberality of this true and unassuming man, and his untiring co-operation, contributed very largely to the up-building of the Methodist Church and her institutions in Winnipeg.

In November, 1870, telegraphic communication with the great outside world was made to us a possibility, and the first messages sent and received were as follows:

"FORT GARRY, November 20th, 1871.
"*Right Honorable Lord Lisgar, Governor-General of Canada:*

"The first telegraphic message from the heart of the continent may appropriately convey on the part of our people an expression of devout thankfulness to Almighty God for the close of our isolation from the rest of the world. This message announces that close—as its receipt by your Excellency will attest it. The voice of Manitoba, uttered this morning on the banks of the Assiniboine, will be heard in a few hours on the banks of the Ottawa, and we may hope before the day closes that the words of your Excellency's reply, spoken at the capital of the Dominion, will be listened to at Fort Garry. We may now count in hours the work that used to occupy weeks. I congratulate your Excellency on the facility so afforded in the discharge of your high duties, so far

as they concern this Province. I know I can better discharge my own when at any moment we can appeal to your Lordship for advice and assistance.
(Signed) "ADAMS G. ARCHIBALD."

To the above dispatch the following reply was sent:

"*To Lieutenant-Governor Archibald, Winnipeg, Manitoba:*

"I received your message with great satisfaction. The completion of the telegraph line to Fort Garry is an auspicious event. It forms a fresh and most important link between the Eastern Provinces and the North-West, and is a happy augury for the future, inasmuch as it gives proof of the energy with which union, wisely effected of Her Majesty's North American possessions, enables progress and civilization to be advanced in different and far-distant portions of the Dominion. I congratulate the inhabitants of Manitoba on the event, and join heartily in your thanksgiving. (Signed) "LISGAR."

During the autumn and winter of 1870 and 1871, I was enabled to keep up several outside appointments as well as to continue the regular services in town, which were now increased by an evening as well as a morning service on each Sabbath, and a regular mid-week meeting for praise and prayer and exhortation. With this increase of pastoral duties and the looking after the finances of the missionaries of the two districts, and the purchasing and forwarding to them of such supplies as they might order, together with the necessary efforts to secure and bring together the required material for church-building in the spring, my time was fully occupied.

Our intention at first was to build both parsonage and church during the summer of 1869, but owing to the fall of the water in the river a considerable portion of our raft from High Bluff failed to reach us until the spring of 1870, when the rebellion was in full blast, with the results already recorded. Thus it was rendered altogether impracticable for us to proceed with our preparations for building until order was restored by the arrival of the troops. In addition to the heavy timbers of oak and poplar and elm, which we required for the frame of the church, and which did not arrive until the spring of 1870, we had to gather from distant points the lumber required, as there were no mills near by for its manufacture, and this circumstance added greatly to its cost. Owing to this fact we were often obliged to resort to the "pit sawing" process, which at the best is a very laborious, tedious and costly as well as unsatisfactory way of getting lumber, both the quantity and the quality being often far from satisfactory. Much of what was obtainable from the saw-mills in the distance was made of "spruce," and badly sawn, and yet sold at prices which may seem well-nigh incredible to those unfamiliar with such surroundings. Mr. Begg, then and for years a resident, in his history of these times, wrote thus: "In the spring of 1871" (when I was preparing to build), "common lumber sold for $70 a thousand feet, and the best quality of dressed lumber brought $100 a thousand."

This should be borne in mind when we come to the figures which show the expenditures incurred in the erection of these mission premises. To economize where practicable, I occasionally purchased from the freighters the "flat boats" which had been used to bring loads of freight down the river, in order to secure the pine lumber used in their construction, and then broke them up myself to avoid the lumber being injured; thus securing, at less cost than I could otherwise, the material required in certain portions of the building. This was decidedly unpleasant and tiresome work, but, under the circumstances, it was warrantable and not "*infra dig.*" "Necessity is the mother of invention" sometimes, and knows no law. The most annoying part of the business to me, I confess, was to be compelled to note the manifest disposition of many of those conscienceless laborers to whom I was paying from two to two and a half dollars a day, to squander the time which was not theirs in smoking and gossiping with such idling half-breed or Indian cousins as might loiter along, while the "pit saw" and its work stood still. Perhaps my patience did not always bear the strain as well as it should, and yet I don't know that under similar circumstances it would behave differently to-day.

CHAPTER XIII.

THE BUILDING OF OUR FIRST GRACE CHURCH.

We do not always "see ourselves as others see us," and so I will quote again from Mr. Begg's history of those earlier days. Thus he wrote: "On the 10th of April, 1871, the Rev. G. Young commenced building operations in the erection of Grace Church, the reverend gentleman superintending the work himself. Mr. Young was a clergyman specially fitted for establishing a church in a new country; he was not afraid of work, and could have been seen, crow-bar in hand, as busy as any of the workmen on that morning assisting to move the heavy timbers used in the construction of the church." If ever that "first Grace Church" building should be taken down it will be found that the foundations of double oak sills and sleepers which we then placed in position were indeed, as Mr. Begg has stated, "heavy timbers." And yet by means of a somewhat ingenious use of a pair of very large Red River cart wheels and axle, with a strong pole and rope, they were suspended separately by self-help, and then hauled from the bank of the river, where they had been landed, to the site of the building, by my spirited and faithful roadster "Polly."

Thus far I had written when the *Guardian* brought me the following account, given in the correspondence of the Rev. Mr. Morden, of the almost complete destruction of my dear old Grace Church by burning. In the near future, I presume, the foundations I helped to lay and the "heavy timbers" aforesaid will be—at least all that is left of them—unearthed and exposed to view, and then unceremoniously dragged away.

"OLD GRACE CHURCH.

"A recent fire has given passers-by on Main Street, Winnipeg, an opportunity of once more seeing a portion of the old Grace Church, which, with the Wesley Hall block, built during the pastorate of the late Rev. Dr. Rice, in 1881, on the site of the parsonage occupied by the Rev. George Young, D.D., and his successor, Rev. J. F. German, M.A., was destroyed a few weeks ago, and along with it the greater portion of the block adjoining it on the south, into which the church had been enlarged. As the enlargement preserved nothing of the appearance of the original building, probably few of the present citizens were aware that it was still standing; but the fire has left a portion of the old lecture-room exposed to view from Main Street, though from the rear it has all the time been an object of interest to people who were here in the earlier days. The blackened ruins are the last of the old Grace Church that anybody will ever see, as the building is too badly damaged to be repaired. The site is too valuable to be long left vacant, hence, no doubt, soon after the building season opens, the last vestiges of the historic structure will be carted away, and a fine business edifice will occupy the ground with which so much of Methodist history is associated. The building of the old Wesleyan Institute, the forerunner of Wesley College, is still in existence, and not much changed in its outward appearance, though scarcely recognizable in its surroundings. The splendid seven-storey Manitoba Hotel now stands where it stood, and the pioneer home of Methodist teaching is to be seen a few doors farther south on the same side of the street. The Institute cannot be said to have grown into Wesley College, seeing that an interval of some years was allowed to occur, during which Methodism was without an institution of learning, and then Wesley College had to begin at the very bottom to work its way up; yet the efforts of Rev. Dr. Young, Mr. Allan Bowerman, M.A., and the Methodists of Winnipeg, who were associated with them in their early educational struggle, had no unimportant relation to the future of the Church. Like the old Grace Church, the work done remains, though it may not be visible to the crowds who pass along the busy and crowded street.

"Winnipeg, Tuesday, February 16th, 1897."

In the early spring of 1871 we solicited tenders for the carpenter work only, leaving the building of the lecture-room as well as the plastering and painting, etc., for separate contracts. And here we were furnished with evidence of the truth of the old copy we used to write after in early boyhood, "Many men of many minds." Three tenders came in, making very diverse proposals. The first offered to do the work according to specifications for $1,900, the second for $1,200, and the third for $600—quite a difference certainly. Messrs. Gardiner & Dawson secured the

BUILDING OF OUR FIRST GRACE CHURCH. 203

contract and commenced the work forthwith, and right honorably did they complete it, and the lecture-room in the rear as well. Mr. Gardiner, at the time of taking the contract, was still doing duty as one of the Canadian volunteers in Fort Garry; but as the time was near when he was to receive his discharge, the commandant kindly gave permission for him to make the contract and also to commence the work. He and his partner, Mr. Dawson, subsequently erected a goodly number of buildings in the town, one of which was the first Zion Church.

The size of Grace Church was 30 x 50 feet, with eighteen-foot posts, and a steep churchy roof, as will be seen from the accompanying illustration, which first appeared under Dr. Wood's administration, in the *Wesleyan Missionary Notices*. The building was well painted throughout, the roof with fireproof paint; the interior wainscotted with well-seasoned basswood and grained oak. When completed it was voted the neatest little church north of St. Paul. Mr. Begg, from whose book I have already quoted, described it as "a credit to the city, and especially to the Rev. George Young, who labored so assiduously to provide a suitable place of worship for his people." The beautiful stained glass windows, prepared by Mr. McCausland, of Toronto, were specially attractive, and bore the names of the several congregations and Sabbath-schools in Ontario and Quebec whose liberal donations were sent to Mr. (now Senator) Sanford, of Hamilton, and by him applied to the payment of Mr. McCausland's bill. The beautiful circular window

FIRST "GRACE CHURCH," AND MISSION PREMISES.

which was placed in the front of the church and admired by all who saw it, whether pagan or Christian, was donated by Mr. McCausland. It was a question with many who saw the windows ere they were packed, as Dr. Wood wrote me, how they could ever be freighted through to Red River in safety; and yet they were so carefully put up in long narrow cases as to bear all kinds of rough usage, in their transportation by steamer and freight cars and Red River carts, without any serious breakage. After the first Grace Church was found too small, and superseded by the erection of the large block known as "Wesley Hall block," the lower flat of which was for rental as stores and the upper as a large hall for worship (which could accommodate a congregation of eight hundred or more), these windows were transferred to a new church, now known as "Wesley Church."

In the unpacking, arranging and putting up of the windows I received much aid from my two friends Messrs. Kennedy and Ashdown, without which I know not how I could have succeeded. Colonel Kennedy was in earlier days a first-class painter, grainer and letterer, and his work on the doors, wainscotting and desk, as well as in lettering the name which was placed on the front gable, was so artistically executed that not a few wondered, when the building was opened, whose handiwork it was that so beautified our little temple. The name "Grace Church" was given by me to this our first Methodist church in Winnipeg in view of what I deemed its appropriateness. There was so much of "grace," both Divine and human, in the disposing and enabling of so many to aid us in our desire to "arise and build," considered in connection with the anticipation that special prominence would be given by all its ministers to the "exceeding riches of His grace" for whose glory the mission had been established and the building erected, that this name beyond all others seemed most fully to harmonize with our feelings at the time. Two other names competed somewhat with this for a season, but preference was finally given, for the reason just indicated, to the one chosen, and "Zion" and "Wesley" were held over for a more convenient season, and then given to the two Methodist churches next built in the town.

When the building was nearly completed, and the opening services were occupying my thoughts a good deal, I was favored with a friendly call (not the first nor the last by any means) from the Bishop—now Archbishop—of Rupert's Land, one of the most scholarly, liberal-minded, godly bishops of the Anglican Church. As he looked through the building and expressed his admiration, I suggested the following programme of an opening service, prefacing it with the remark that while he would much oblige me, as well as many others, by its acceptance, still that I should not feel myself aggrieved should he deem it inconsistent or unadvisable to do so. The proposal was that he should conduct the opening service and preach the sermon precisely as if in one of his own churches, allowing me the privilege of a fellow-worshipper and a hearer—a proposal, certainly, I would

BUILDING OF OUR FIRST GRACE CHURCH.

not have made to any other minister in all the North-West. The good bishop thanked me in the kindliest manner, and assured me that personally, if circumstances were favorable, it would afford him great pleasure to accede to my wish, but as he was just then preparing to leave for England, and many duties and cares were pressing, he felt that he must beg me to excuse him from undertaking the service. So much for catholicity on both sides.

The 17th of September, 1871, arrived at last, and was indeed a red-letter day in our history in Winnipeg. The pastor preached at 10.30 to a crowded congregation from Eph. ii. 7: "The exceeding riches of His grace." The Rev. M. Robison preached at 2.30, and the pastor occupied the pulpit again in the evening. Many of our friends who had hoped to worship with us in these opening services were prevented by the prevailing "Red River fever," some of them sick nigh unto death, so that we felt compelled to postpone for a season the concert and soiree for which preparations had been made.

The collections at the opening services amounted to $122.12, and the net proceeds of the concert held December 6th, 1871, were $267.50. The amount collected by myself and two or three helpers, among the military in Manitoba, was $1,366.87, and subsequently by Colonel Kennedy and Mr. Ashdown, $250, making in all for Winnipeg and the adjacent neighborhoods $1,616.87, to which if we add the proceeds of Dr. Punshon's lectures and the collections made on the Conference Sunday, and the excess of our Sunday collections over running expenses, we have a total of

$2,100.16, which I think will be considered, in view of the circumstances, as exceedingly gratifying and creditable.

The accompanying kindly references by Dr. Wood in the *Methodist Missionary Notices* of October, 1875, will be appreciated:

"The mission was begun by the Rev. Geo. Young, in 1868. Bro. Young gave up his pastoral charge of the Richmond Street Church and congregation, Toronto, and the Chairmanship of the District, in response to an invitation to begin this new enterprise. True, there had for a long time been Wesleyan missionaries to the west and north of Fort Garry, the former one thousand miles away and the latter five hundred, but these principally labored among the Cree and Stoney Indians. A change in the relationship of these vast territories from the Honorable Hudson Bay Company to the Home Government and the Dominion of Canada, would naturally throw open for immediate settlement the fine lands on the Red River, the Assiniboine, with other attractive sections, now embraced in the Province of Manitoba; to prepare for the movement, Bro. Young began his labors.

"A valuable and commodious site, in what will become a city of large dimensions, was generously presented to the Society by the Honorable Hudson Bay Company, and on this, with indefatigable labor, and for the first two years with a good deal of social inconvenience to his family, he erected Grace Church, with its school-room and comfortable parsonage and out-buildings. The heavy frame of timber between the two buildings bears up a fine-toned bell, given by the Sabbath-school at Oshawa, as the inscription cast upon the external surface points out; this bell pealed

BUILDING OF OUR FIRST GRACE CHURCH. 209

forth its notes of welcome when Colonel Wolseley and the British troops marched into Winnipeg to put down the Riel rebellion.

"In the year just closed there were eight Methodist ministers among the settlers in Manitoba. In the past seven years eight sanctuaries have been built, societies organized, and the ordinances of religion maintained with much regularity. The grasshopper plague has diminished the ability of the people to sustain the cost of these missions, but we are anticipating more fruitful harvests, and a tide of greater prosperity pervading the whole Province. Attached to the sanctuaries and 'preaching places' are two hundred and seventy-nine Church members, with ever increasing congregations."

The large donations from the kind friends in the east, which so greatly encouraged us, and without which we could not have built as we did, nevertheless were much less than they ever imagined, because of the enormous freighting and other charges which came along with them, and which I had to meet ere the goods were delivered. The freight from Canada at that date through the United States, *via* rail and steamer and ox or pony carts, generally ran up into the neighborhood of $10 a hundred, and when the weight of the strong packing-cases had to be added and paid for at the same rate, it can easily be seen why the expenditures were not smaller. The constant worry I experienced over these excessive but unresistable charges was far more wearing on me than all the hard work involved in the handling of the materials until they became a part of the building.

The following, communicated by the late Dr.

Stafford to a paper since then discontinued, will indicate his views of the situation in the times of which I write. At the date of his writing he was the popular pastor of the present costly Grace Church in the City of Winnipeg:

"Very few even of Dr. Young's intimate friends know what an experience he had from his arrival in Winnipeg in the summer of 1868, till the fall of 1871 saw the completion and dedication of Grace Church. A coolness, not arising from indifference on the part of other churches, was overcome by patient endurance and by such prudence as he had manifested before in many fields of labor. There was lack of church accommodation. A room was rented for a time till a parsonage was ready, which did double duty for preaching place and residence. The rebellion broke out. The missionary was simply loyal, and his record throughout these troublous times is so much a matter of history that no mention need be made of it here. After the rebellion, Grace Church, which had been indefinitely delayed, was pushed forward to completion. The share he had in this, bearing the expense personally in a great measure and toiling with his own hands to bring the material and aid in the erection, is known fully only to those who aided him in the task, and have shown the same willingness to speak of the work. A small congregation of faithful friends gathered in and steadily increased in numbers. Still, many journeys had to be undertaken in various directions to establish or visit missions, and the rapid growth of the city, from 1872 to 1876, required every effort to visit newcomers, look after the sick, provide for the poor, and bear a share in the various educational, religious and temperance movements then exciting attention in the new city."

The following report of the soiree already referred

to, which I quote from *The Manitoban*, may not be uninteresting, especially as it gives the names of several ladies and gentlemen who so kindly contributed to our aid in that time of need:

"A very successful soiree, in aid of the building fund of Grace Church (Wesleyan Methodist), Winnipeg, came off on the 6th inst. The church, which is a handsome, comfortable structure, was pretty well filled, there being, probably, 250 persons present. The evening's entertainment opened with tea and cakes in the school-room attached to the church,—the ladies, who were mainly instrumental in getting up this part of the affair, presiding over the refreshment tables; and these, we may observe, were well loaded with eatables of a most appetizing description. This was succeeded by music, and addresses delivered by the Rev. Mr. Young, Rev. John Black, Rev. Professor Bryce, Rev. Mr. Robison, and Mr. Edwards. The choir, with Capt. Kennedy as leader, was composed of Mrs. Young, Mrs. Lusted, Miss McDougall, Miss Linton, Miss Crozen, Miss Chambers, Miss Hodgkiss, Miss Walkley, and Messrs. Ashdown, Emslie, Hackett, Kellond, John Kerr, David Young and George Kerr. Some choice solos, duets, and chorus pieces were rendered in excellent style, especially a couple of solos by Mr. Blanchard.

"In the course of Rev. Mr. Young's remarks, he gave some statistics regarding the mission property, as of much interest. The site for the mission was, he explained, granted by the late Governor McTavish, of the Hudson Bay Company. The total expenditure for all the mission buildings, consisting of Grace Church, the first Zion Church, with school, parsonage, house for the man who takes care of the premises, barn, stable, was $7,318.33. The receipts from all sources amounted to $4,475.56." The deficit was provided for later on.

CHAPTER XIV.

THE FENIAN RAID OF 1871—A FIZZLE AND A FARCE.

VERY soon after that sunny Sabbath when Grace Church No. 1 was opened for worship, we were surprised by the sudden gathering of lowering clouds which seemed to threaten an oncoming storm. Rumors were circulating freely in the community to the effect that General O'Neil, of Fenian notoriety, was again working up a raid on the pocket-books of the confiding Irish servant-girls of the neighboring republic in order to secure funds to enable him to deal a stunning blow to England through Canada, and that by means of a carefully planned invasion of her distant and newly acquired Province of Manitoba. Several circumstances seemed to conspire to promise him a far easier task and much greater success than he had hitherto realized, in this invading business. It has been stated by O'Donohue, Riel's ex-treasurer, that he was assured by the French half-breeds of Manitoba of a friendly reception and their hearty co-operation. Added to this, he was confident of an ample supply of brave men, whose hatred of all that was British was undoubtable, and who had been employed in the construction of railways in the neighboring State of Minnesota, and were just then being discharged. Of arms and ammunition it was reported that he was sure of an abundant supply, inasmuch as the United States Government had kindly returned all that had been seized after their former raids. It was not therefore surprising that this rather over-sanguine individual should be easily persuaded to undertake the liberation of poor oppressed Ireland after this rather circuitous fashion. In a letter from O'Donohue to the Speaker of the House of Commons at Ottawa, dated St. Paul, Minnesota, February 26th, 1875, he stated emphatically that he could prove by documents in his possession "that the so-called Fenian invasion was a misnomer, and that the movement was simply a continuation of the insurrection inaugurated in 1869-70 in the Red River Settlement, and with the same avowed intention and by the same parties." These statements, as was to be expected, were indignantly denied by some who were anxious to save the French half-breeds from this suspicion. A competent authority, however, took very different ground, and assured us that he had carefully investigated the matter, and that he could see no reasonable grounds to doubt but that Riel did fan the movement at the first, and that it was only after the raid had failed, and the valorous O'Neil had for the third time sought and found safety in the arms of a United States marshall, that he came to the conclusion that "discretion was the better part of valor," and so hastened to offer his services and those of his following to Governor Archibald. And in harmony with this view it may be proper to note another fact showing that this miserable movement was no impromptu act.

At the trial of Lepine, in 1874, one of the loyalist ex-prisoners swore that when he was put in prison with the others, Lepine took from him his pocketbook, containing $300 in money, and that after being released he visited that worthy's quiet home, and asked for his money, but was coolly told that he "could not get it," and furthermore that he had better keep quiet, for the Fenians were coming with O'Donohue, and that it would be better for him to say nothing more about it. Well, the Fenians, at least a few of them, came ere long with O'Donohue, but the $300 never to this day returned to the pocket-book of that loyalist.

At about 7 a.m. on the 5th of October, 1871, the raiding force, a mongrel sort of thing, and numerously generalled by O'Neil, Donnelly, Curry and O'Donohue, and I don't know how many others, with about thirty-five "rank and file," crossed the boundary and attacked, and did really capture, the undefended trading-post of the Hudson Bay Company, which was commonly known as a fort. The *modus operandi* in this wonderful achievement will be best seen from the sworn testimony of Mr. Watt, who was then in charge of that post:

"W. H. Watt, sworn and examined by the Attorney-General—

"'Am in charge of the Hudson Bay Company's post at Pembina. About half-past seven on the morning of the 5th of October, a party of armed men took

THE FENIAN RAID.

possession of the place in the name of the Provisional Government of Red River. I was taken prisoner while in bed and held until our release by the American troops between two and three o'clock p.m. The men who took the place were armed with rifles and bayonets, and some with side arms. Prisoner was one of them; did not know any in command of the party till next morning. Saw O'Donohue, O'Neil, Curry and Donnelly there. They were called generals, colonels and commanders-in-chief. (Laughter.) The Hudson Bay Company's fort is on British territory. While I was prisoner there were acts of robbery committed. A great quantity of provisions was taken out of the store and loaded into waggons in the square of the fort. They plundered the place while there and made prisoners of the people of the fort. They placed sentries on the gates and made themselves perfect masters of the place. Witness then narrated the arrival of the United States troops, and said that when Curry and O'Neil heard of it, the former said that the waggons with the plunder must be got out. That was Curry's last order before he fled with the rest. The rank and file were already (continued witness) nearly all gone—some on horseback and some on foot—prisoner along with the rest. They scattered in all directions. While the Fenians were in the fort the commands were given in English, by all the four officers; counted thirty-seven armed men inside the square at one time. Saw the witnesses brought in prisoners by the Fenians, but not prisoner at the bar. He was with the body of armed men who took the fort, and armed like them. While the armed men held possession of the fort, their officers told me they had taken it in the name of the Provisional Government of Red River, and that they were going to take Fort Garry also. The Fenians crossed the river after they fled from the troops. When the Fenians were apprised by the horsemen that the United States troops were upon them, I looked into the square of the fort and saw a great commotion among the Fenians. Each one ran hither and thither—some escaping by one gate and some by another. I soon found myself without a guard. All the generals and colonels had skedaddled except one man.'

"To the Attorney-General—

"'That one man was O'Donohue.'"

The reason of this friendly intervention of the United States troops has been given by the United States Consul, the late Consul Taylor, in the following statement: The consul says that he obtained information early in September, 1871, of the probability of a Fenian attack upon Manitoba, which he communicated to Governor Archibald and his ministers, and received an assurance that neither the Manitoba authorities nor the Canadian Government would object to a movement of American troops across the international boundary for the suppression of a violation by Fenians of the Neutrality Laws of the United States. On the 11th of September a full statement of the situation was forwarded to Washington. On the 19th of September orders were sent to Colonel Wheaton to make the proposed armed intervention, which he gallantly executed, and under date of October 5th was able to communicate the capture. The 100,000 more cut-throats who were to follow O'Neil and company never came.

For the service to both countries Colonel Wheaton and Consul Taylor received through the Department of State, by Sir Edward Thornton, the thanks of the British Government.

Major Mulvey, then the editor of *The Manitoba Liberal*, was in command of a company of volunteers who went to the front to repel the invaders, and thus wrote concerning the raid:

"In our last issue we stated that a Fenian invasion of the Province had taken place. Upon the strength of the Governor's proclamation we made the assertion. But at the time of its issue, men in a position to know positively asserted that it was no Fenian raid —that it was nothing more or less than a projected rising of the supporters and friends of the old Provisional Government. Men who had carefully watched the conduct of Riel in this Province since last Christmas, and who had heard his seditious harangues outside of chapel doors on Sundays, knew better what was in the wind, and notified the authorities accordingly, who treated the information with indifference. Now it is ascertained that O'Donohue was aided and abetted by Riel and his friends in this Province, and was told time and again that the French population in this country were ready to take up arms on his side. The fort was taken possession of, not in the name of the Fenians or Irish Republic, but in the name of the Provisional Government of Red River.

"VOLUNTEERING AMONG THE ENGLISH.

"As soon as the Governor's proclamation was issued calling upon all classes and political parties to 'rally around the flag,' a public meeting was called in Winnipeg and largely attended. By six o'clock the following morning nearly three hundred men from

THE COMMANDANT ADDRESSING THE RECRUITS AT FORT GARRY.

Winnipeg alone were enrolled, marched to the Government House and their services proffered. Before the sun set the following day the men who at first declared they would never again shoulder a musket were on their way knee deep in mud.

"DEPARTURE FOR PEMBINA.

"On Friday, at 1.30 p.m., an order was issued to the Winnipeg company to assemble for parade, and inside of an hour they paraded ninety strong. At three o'clock they were ordered to equip themselves and to be ready to march at four. Although there is considerable difficulty in providing men with munitions of war and necessaries for the route, yet through the exertions of Major Irvine and Major Peebles and the company officers, they were equipped and ready before the appointed time.

"Many of our citizens closed their places of business, amongst whom may be mentioned Davison & Miller, of the Manitoba Hotel, and Dawson & Gardiner, contractors; in fact, almost every man of the company left at great personal sacrifice. No inducements could prevail on Mr. Farquarson and Mr. Armstrong, two aged men, to remain behind.

"At five o'clock the little expedition, numbering two hundred men and twenty teams, moved off from the fort across the Assiniboine.

"In the pelting rain the men had to stand for nearly three hours waiting for the whole to cross that abominable ferry. The Winnipeggers had only fifty-five blankets for eighty-eight men, and these were wringing wet, so that the comfort of the first night's campaigning was not very agreeable. But the men were in the best of spirits. The roads were nearly impassable, and we had scarcely marched two miles ere the teams got off the road, so we threw out a line of skirmishers to find it, and when they came to a ditch they shouted out to the driver 'right' or 'left,' as they were unacquainted with the teaming phraseology of 'gee' and 'haw.' We succeeded in making five miles of as miserable a march as ever soldiers made, when the sound of the bugle told us that we were to pitch tents for the night.

"On the wet ground, covered by a single wet blanket, the gentlemen soldiery of Winnipeg spent the first night."

I deemed it my duty to join them next morning, my son having done so already.

"The little expedition halted the following day at Stinking River for some five or six hours. Here we ascertained that O'Donohue was taken prisoner and released again. The men began to doubt the probabilities of getting a chance at the Fenians this time, and this threw them into a state of bad humor. After travelling the following day to Larocque's in St. Agathe, where we remained over night, we retraced our steps and arrived home on Tuesday afternoon after a five days' campaign, sorely disappointed at not seeing the face of a Fenian.

" FRENCH VOLUNTEERING.

" Before leaving the fort and while on our way we heard a great deal about the French volunteers. Well, we could not find a man who saw a French volunteer on the way, further than a few men under that well-tried and sterling loyalist Wm. Dease, and a few scouts from Winnipeg under Captain Plainval.

"On the 3rd of October the proclamation was issued; by next day it was nobly responded to by the English; and on the eighth, when, as far as is known, the danger was entirely past and not a Fenian remained in the country, the French offered their services—what patriotism!

"Before the men dispersed, they halted at the parsonage, and gave three hearty cheers for the Rev. George Young, their worthy chaplain, who, through commendable self-denial, accompanied the little expedition from the start, and who preached on Sunday a most eloquent sermon. Too much praise cannot be given the reverend gentleman, for, if there be one man who has acted a soldierly, manly part in the affairs of this country, that man is well-known to be the Rev. George Young."

In the midst of these excitements, a correspondence of the Lieutenant-Governor with Priest Ritchot, of St. Norbert, seems worthy of a place in these records, inasmuch as it throws some light, by obvious implications at least, upon matters under review:

"ST. BONIFACE, 5th October, 1871.

"*To His Excellency the Lieutenant-Governor:*

"May it please your Excellency,—In the conversation which I had the honor to hold with you yesterday we both agreed that it was proper to secure the influence of Mr. Riel to direct his compatriots in the present state of affairs, and prevent them taking a false course.

"Upon deep reflection, I take the liberty of remarking to your Excellency that inasmuch as Mr. Riel is in such a position that he cannot act openly as a citizen, I do not believe that he should place himself at their head unless he had some guarantee that his proceedings would be looked upon with favor by your Excellency.

"Consequently, I beg leave to ask of you some

assurance which will shelter him from any legal proceeding, at least for the present (*pour la circonstance actuelle*).

(Signed) " N. J. RITCHOT.

" P.S.—Being about to leave immediately for my parish, I beg to request your Excellency will kindly give an answer to the bearer, who will at once bring it to me. (Signed) " N. J. R."

" GOVERNMENT HOUSE, October 5th, 1871.

" REVEREND SIR,—Your note has just reached me; you speak of the difficulties which might impede any action of Mr. Riel in coming forward to use his influence with his fellow-citizens to rally to the support of the Crown in the present emergency.

" Should Mr. Riel come forward as suggested, he need be under no apprehension that his liberty shall be interfered with in any way; to use your own language, ' *pour la circonstance actuelle.*'

" It is hardly necessary for me to add that the co-operation of the French half-breeds and their leaders in the support of the Crown, under present circumstances, will be very welcome, and cannot be looked upon otherwise than as *entitling them to most favorable consideration.*

" Let me add that in giving you this assurance with promptitude, I feel myself entitled to be met in the same spirit.

" The sooner the French half-breeds assume the attitude in question, the more graceful will be their action and the more favorable their influence.

" I have the honor to be, Reverend Sir,
" Yours truly,
(Signed)   " H. G. ARCHIBALD,
" *Lieutenant-Governor.*

" Rev. Pere Ritchot,
"St. Norbert."

Messrs. Riel, Lepine and Parenteau wrote to Governor Archibald as follows:

"St. Vital, 7th October, 1871.

"May it please your Excellency,—We have the honor of informing you that we highly appreciate what your Excellency has been pleased to communicate to Rev. Mr. Ritchot, in order that we might be better able to assist the people to answer your appeal. As several trustworthy persons have been requested to inform you, the answer of the Metis has been that of faithful subjects. Several companies have already been organized, and others are in process of formation.

"Your Excellency may rest assured that, without being enthusiastic, we have been devoted.

"So long as our services will be required you may rely on us.

"We have the honor to be, etc., etc., ...

(Signed) "Louis Riel.
"A. D. Lepine.
"P. Parenteau.

"To the Honorable G. Archibald, Lieutenant-Governor of Manitoba."

To this the Governor caused the following answer to be made:

"Gentlemen,—I have it in command from His Excellency the Lieutenant-Governor to acknowledge the receipt of your note of this morning, assuring His Excellency of the hearty response of the Metis to the appeal made to them in His Excellency's proclamation.

"You may say to the people, on whose behalf you write, that His Excellency is much gratified to receive the assurance which he anticipated in his communication with the Rev. Pere Ritchot, and which your letter conveys, and that he will take the earliest opportunity to transmit to His Excellency the Governor-General this evidence of the loyalty and good faith of the Metis of Manitoba.

"His Excellency will be pleased to be furnished, as soon as possible, with a nominal list of the persons in each parish who desire to enroll in active service in the present emergency.

"His Excellency will rely upon their readiness to come forward the moment they receive notice.

"I have the honor to be, gentlemen,
"Your obedient servant,
(Signed) "W. F. BUCHANAN,
"*Acting Private Secretary.*

"To MM. L. Riel, A. D. Lepine, Pierre Parenteau."

The day following the date of this last letter an incident transpired which called forth a good deal of sharp criticism. I quote again from the *Liberal:*

"THE GOVERNOR AND RIEL.

"We briefly referred in our last to the fact that on Sunday afternoon, the 8th inst., the Lieutenant-Governor was sent for by Louis Riel, who, with about one hundred of a gang who aided him in his villainies of 1869 and 1870, took up a position on the east side of the Red River, opposite Fort Garry. The summons was duly and expeditiously answered by His Honor's appearance among them, and in the blaze of day, and within a gunshot of the spot where Thomas Scott was murdered, the Queen's representative shook hands with the murderer. It will be seen from other columns that Riel, on hearing of O'Donohue's failure at Pembina, decided, instead of going to join that worthy, as was his original intention, on offering his services to Mr. Archibald. The acceptance of his services was in entire accordance with the Lieutenant-Governor's policy. We cannot find language to express the deep humiliation created in the minds of the people who witnessed or heard of this climax of insult to loyal men in the Province."

The results of this correspondence and hand-shaking were such as might have been anticipated. These well-mounted Metis, headed by Riel and Lepine, now volunteered their services as scouts to guard the frontier against further raids that might be attempted, of which there was not the remotest danger. Their offer was made for a widely different purpose; it was, however, accepted forthwith (shall I say by the unsuspecting Governor?), and as soon as duly supplied with provisions, etc., etc., they left to go where they pleased and enjoy themselves as they well knew how to do. A detachment of this somewhat belated scouting force paid a visit to a small settlement of loyal Protestants at Boyne River, sixty miles distant from Winnipeg, where I was accustomed to hold services and do pastoral work. The object of their visit seemed to the settlers to be to terrorize, in order to induce them to promise to give up their "claims" in this pleasant and well-wooded locality and go elsewhere in quest of homes. They were told that they were authorized to stake out claims for themselves in that section, and that they would return before long and build their houses on them. At my next visit to the settlement, when this was reported to me, I advised the people, who were considerably disturbed by this visit from the "scouts," to rest quietly and await further developments. As I was returning across the forty-mile stretch of unoccupied prairie, I saw in the distance quite a number of these mounted volunteers who where provisioned to guard the frontier, but who, having tired, I suppose, of their hardships and privations in soldiering, were then "homeward bound." They never returned to disturb the Boyne River settlers, and it was well for themselves that they did not.

Thus ended the farce that followed the fizzle, and yet the two combined occasioned another "call to arms" in Ontario, and another heavy expenditure to the Dominion Government, in the sending out of a second expedition under Captain Scott to reinforce the company in Fort Garry, and so to be the better prepared to deal with either raiders or insurrectionists that might require attention. This expedition of two hundred men left Collingwood on the 21st of October, 1871, reached Port Arthur on the 24th, and arrived within twelve miles of the North-West Angle of the Lake of the Woods on the 12th of November, where they were compelled to leave their boats and march across the newly formed ice to the road leading to Fort Garry, and proceeding thence, in intensely cold weather, arrived at the fort on November 18th— a marvellous march certainly under such circumstances—110 miles in a little over four days. The journey from Collingwood to Winnipeg was performed in eighteen days.

THE FENIAN INVASION OF MANITOBA, IN TWELVE TABLEAUX.

(From the "Canadian Illustrated News," Nov. 4, 1871.)

In January, 1872, Riel and Lepine consented to retire from Manitoba, and of course cease agitating the people for a time, in consideration of receiving each the sum of $1,600, while provision was to be made for their families for a period of not less than a year. They had found it so profitable to agitate and cause an insurrection, and then to seize the fort and its contents of goods and food, and liquors and money, and then to imprison many of their former neighbors and confiscate horses, sleighs and robes, and even money, in 1869 and '70, that now in 1872 they seemed to think that their demands for almost any sum, as an inducement to retire, should at once be met.

So much for the "peace at any price policy." And what seems almost incredible, this was being done in the same Dominion in which and while a reward of $5,000 was being offered for their arrest; a portion of which, if not all, was paid subsequently to those who took part in the arrest of parties implicated to some extent in the murder of Scott. In his restless ambition for position and power, Riel returned to Manitoba and was elected by these loyal (?) Metis to represent Provencher in the Dominion Parliament.

On the 30th of March, 1874, he appeared at Ottawa, and, signing the roll of the House, quickly vanished, and on the 16th of April he was duly and deservedly expelled.

A revelation, both encouraging and admonitory, followed this contemptible fizzle:

First.—The loyalty, bravery and reliability of the Protestant sections of the population were revealed as never before.

Second.—There was also a fuller disclosure of the extent to which the Metis were controlled by unpatriotic influences than many had hitherto suspected.

Third.—That the real motive of those who combined to bring about this raid and the consequent disturbance, was not so much conquest as intimidation, in order to an amnesty for Riel and Lepine and their coadjutors in rebellion and crime, and for "better terms" for the French half-breed element. In this I doubt not they acted under dictation. The volunteers, whether Canadians or natives, who rallied around the old flag and followed it to meet the foe, required no urging from their clergy to induce them to take up arms for the defence of the country, and certainly they received no instructions to clamor for "better terms" before consenting to do so. Had all pursued a similar course, a better state of things would have speedily obtained throughout the country.

CHAPTER XV.

THE FIRST MANITOBA MISSIONARY CONFERENCE.

IN accordance with our request, the Board of Missions appointed a deputation to visit Winnipeg and meet, for consultation, etc., the missionaries from the interior, who should be called together for that purpose. On the 16th of February, 1872, I received the following telegram from the Mission Rooms, Toronto:

"Summon missionaries of both Districts to meet deputation, Punshon, Wood and Macdonald, August first, at Winnipeg.
(Signed) "WOOD AND TAYLOR."

Of course I did as bid, and the brethren were not disobedient to the authoritative summons. Of the deputation, Dr. Wood was the first to arrive, and a most trying trip for one of his age he had from Moorehead to Winnipeg by stage. Two days and two nights it took, amid dust and mosquitoes, for the old tumble-down rig to bring its passengers through. The good doctor arrived at our parsonage at midnight very much exhausted, and next day wired Dr. Punshon and Mr. Macdonald at Moorehead to be sure and

FIRST MANITOBA MISSIONARY CONFERENCE.

connect with the steamer on Red River and not come by stage. And it was well for them that they heeded his warning.

As the missionaries and the other members had not yet arrived, Dr. Wood, after resting for a few days, accompanied me on a trip to Portage la Prairie, High Bluff and Poplar Point, which involved a drive of 120 miles, in order that he might personally look over the ground and judge of the present condition of the work and its future prospects. Services were held at several points, and the doctor returned, pleased with the country and the people he had met and the prospects.

Soon after our return the missionaries from the regions beyond reported at the parsonage, as did the remainder of the deputation. All were in advance of the time appointed in the summons sent us over the wires, and therefore, instead of August first, our conference opened on July 26th, 1872, in our first Grace Church. During the few days following, ere the brethren separated, we enjoyed the great privilege of hearing two of Dr. Punshon's inimitable lectures, which were well attended and highly appreciated by the people; he also preached on the Sabbath in the morning, Dr. Wood preaching in the evening. By all it was accounted a rare privilege indeed to hear these lectures and discourses from such honored and gifted ministers.

For a description of the conference and its work I cannot do better than quote the report presented to the Board of Missions by the deputation on their return to Ontario. The report was presented at the annual meeting of the Board, held on this occasion in the town of Brockville, and was as follows:

"REPORT OF THE DEPUTATION APPOINTED TO VISIT MANITOBA.

"By the President's direction, the missionaries in the Red River and Saskatchewan Districts were summoned to meet the deputation at Winnipeg on the 1st of August. Through the good providence of God the whole of the brethren were in Winnipeg—with the exception of J. Sinclair, native teacher at Oxford House—on Tuesday, the 23rd of July. One party had been travelling twenty-five days, and another twenty days. These were from the Saskatchewan District, who, having their horses and travelling equipage, preferred camping on the prairie, in the vicinity of the town, during the whole of their stay, choosing the air and freedom of such a home before the best accommodation they could have in the houses of friends who would willingly have received them as guests for their works' sake.

"The deputation being completed on the 25th, by the arrival of Messrs. Punshon and Macdonald, the following are the names of the members who constituted the meeting, which began its conversations upon the state of the work of God in this vast country, on the morning of July 26th, 1872, in the Wesleyan Church, Winnipeg, Province of Manitoba:

"The Rev. W. Morley Punshon, LL.D., President of the Conference; Rev. E. Wood, D.D., Secretary of the Missionary Society; and J. Macdonald, Esq., Treasurer of the Society, deputation from the Committee and Conference. Rev. George Young, Winnipeg, Chairman of the Red River District; Rev. George McDougall,

Edmonton House, Chairman of the Saskatchewan District; Rev. Michael Fawcett, High Bluff; Rev. Matthew Robison, High Bluff; Rev. Henry B. Steinhauer, White Fish Lake; Rev. Peter Campbell, Victoria; Rev. John McDougall, Woodville; Rev. E. R. Young, Rossville, Norway House; Rev. A. Bowerman, Winnipeg. A candidate for the ministry, George Edwards, employed by the Chairman, was also present.

"After religious exercises the first question which engaged the attention of the meeting was the spiritual state of the several missions. The deputation heard, with pleasure and gratitude to Almighty God, that at all the stations occupied by the Society the 'signs' of true evangelical prosperity exist. This they attribute, in connection with the Holy Spirit's influence, to the devotedness of the missionaries to their high calling, other testimony than their own being given that they pay no more attention to the secularities of life than what they are compelled to do from a sense of duty in providing for the wants of themselves and families, and presenting an example of industry in their domestic arrangements for the converted Indians to imitate.

"The congregations in Winnipeg vary much, as the people arrive and depart to other locations. The building will easily accommodate 250; at times the place is crowded with a devout assemblage. The means of grace peculiar to us as a Church have been established by Mr. Young, and are much appreciated by the more spiritually minded. Up to the time of the visit of the deputation, the only weekevening service among Protestants in the town was held by Mr. Young. Besides supplying Winnipeg, the missionary has extended his visits occasionally to a distance of sixty miles—hence Boyne River, Sturgeon Creek, Headingly, and Victoria Settlement are places where he has been welcomed as a minister of Christ. Now that an assistant has been given him, and the population at these appointments being rapidly on the increase, the prospects of usefulness are very cheering.

"The High Bluff Mission was visited, embracing Poplar Point and Portage la Prairie Mr. Robison's labors here have been greatly blessed. The people highly appreciate the ordinances established among them. In addition to the two churches already built, preparations are being made for one at Gowler's and another at the Portage. Mr. Fawcett has entered upon his labors here in a cheerful and self-denying spirit. The deputation regret the inconveniences he and his truly devoted wife had to endure for the want of household accommodation. Should success attend the efforts made for the erection of a parsonage, or the hiring for the time being of a house to shelter themselves, we may anticipate continued prosperity in the discharge of his ministerial duties, and of those associated with him in this truly missionary field.

"Settlements are forming beyond the Portage, which have already been visited by the Society's missionaries, and as these extend and increase in numbers they should secure our practical sympathies by sending to them additional laborers.

"The statements of the Rev. E. R. Young respecting Norway House Mission were full of encouragement. Far away from the many allurements to evil which beset other Indian communities—especially in Ontario —these converts display a consistency of deportment, attention to the means of grace, and practical remembrance of religious instruction, which result in an intelligent growth in Christian knowledge and experience. Beside visiting Oxford House, and administering the ordinances to the members of the Church there, which is more than two hundred miles northeast of his own mission, his visits to Nelson and Berens Rivers have been attended with great success. At one time he met at Nelson River 250 Indians: of these 110 have been baptized, seventy of whom were adults. Several of these were at Winnipeg, and sought an interview with the deputation for the purpose of entreating them to send a teacher to their people. Two of them belonged to bands five hundred miles still farther north. The whole region is purely a fur-bearing country; the people are unsettled and migratory in their habits, and yet hundreds of them are calling for that knowledge which can only be imparted by the Bible and the servants of God. The most feasible plan for supplying these wants, as it appeared to the deputation, would be to employ one or more native agencies, and allow the missionaries at Rossville to direct their labors, and administer the ordinances of religion at their gatherings each year for purposes of trade. The months of April and May, and August and September, are the best times of the year for meeting large numbers of Indians at Nelson River and other places. Norway House is 340 miles north of Fort Garry; and Berens River, where the Hudson Bay Company have a trading post, a little more than half way to the Rossville Mission, being on the eastern shores of Lake Winnipeg, 180 miles distant. Connected with this is Pigeon River, the residence of a small band, ten miles by water and six by land from Berens River. There are 250 Indians, all accessible to your missionary, sixty-eight of whom have given in their names for Church membership, and ten of whom Mr. E. R. Young pronounces to be soundly converted to God. The land in this locality is very good for settlement, and the fisheries inexhaustible. As Rossville is becoming overcrowded, and the soil there for agricultural purposes only limited, if the Society establish a substantial mission at Berens River, having the same spiritual advantages which are enjoyed at Rossville, no doubt a number of Indian families would make Berens River their home, and thereby constitute a growing, healthy mission station, midway between Red River and Norway House. The Indian will leave his hunting and trapping and hesitate not to travel 150 miles, if necessary, to attend sacramental service: and that, too, without any reliance upon ritualistic merit, but purely from the love of Christ in his heart, and obedience to the law of his Divine Master. It was reported to the deputation that for the want of ordinances once enjoyed at a mission station five hundred miles away from Rossville—transferred some years since by the parent Society to another branch of the Church of Christ—thirty-five members had removed the whole of this distance to Rossville for no other reason than that they might enjoy class and prayer-meetings, in addition to what they called a different ministry, without which they declared they could not live.

"From the long period of time Oxford House has been left without an ordained missionary, there are not the same gratifying features of life and vigor existing there which we all earnestly desire. In the judgment of the deputation, this post should immediately receive the appointment of a minister in full standing. Whilst approving of the appointment, by Mr. E. R. Young, of the excellent brother now at Berens River, yet the authorities of the Church would act quite in accordance with the importance of the work if they appointed an ordained man to take charge of this station, and for which, in addition to the free-will offerings of generous and esteemed friends, it is hoped the committee will make suitable appropriations.

"Lengthy conversations were held upon the religious state of the work at Edmonton House, Woodville, Victoria, and White Fish Lake—Saskatchewan District—from which the deputation received favorable impressions of the present healthy and prosperous condition of all the missions. The two day-schools have received much support from the Hon. Hudson Bay Company's officers, and the settlers who have located where these are in operation. The deputation are convinced that the brethren there are truly devoted to their work; and whilst they have been preserved amidst many dangers in their frequent and laborious journey, God has graciously owned their testimony of the truth as it is in Jesus, so that the Cree and the Stoney join their songs of praise for converting grace with their more favored brethren, 'the pale faces.' The deputation commend to the committee a new post selected by the Chairman, of the Bow River, as a most favorable point to operate among the Blackfeet, whose disposition to receive a missionary is now very earnest, but whose wants cannot be fully met until another missionary is sent to that District, which they hope will not fail to be done early in the ensuing spring.

"Upon the subject of education, the deputation desire to draw the attention of the Church to the desirableness of an early effort to establish a college at Winnipeg. Mr. Macdonald was requested to name this to Governor Smith, from whom he received the assurance that if the Wesleyan Church entered into this enterprise the Hudson Bay Company would provide gratuitously sufficient land for this purpose. A day-school should also be established at Oxford House, Woodville, and Edmonton House.

"The deputation feel much indebted to Governor Smith for the great courtesy and hospitality which they received from him during their stay at Fort

Garry, and for the interest which he and other officers of the company showed, especially in the trouble and expense incurred in fitting up accommodations in their commodious new warehouse for Dr. Punshon's lecture on the evening of the 30th of July. This large and respectable assemblage was presided over by His Excellency Governor Archibald, whose attendance at the ordination service, in addition to this, evinced a catholicity of spirit encouraging to all laborers in the Church of Christ. The proceeds of this lecture, and one delivered in the Wesleyan Church on the previous Friday evening, when Jas. W. Taylor, Esq., American Consul, presided, were generously presented by the President toward the liquidation of the debt upon our church and parsonage. The religious services excited much interest in the settlement, and were seasons of profit and delight.

"In conclusion, the deputation congratulate the committee on having brethren in these Districts of whom gentlemen in high authority speak with great respect, and hold them in much esteem as Christian ministers; and for them and their work they bespeak a continued manifestation of that confidence, sympathy, and liberality which have hitherto marked all their dealings with those new and distant missions. Considering the vast extent of their work, their appeals for a few extra grants are not very large, to which it is hoped a cheerful response will be given. They would also press upon the attention of the committee the following resolution, being deeply convinced that great good will result from its being practically, and at an early day, complied with:

"Moved by the Rev. George Young, seconded by the Rev. George McDougall, 'That it is the unanimous judgment of this meeting that the remoter missions of these Districts should be visited by an officer of the Society, or a senior member of the Conference; and we earnestly solicit the General Committee to make arrangements for this desirable object as early as practicable.'

"In the accomplishment of so long a journey, the deputation would gratefully acknowledge their indebtedness to the goodness of God in preserving them from harm. Two of them experienced a remarkable deliverance from imminent peril on the waters of Lake Superior, in interposition of Divine mercy to many others embarked in the same steamer with Messrs. Punshon and Macdonald, which resulted in voluntary thank-offerings that will greatly assist in the erection of Providence Church in Prince Arthur's Landing, commemorative of their marvellous rescue, and their heartfelt gratitude to Almighty God."

I deem it appropriate to insert here the concluding paragraph in the Minutes of the Conference which was taken by myself as Secretary:

"The business for which the missionaries had been called together having been finished, appropriate and affectionate farewell addresses and counsels were given by the lay Treasurer, Mr. Macdonald; the Rev. Dr. Wood and President Punshon, after which the 539th hymn was sung and the Divine blessing invoked upon the missions throughout, as well as upon the missionaries in their long, tiresome and perilous journeys, and their flocks in the distance. The meeting closed with the benediction from the President."

The following extracts are from addresses given at the Brockville meeting by the late John Macdonald, Esq., and the late Rev. Dr. Punshon:

Mr. Macdonald said: "It may be expected that I may have a few words to say about the Red River, being one of the deputation to that distant part of our work. Time was when a visit to that land, the Red River of the North, meant a long and fatiguing journey. To reach it from Toronto it was necessary first to go to Montreal, to follow the old canoe route of the Hudson Bay Company, by water and portage, to be bitten and tortured by mosquitoes, as our good President was, to reach that land maimed and wounded, and then to be shut out from civilization for years, perhaps for many of them. The journey itself was one which could be undertaken only by those of rugged constitution, those having great powers of endurance, and these would be abundantly called into exercise before he reached the end of his journey. The land itself was a sealed land, apart from the traders of the Hudson Bay Company; none but some hardy venturer undertook that journey, and he, when he ventured, became as much an object of wonder as he would have been had he been an Arctic explorer; and should he furnish a paper on that country less important than it is in the power of the members of this deputation to furnish, he was as certain as he was a living man to be made a member of the Royal Geographical Society. All this is now changed. We came back not to find that we were objects of wonder —not to be feted or made members of the Senate, for contributions which we have made to the existing knowledge of that country, but to find that we are only ordinary mortals; that we have done only what you may do, and do so quickly that your friends will scarcely notice your absence. The land is no longer a sealed land; you can now reach it by lake and railroad in a few days; and although our visit has been so recent, yet since then railroad communication has been extended within seventy miles of Fort Garry; so that now even an invalid can go there and not only be none the worse, but much the better for the journey. Sir George Simpson, in a work which he published of a 'Voyage Round the World,' spoke of that district as amazingly fertile, very salubrious, and large enough to receive the millions from the overcrowded cities of the Old World. When examined before a select committee of the British House of Commons, he withdrew any statement of the kind, and represented it as unfit for settlement, and the climate so uncertain as to render the growing of grain very precarious. The Hudson Bay Company, I have no doubt, discovered, ere this, that their interest lies in diffusing information about the country, not withholding it, and that in proportion as the land is opened up their own interests will be promoted. Well, I will not detain you with the journey down the river, beautiful as it is; of the tortuous windings of the river, so many that a distance of two hundred and fifty miles by land is extended to about seven hundred miles by river, where all the bends in the river are so alike that you cannot tell one from the other, and all so beautiful that despite the unvarying sameness you can look at them day after day without tiring, and feel that

'A thing of beauty is a joy forever.'

Nor am I going to speak to you about the boundless prairie, stretching away for a thousand miles, and I cannot tell how much farther—and fertile as boundless. Nor am I going to speak of the climate, charming as that was when I was there, and pleasant and healthful as I was told the winters were. Nor am I going to speak of the political opinions that prevail, for I hold that a Society like this should have nothing to do with political parties. Their work is to do good to the bodies as well as to the souls of men, without reference to their politics, nationality or creed. My remarks must have reference only to our work there.

"You will remember that the effort for the building of the Fort Garry church originated at the meeting of this committee in Guelph four years ago. That was the first meeting of this committee at which the President sat, and his name was at the head of the subscription list. Very wise was the election of the Rev. George Young for that work, who has so labored as to have secured the confidence of all classes of the community. His circuit to-day is one of the most desirable in the Dominion. The church property itself is a beautiful property; the church, as chaste as any that I have seen in any of the rural districts. The windows are all of beautiful stained glass, and four designs in the centre show that they have been the gifts of the Sunday-schools from Main Street, Mount Zion, Centenary, Hamilton; North Street, London; Ottawa, Brantford, Picton, and Quebec. I do not remember seeing Brockville, but any neglect there you purpose, I am persuaded, correcting now. Of the church itself, an Indian who came with Rev. E. R. Young from Norway House said, on seeing it, 'This is very beautiful. I am going to heaven, and I hope it will be as beautiful as this.' At the request of the other members of the deputation, I brought under the notice of the Governor of the Hudson Bay Company, the Hon. Donald Smith, the matter of a grant in Winnipeg for an educational establishment, and with the same princely conduct which marked all the other acts of that Company toward the members of the deputation, Mr. Smith said a suitable grant would be given; in fact, all that would be needed; and when you are told that fifty-feet lots were sold in Fort Garry, while we were there, for two thousand dollars, you will understand that such a grant means money. If we are to do our work there as we should, we must have our educational establishment. The Church of England has one,

The Free Church has one. We should have one. We want about $3,000 to commence this work, and we have good hope that we will get it to-night. I was in hopes, sir, that you would have the honor of commencing this work, as Oshawa had the honor—that is the Sunday-school—of contributing the bell, the only one in Winnipeg. And let me say of this bell, that it not only calls to the house of God, but during days of darkness, when the land was in the midst of a rebellion, it rang out not only sounds of deliverance to the settlers, but sounds of welcome to our volunteers who came to their help. Well, sir, I have in my hands a note about this scheme: If it be true (and you as a politician will know whether it is or not) that one vote before twelve o'clock is worth two after, then what I am about to announce will have an important bearing upon this effort. Mr. John Torrance, who, I regret, is unable to be with us, writes me with a readiness and liberality which characterize all his efforts in connection with our funds, to put him down for $250. That is a good commencement, and, I think, assures us of the result. The resolution with which I am entrusted has matter enough to enable one to speak for a month; it speaks of 'gratitude to God, spiritual success, enlarged income, Divine promises, providential openings, and increased liberality.' Now, upon this I must only venture a few words: Why the increased wealth which is flowing in so abundantly to Christ's people? Is it to make them increasingly sordid? Is it to lead them to say that they have much goods laid up for many years? What does the remarkable prosperity of the past few years—the most remarkably prosperous, perhaps, the world has ever seen—say to us? 'Speak to the people that they go forward.' . . . I am to be followed by the President, and must not longer detain you, but trust that this evening we shall raise the amount we require for this institution.

The Rev. Dr. Punshon, in seconding the third resolution, said: "My friend Mr. Macdonald, in moving this resolution, said it was one on which a speech might be made for a month. But I am not disposed to make a speech to-night, and were I so disposed, the taste and temper of this congregation are not, at this hour, disposed to listen. But one thing you have the opportunity of doing, under the influence of what you have heard—that is, to follow up the challenge given in reference to the proposed institution at Manito*ba*. I must say, I don't like this pronunciation of Manito*ba*, this Frenchified mode which some purists have adapted. But Mr. Macdonald has really stolen my speech. I have been dwelling on the hope of giving some account of my visit, in company with him and with Dr. Wood, to the Red River country. In this, however, he has anticipated me. I may just note, with respect to our country, that while it was interesting, it was a most eventful journey. We were mercifully delivered from the disaster of shipwreck after we had crossed from Sarnia, and were approaching the opposite side. I shall not soon forget what I then witnessed of the wonders of the Lord on that wonderful lake. After reaching Duluth, we proceeded by the Northern Pacific Railroad. From what we witnessed in this land journey, and from a sense of duty to carry out the advice of Mr. Wesley, to 'go not only to those who want us, but to those who want us most,' there are many places through which we passed in the United States to which we should send missionaries. Of these I may mention Brainard, a village on the bank of the Mississippi. I cannot tell whether or not it is named after the celebrated missionary, and therefore predestinated to be missionary ground. It is a little city in a forest. Each inhabitant seems to have cut away the trees only that were required to give space for his house. Thus there were presented vistas most picturesque and beautiful. This town dates from a year ago last month, and has now about eight hundred inhabitants. We passed through it twice, once on our outward journey, and again, after an absence of three weeks, on our return, and in that short time one man had been shot, one stabbed, and two Indians were tried by Lynch law, and strung upon tall trees in front of a saloon, with the appropriate name of 'The Last Turn.' We certainly might send missionaries there with advantage if we had the means, if only to teach them reverence for human life. Then there was the town of Moorehead, of which Dr. Wood has a pleasant and salubrious remembrance. There every second dwelling is a gambling-house, a dance-house, or a saloon. There is no church, no school, no Sabbath, every one carries arms, and as one of their own citizens remarked, 'It is a dull day which passes without a shooting.' Possibly some missionary effort might not be wasted there. You may imagine that travelling is not altogether pleasant in these parts. I say nothing of the voyage down the Red River for seven hundred miles, nor of the mosquitoes—as blood-thirsty cannibals as ever stuck spears into human flesh—nor of the discomfort of the steamboat, nor of the tortuous character of the river, which winds so persistently and so extremely, that we passed by a man's house on two sides of it, and were half an hour by the watch in getting from one side to the other. I pass on to notice our work. Our first Sabbath in Winnipeg was a high day. First, we had a love-feast in the morning, starting in good Methodist fashion; then, in the forenoon, I preached, after which the ordination of the Rev. John McDougall took place. In the afternoon we held a missionary meeting. In the evening Dr. Wood occupied the pulpit; and this remarkable day closed with the administration of the Sacrament of the Lord's Supper, at which were present Christians of all colors, white and red and yellow, all animated by the one hope, and rejoicing in the one Saviour. We were made glad in witnessing these results of missionary toil."

As the result of this Conference the Mission Rooms became not only better acquainted with the vastness and importance of the work in which we were engaged, but with the necessity of increasing the staff of laborers, as well as the appropriations to these toilers in order to secure greater progress.

After the many allusions in the preceding remarks of Mr. Macdonald and Dr. Punshon *re* the Red River of the North, the following correspondence and poem will not be, to many at least, void of interest.

THE BELLS OF ST. BONIFACE.

In a poem by John Greenleaf Whittier, "The Red River Voyageur," there is a beautiful allusion to the "bells of the Roman Mission," now the Arch-episcopate of St. Boniface, "calling to the boatman on the river and the hunter on the plain," and invoking at the close of life's voyage "the signal of release in the bells of the Holy City, the chimes of eternal peace." Archbishop Tache, returning from his late visit to Montreal, was reminded by Lieutenant-Governor Schultz that the 17th of December was the eighty-fourth birthday of the poet, and His Honor suggested that the anniversary should be greeted by a joy-peal from the tower of the cathedral of St. Boniface. His

Grace cordially concurred, waiving the usage that the bells should cease their chimes after the Angelus, and the graceful tribute was directed and rendered at midnight with the last stroke of the clock ushering the natal day. Mr. Whittier, having been informed of the incident by U. S. Consul Taylor, addressed the following letter to Archbishop Tache, who kindly consented, at our request, to its publication, as follows:

"NEWBURYPORT, MASS., 3 mo. 5, 1892.

"*To Archbishop Tache:*

"MY DEAR FRIEND,—During my illness from the prevailing epidemic, which confined me nearly the whole winter, and from which I am but very slowly recovering, a letter from the U. S. Consul at Winnipeg informed me of thy pleasant recognition of my little poem, "The Red River Voyageur" (written nearly forty years ago), by the ringing of "The Bells of St. Boniface" on the eve of my late anniversary.

"I was at the time quite unable to respond, but I feel that I should be wanting in due appreciation of such a marked compliment if I did not, even at this late hour, express to thee my heartfelt thanks. I have reached an age when literary success and manifestations of popular favor have ceased to satisfy one upon whom the solemnity of life's sunset is resting; but such a delicate and beautiful tribute has deeply moved me. I shall never forget it. I shall hear the bells of St. Boniface sounding across the continent, and awakening a feeling of gratitude for thy generous act. With renewed thanks, and the prayer that our Heavenly Father may continue to make thee largely instrumental in His service, I am,

"Gratefully and respectfully,
"Thy friend,
"JOHN G. WHITTIER."

Thinking it possible that the poem which had been the occasion of this exchange of delightful greetings may be unfamiliar to some of our readers, and knowing that it will be welcome to all, it is here republished :

"THE RED RIVER VOYAGEUR.

" Out and in the river is winding
  The links of its long, red chain,
Through belts of dusky pine land
  And gusty leagues of plain.

" Only at times, a smoke wreath
  With the drifting cloud-rack joins—
The smoke of the hunting lodges
  Of the wild Assiniboines.

" Drearily blows the north wind
  From the land of ice and snow ;
The eyes that look are weary,
  And heavy the hands that row.

" And with one foot on the water,
  And one upon the shore,
The Angel of Shadow gives warning
  That day shall be no more.

" Is it the clang of wild geese,
  Is it the Indian's yell,
That lends to the voice of the north wind
  The tones of a far-off bell ?

" The voyageur smiles as he listens
  To the sound that grows apace ;
Well he knows the vesper ringing
  Of the bells of St. Boniface.

" The bells of the Roman Mission,
  That call from their turrets twain,
To the boatman on the river,
  To the hunter on the plain.

" Even so in our mortal journey
  The bitter north winds blow,
And thus upon life's Red River,
  Our hearts, as oarsmen, row.

" And when the Angel of Shadow
  Rests his feet on wave and shore,
And our eyes grow dim with watching,
  And our hearts faint at the oar,

" Happy is he who heareth
  The signal of his release
In the bells of the Holy City,
  The chimes of eternal peace."

CHAPTER XVI.

DR. LACHLAN TAYLOR'S WONDERFUL TOUR AMONG THE MISSIONS IN THE "GREAT LONE LAND."

THE incorporation of the following most interesting account by our now departed brother, of his long tour of "inspection," will, I am sure, gratify large numbers, many of whom have never before enjoyed the opportunity of reading it. He and his fellow-traveller, George McDougall, have long since rested from their toils for the Master:

"In pursuance of the important object of the mission to which I was appointed, I left Toronto May 5th, 1873, *en route* for Manitoba and the great North-West. Arriving at Chicago the following morning, we remained a few hours examining the growth and progress of the city, and the marvellous and incredible rapidity with which its miles of ruins by the disastrous conflagration are being restored; the city rising from its ashes with far more than its former magnificence and splendor.

"We left in the evening for St. Paul, and thence by the North-Western and the great North Pacific Railway for Moorehead on the Red River. On arriving, we found that we were most fortunate in the time spent in Chicago, as it abridged by so many hours our stay in Moorehead. The steamer having got in a few hours before us, would have to discharge her cargo and take on a large freight before we set out for our destination, but, on the whole, limiting our stay to ten or twelve hours in the meanest and muddiest village we met in all our travels, and the crossing of whose principal street when we were there, was like crossing the Rubicon, for none wanted to repeat or try it again.

"The Red River is one of the most tortuous and crooked rivers in America, sometimes almost doubling upon itself like a great boa constrictor, running nine hundred miles from its source in Dakota to where it empties into Lake Winnipeg, falling only two hundred feet in six hundred miles; its valley being twenty thousand square miles, a territory as large as both the States of Vermont and New Hampshire, and, like Manitoba generally, the richest soil I have seen since I left the banks of the Nile; and as the heavily-laden steamer, towing two scows loaded to the water-edge, moved slowly on, and the river being very high, we had a fine chance when we came to our own country of surveying the prairie from the upper deck, which contrasted favorably with Minnesota and Dakota, being more elevated and dryer, and if only half cultivated, would wave with golden grain and garnered harvests, richly rewarding the tillers' toil.

"On May 14th, the ninth day after leaving Toronto, we sighted Fort Garry and the thrifty and prosperous little town (now the city) of Winnipeg. We were still more delighted to have pointed out to us as we neared, what they called Mr. Young's church, which, with its neat red roof, is one of the most conspicuous objects in the little city, the future metropolis of the great North-West. I was highly pleased, as our noble deputation the preceding year must have been, to find that Mr. Young, in securing the large and valuable lot on which the premises stand, had made the very best selection he could have done, as it is, from the growth of the town towards the fort, in the very heart of the city, and must be very valuable in the coming time.

"When we landed we received a cordial salutation from our esteemed brother, and a hearty Methodist welcome from his family, and felt at once all the comforts of a home. I preached on Sabbath morning to a congregation of nearly three hundred, and we took up a collection for the Missionary Society. Addressed the large and interesting Sabbath-school in the afternoon, whom I found well up in Bible history; and my friend Bro. Armstrong preached a most effective and practical sermon in the evening. As all the facts connected with our important cause here were so well put in the report of the deputation of last year, as well as the facts communicated by Bro. Young himself during his recent visit, I need not enlarge; but bear my testimony to the wisdom of the choice that was made in selecting him for his present position. I was highly delighted to find that he was regarded by all as a first-class representative of our body on any and every occasion, both in the pulpit and on the platform; and it gave me great pleasure to see his unwearied devotion to the interests of every missionary in the work in the whole country; in many cases anticipating their wants and studying in every way to promote their welfare. The firm and manly stand he took during the dark and perilous days through which the infant colony passed, when traitors were in the ascendant, and his magnanimous and Christian heroism in standing by the side of poor Scott, tying at his request the bandage tighter over his eyes and administering to him what consolation he could, and breathing the name of Jesus in his ear a minute or two before he was shot, have given him place in the affections and memories of the people that will not be forgotten during the present generation.

"Bro. Young drove me to two of his out-stations, Stoney Mountain and Headingly, where we found twenty-eight hearers at the former, whom I addressed, and twelve at the latter, to whom Bro. Armstrong preached, and I closed with an exhortation. At some of these places it is emphatically the day of small things, but our Church from the beginning, true to her character, must be the pioneer and carry the message of life to those that will be scattered abroad over that land of magnificent distances. . . . .

"Embracing the first opportunity, we sailed the following Thursday in the boat of a private trader (as it was uncertain when the Company's boats would be ready) for Norway House, which we reached in thirteen days and a half, time enough to cross the Atlantic, although it is only about 360 miles. This was the most uncomfortable voyage I ever performed, for the following reasons :—First, an open boat without any chance of walking or promenading, or exercise, and obliged to sit all day in a space about six feet by eight, and as we were voyaging in the very worst time of the flies, when we went ashore either for cooking meals or camping for the night, millions of mosquitoes were ready to pounce upon us, and whose voracious powers no language could describe. Our digestive organs got sadly out of order, and we could sympathize with our esteemed brethren, the missionaries and their families, who have had to take a similar voyage to reach that field of self-denying toil and labor. On the fourteenth day from Winnipeg, sailing on slowly on a beautiful little lake called Mission Lake, the master of the boat exclaimed : 'We are only about half-a-mile from Mr. Young's house,' and never was intelligence received with more joy by an Atlantic voyager after a stormy voyage, than we received the welcome announcement, and soon that joy was heightened by our kind reception at the parsonage, although we arrived at an unseasonable hour. Mr. Young was soon up, and after a comfortable supper, with Christian family comforts, we conversed till full dawn, and then went to rest. On Sabbath morning we heard the bell ring at half-past six for the morning prayer-meeting; it rang again for Sunday-school at nine. As the mission premises are located on an elevated point of land, almost surrounded by water, it was a grand sight, that glorious Sabbath morning, to stand and see boats approaching in every direction, some rowing, some paddling, some sailing, from the tiny little bark canoe, to the "Lady of the Lake," rowed by eight stalwart Orkney men and Highlanders, having on board the officers of the Hudson Bay Company, from the fort; and all if not flying as a cloud and as doves to their windows, yet coming on the wings of the wind as ships to their haven, and voyagers to the port of peace—the sanctuary of God. I preached at eleven o'clock to nearly four hundred, including officers and employees of the Hudson Bay Company, Orkney men and a few enthusiastic Highlanders, and some half-breeds. But the large majority were Indians, members and adherents of our Church, and seldom have I witnessed, either at home or abroad, such devout attention to the word preached and such a spirit of devotion in the congregation—that indescribable something that pervades the service, felt alike by both preacher and hearer, when praying hearts are lifted up in communion with God. Upwards of one hundred and twenty partook of the Lord's Supper in the afternoon, and a few had come over twenty miles to be present. The preceding Sabbath, when we were expected, and before the large brigade of boats had left, upwards of two hundred and twenty had communicated, and although we were deeply sorry that we failed to reach them, yet we did our best to get there, and could do no more. In the evening we crossed to the fort, and had service in the neat room fitted up as a church by the Company. My esteemed fellow-traveller, Mr. Armstrong, preached, and we felt it was good to be there. We spent a couple of hours in the Mission School, and found a fine school with sixty-five scholars in attendance. We heard them read the Scriptures, both in English and in Cree, in the syllabic characters, and also heard them examined in No. 1 Catechism, and was delighted at the accuracy of their answers in English to some of the most difficult questions, especially as they speak and think in Cree, although they may know a little English. Brother Young gave out some hymns in Cree, which they sang charmingly, and their writing and the cleanness of their copy books would compare favorably with those of any school in this favored Province. When I looked at the prosperity of the mission and the school, and cast a retrospective glance up to the days of the devoted James Evans, I could not but reflect on what immense benefits have been bestowed on that people and their children by the Wesleyan Missionary Society, and at the same time exclaiming, as I did after the Sunday morning service: Much as the parent Society, as well as our own, have expended on this mission, it is repaid a thousand times in the sound conversion, consistent lives, and happy deaths of these simple-minded followers of the Lamb. It is doubtless the finest Indian mission in the Dominion, if not in America.

"24th (Tuesday), enjoyed a strong breeze and a favorable wind from the south. Accompanied by my brethren, Messrs. Young and Armstrong, we embarked with a fine brigade of three boats of the Hudson Bay Company, all manned by our people, for Oxford

House, some two hundred miles distant. On this voyage we saw a most remarkable proof of their gifts and piety. Supper done, at the call of their pastor, the crews of the three boats came together, a hymn was sung, given out in English and Cree; and the commodore of the fleet, Bro. Cochrane, led in prayer, and one of the ministers followed us in a short one in English; and Bro. Young informed us that if we sailed for ten days he could call on a fresh one each time to lead our devotions, out of a company of twenty-six men. Where would you find such boat crews on the waters of the globe, such a majority that could lead fluently and appropriately in prayer? more in proportion than in any of our city churches. The company at devotion would have been a grand scene for an artist. The grave and devout appearance of the worshippers, prostrate with their faces to the ground; the ministers in the same position; the two tents representing pilgrim life; the camp fires burning; and the charming background of poplars, firs, spruce, and larch, would make a picture fit to fill a niche in any gallery in the world. And, what the artist could never touch with his pencil or his brush, the deep emotion and peace of souls in communion with God, and the felt consciousness of the Divine presence. After a most wonderful voyage, in which I saw specimens and examples of navigation that I never saw equalled, we arrived at Oxford House, beautifully situated on Oxford Lake, one of the finest in America, and received a cordial welcome from the gentlemanly officer in charge, C. Sinclair, Esq.

"On Sabbath morning I gave them 'Walks about Jerusalem,' applying it spiritually, and Mr. Sinclair, our evangelist there, interpreted; but unfortunately, one of my finest points on the prayer-meeting in the garden of Gethsemane, under the magnificent olive, was shorn of its glory in one particular, by Bro. Young hearing him translate the olive as a greasy tree or stick, and for the moment to me ignorance was bliss, and I passed on—or had I known it I certainly would have said: Can you not do better than that? If not, pass it by. Bro. Young gave them an instructive address in the afternoon, after which we had the Sacrament of the Lord's Supper, and baptized several children. Though all were glad to see the visitors, and there was a general rally for miles around, making a congregation of about sixty, yet we found the cause in a low and depressed state, and the general aspect and condition of the mission most unsatisfactory. An evangelist who cannot administer the ordinances must always be placed at a disadvantage, especially where there are a number of church members, and this was not an exception. Again, the members and adherents were divided between the old locality, or head of the mission, at Jackson's Bay, and the fort, eighteen miles distant— the large majority being at the fort—and anxiously desiring the removal of the church and mission thither; but three or four families pleading for things to remain as they were, regarding it as a better place for their fishing, with small patches of arable land where they raised a few potatoes, arrangements were made for the removal of excellent materials which the assistant had prepared and erected for a new church, ready for the plates, from the bay to the fort; and the erection there of the new premises; and for the school-house at the bay to be fitted up for a little church, which has been done, and will more than accommodate the few that are remaining. It is to be hoped that ere long the few still at the bay will come to the fort, and not only save the missionary fatigue and labor, but enable him to concentrate his efforts with greater success where they are most needed. An old local preacher, however, named Daniel Belton, visited us, and in an eloquent oration (as understood by Bro. Young and Mr. Sinclair), set forth their claims, and his whole manner and bearing commanded our unqualified admiration. They complained that they had had no school for eight years, but now they will have a faithful and effective man from Norway House, and who will, we believe, make a most successful helper. From the spirit and courage which our Brother German manifests and in which he enters on his work, we believe Oxford House Mission has entered on a new era of spiritual prosperity.

"As we could not wait for a couple of weeks till the first brigade, which was expected, returned from York Factory, we were obliged to hire two small bark canoes, manned by two men each, with one of ourselves in the centre of the tiny craft with his paddle, for the return journey to Norway House, and although one sitting in his easy chair in a parlor may admire Longfellow's description:—

>"And the forest life is in it,
> All its mystery and its magic!
> All the lightness of the Birch tree,
> All the toughness of the Cedar,
> All the Larch's supple sinews,
> And it floated down the river,
> Like a yellow leaf in Autumn;
> Like a yellow water-lily."

Yet it is much more practical, and another thing, when crossing a lake twelve or fifteen miles long, in a pretty stiff breeze, and only nine or ten inches above the water. The Superintendent of Norway House seemed in his element, and the Indians said the visitor could paddle pretty well.

"After four days' hard paddling we arrived at Norway House, and found all well. Although complaining next day, I had a comfortable Sabbath and preached at the fort in the evening. Next day we bade our friends adieu, and Bro. Semmens and myself sailed with the same trader with whom we went out, arrived safely in Winnipeg, where I found my guide, companion, and famous fellow-traveller, for the prairie and the great North-West, Bro. John McDougall, had been waiting patiently with his men for three weeks for my arrival.

"Our dashing, unbridled native steeds being collected from their great unfenced pasture field—our little stores purchased and packed as necessary to be secured before you start on your journey through 'The Great Lone Land' as if you were part of an Eastern caravan—our carriages, an ordinary Ontario waggon and two buckboards; a small party of three men, subsequently increased to six, started from what is now the City of Winnipeg, on a tour of two thousand miles, and ten weeks' continuous travel, to visit all the important points where our missions have been or may yet be established, and explore generally the largest and grandest division, although the least known, of our glorious Canadian Confederation.

"From Rat Creek, and Messrs. Grant's and McKenzie's farms, the present *ultima Thule* of civilization on the great highway to the Saskatchewan, we saw only one house, and that uninhabited, till we reached Fort Ellice, on the bank of the Assiniboine—two hundred and thirty miles from Fort Garry—where we received a Highland welcome from Mr. McDonald, the gentlemanly officer in charge. Having rested and recruited, we set out for the next grand stage, and saw not a house till we came within eighteen miles of Fort Carlton, which is three hundred and seven miles from Fort Ellice, almost as far as from Toronto to Montreal, without seeing a human abode, civilized or savage, and passing nearly the whole of the distance through a most picturesque and charming country. Here two or three of our shoeless horses began to get footsore and we had them shod, also sundry repairs to some of our gear and trappings. We travelled one hundred and sixty-seven miles farther, when my active companion, leaving the man and myself to cook and prepare our dinner, communicating by signs, mounted one of the best saddle horses, and from what is termed the guard of Fort Pitt, galloped off to the fort, and in the course of two or three hours returned, accompanied by the Chairman, Brother George McDougall, and a servant, Brother Peter Campbell, his boy and another boy that came with them, which threw a new element of life into our party; and after mutual congratulations we went on our way rejoicing. Nearly one hundred miles farther and not very far from the royal little Victoria, we turned our faces directly north, leaving the boys in charge of the tent and baggage, and rode forty miles on horseback to White Fish Lake Mission, which, in one day on a native horse, without having had practice for some years, made sleep sweet on the hard floor with my coat for a pillow. Here we were much disappointed to find the neat mission house locked, and the missionary and his family, and the teacher and his family, with the large majority of our people, women and children, away hundreds of miles on the plains hunting the buffalo. But we found the *locum tenens* of the place, Benjamin Sinclair, who was overjoyed to see us, and he hardly knew what to say, or how to express himself, when I presented him with the $120 from the Committee towards making up his loss when the canoe upset with himself and Peter Jacobs. His conversion, as related by himself, is intensely interesting. While my friends were getting the horses ready, I went to the church and rang the Toronto bell, which was presented by our esteemed colleague, Mr. Macdonald, and in ten minutes we had seventy of a congregation; Brother John McDougall interpreted with great earnestness, and we had a time of refreshing from the presence of the Lord. This mission, located at 54° north latitude, more than eleven degrees north of Toronto, was commenced in 1856, by the excellent brother who has been the pastor from the commencement till last June, when he was appointed to Woodville. During his seventeen years, God has given him great success; the membership being one hundred and eighteen, and the congregation about two hundred, with a school of sixty children. The premises are a plain log church, thirty by twenty, a mission house with five rooms, and a kitchen, neat and comfortable, and a stable that answers the purpose, and all erected with the missionary's own hands, with what help the Indians could give him, and without expense to the Society. The mission lot, of five or six acres, may be cultivated, for the soil is as rich as Solomon's gardens. There is a lake at the door abounding with the finest fish in America. Many happy deaths might be named connected with the history of this mission if our space would permit.

"The next mission in order is Victoria, picturesquely situated on the Saskatchewan, 54° north latitude, and, by odometer, eight hundred and sixteen miles from Fort Garry. We received a warm welcome from Mrs. David and Miss McDougall, and then passed on to our comfortable home with Brother Campbell's family in the parsonage. This mission was commenced by Bro. George McDougall, in 1862, beginning with a large body of Crees, professed adherents of our Church, and therefore classes were organized in a short time. A church and mission house was built in two years, which cost $2,000, which was all defrayed by local contribution and personal effort. There are about ten acres enclosed, which is considered the mission lot, although in reality there are no bounds to the north till you reach the Arctic circle. The mission-house has eight rooms, four above and four below; a fine garden, a snug little church, which must soon give place to a larger one, as it will hold only about one hundred and fifty; and a bell to summon the worshippers at the hour of prayer.

"In the garden we saw the mournful monuments of the tidings we heard in this land, in the four graves—three of Bro. McDougall's daughters (two his own, and the daughter of Ogemawahsis, adopted), and Bro. John McDougall's first wife; and the tragic details of the former; the death of the three by small-pox, and the father and son putting the lovely daughter and sister in the coffin—digging the grave themselves and covering it—none daring to come near to aid or administer consolation. Poor Mrs. McDougall kept up till the last one was gone, and then she swooned, and did not recover consciousness for some forty-eight hours.

"Our services on Sabbath were well attended, although the large majority of the Indians were away hunting the buffalo. The half-breeds of the fine little settlement and the employees of the Company made quite a congregation. English sermon in the morning, a talk of an hour and a half on the Holy Land, translated into Cree, in the afternoon, and a fine Cree service by Bro. John McDougall, in the evening, filled up this delightful Sabbath. Membership seventy, thirty of whom were received on trial in the revival last spring, under the labors of Bro. Campbell; ten removals and four deaths during the year; and when the Indians are at home the congregation is about one hundred and twenty; sixty children in the school during the week, and sixty-five on the Sabbath; and the school, taught by a gentlemanly, well-educated half-breed of the name of McKenzie, a local preacher in our Church and a good man. Of the many remarkable and happy deaths that have occurred in the history of the mission, a few might be cited did space permit.

"The next mission in order was Fort Edmonton, for which we set out on Monday (for Mr. McDougall meant business), after bidding adieu to our kind hostess, Mrs. Campbell, in whose comfortable house we were as much at home as in many of the mansions of the older Canada, and reached the second day before tea time, seventy-one miles distant. The second day in the afternoon, while passing through a magnificent section of country, looking like an English park, with beautiful groves of aspen and fir in the distance, and some twelve or fourteen miles from Edmonton, we met the Chief Factor, Mr. Hardisty, Mr. McDougall's son-in-law, and his second son-in-law, the son of the Hon. John Young, of Montreal, Mr. Leslie Wood, and Mrs. Hardisty, Mrs. Young and Mrs. John McDougall, who had a most luxurious spread on the beautiful sward, Canadian pic-nic fashion, to which we were welcomed and invited in the style which characterizes the princely benevolence of the officers of the Hudson Bay Company.

"After a quiet evening and rest of one night only, we set out next morning for Woodville, fifty-six miles south south-west from Edmonton, travelling by buckboard and on the saddle, and arriving the second day in time for a social service at the mission house in the evening. Here we were on the ground of, in some respects, the finest band of Indians in all the territory that stretches from Fort Garry to the Rocky Mountains, "The Stonies," and although located in one of the finest situations in all that country, yet the Bow River valley, where Bro. John McDougall has gone, is to be their future home. The mission was named after my esteemed colleague, Dr. Wood, and he would be proud of it if he saw it. Pigeon Lake, on whose bank the premises stand, is one of the very finest lakes in America; from fifteen to twenty miles long, and from six to eight miles wide; and if located in Europe, would find its place in the fellowship of Como, Maggiore, Lucerne, Windermere, or Loch Lomond. It is swarming with white fish of A1 quality, that can be caught at any season of the year, and as many as five hundred have been caught in a day, averaging four pounds each. This mission was commenced by Bro. John McDougall, in 1864, who built the little mission house and church with his own hands, with such help as the Stonies could give him. The Mountain Stonies, as a tribe, are our members, or adherents, and the old ones have remained faithful since the days of the devoted Rundle, thirty years or more; but some have fallen asleep.

"Edmonton is next in order. The devoted Rundle made Edmonton his headquarters, and from which he went forth on his evangelistic tour to the surrounding tribes. When he left there was a vacancy of seven years, when Brother Woolsey was appointed, who remained nine years, labored faithfully and was much beloved and respected; but no premises were erected and no class formed, and the services were held in the fort. Then they were only occasionally visited after Brother Woolsey left, for six or seven years, till Brother George McDougall went and properly established the mission, and of his perseverance and success we cannot speak in too strong terms, and must ever command our highest admiration and praise. Now there are twenty members; a congregation of about sixty, and constantly increasing; two services on Sabbath and one during the week, and as it is a grand centre it is of the utmost importance

that it be properly sustained. The new church, which
we dedicated, is a neat building, well finished; the
work having been done by the Rev. Benjamin Jones
in good style. The dimensions are thirty-two feet
long and twenty-four feet wide, and all the pews were
let before it was dedicated. The mission-house has
five rooms, with a large kitchen; and the premises
cost at least $3,000, only $500 of which was granted
by the Society. The lot joins the fine property of the
Company (who own three thousand acres in a block)
and is fifty rods frontage on the Saskatchewan, and
runs back or north to some imaginary line between
that and the North Pole. The whole of that region
covers one of the finest and largest coal beds in the
world. The services on Sabbath were: sermon and
dedication in the morning; sermon in Cree in the
afternoon, by Brother J. McDougall; and Brother
Campbell preached an excellent sermon in the evening. Preparations being all made, stores purchased,
Brothers George and John McDougall, Brother Snyder,
a young man who is entering our work, the visitor,
William the servant, and a Cree Indian that joined
us subsequently, crossed the Saskatchewan—in all, six
men and eleven horses, for a journey of about eight
hundred miles and over four weeks' constant travel,
to survey that grandest section of the field for future
openings, the new mission field in the magnificent
Bow River valley, Morleyville, and especially to see
the various tribes of Indians on the plains, in their
numbers and strength, and judge of the mission work
yet to be done by our beloved Church, which has,
from the beginning of her history, taken the lead in
benefiting those original masters of the soil who are
fast melting away. We met four camps of the Crees,
with each of whom we had service, and then came to a
camp of forty-three or forty-four tents; held a service
in the evening and another in the morning, with a fine

audience, and afterwards had council with them for over three hours. Three days afterwards, as we were journeying over a magnificent treeless prairie, a scout from the savage and ferocious Blackfeet, who were camped in their strength a short distance from us, galloped into their camp and sounded the alarm that 'American traders' were approaching. As they were in a valley hidden from us, we knew nothing till we saw some sixty men, armed to the teeth, and mounted on swift horses, approaching on the full gallop, bent on blood, and with a solemn resolve to kill us, before they would allow us to enter the camp, and exhibit, as they supposed, our wares for sale. But when they ascertained that, instead of being a party of those outlaws who have injured them in every possible form, we belonged to their country and to their Great Mother across the big waters, and were missionaries and men of peace, we were marched into the chief's tent, where, much to our physical discomfort, we spent that evening, the whole of the next day, being the Sabbath and Sabbath night, and departed next morning in peace, after a general shaking of hands, and in their way friendly good-bye. We held a religious service in the afternoon, and when we knelt on the ground to pray, they gazed at us with intense amazement and all the expression of wonder at our mode of worshipping the Great Spirit. When we reflected on our signal deliverance, we raised our hearts in devout thanksgiving and praise unto God, and realized perhaps as we never did before, 'For the angel of the Lord encampeth round about them that fear Him and delivereth them.'

"Tuesday, after leaving the Blackfeet, we descended into the splendid Bow River valley, and the next day camped within five miles of the location of the future Morleyville, doubtless the most romantic and grandest site for mission premises in all our work, if not in all America. Fronting on the Bow River is the main branch of the South Saskatchewan, a clear rapid stream swarming with fish, flanked and surrounded by the chain of foot hills, which constitute the Propylon, or majestic gateway to the Rocky Mountains, thirty or forty of whose giant peaks can be seen from the mission-house door, having on their northern shoulders the snows that never melt; and in a clear morning, as the rising sun successively gilds the peaks according to their altitude or position, the scene is one of indescribable beauty, sublimity and grandeur. Between the foot hills and the mountains are wide vales or wadys from fifteen to twenty miles wide, where horses and cattle graze and fatten the winter through; and to this desirable spot, having a reserve twenty miles on each side of the Bow River, the Stonies have promised to come in a body, and it is hoped that the Blackfeet who, to the present, have been restless roamers, will be induced to come there also, for there is room enough for all. The committee have made provision for two interpreters, and no church was ever blessed with a better agent, or a man possessing higher qualifications for that work, than Brother John McDougall.

"Ten days after, we reached Fort Benton, the head of steamboat navigation on the Missouri, hoping from information previously received that Bismarck, where the Northern Pacific crosses the river, was not a very long distance from us, but, alas for our ignorance of the geography of the great North-West! that land of magnificent distances, for we found that it was more than one thousand miles by the river and between seven and eight hundred by land, and either was dangerous unless there was a large party, for the meanest and most treacherous of all the Indian tribes occupy those regions."

CHAPTER XVII.

OUR EARLY EDUCATIONAL MOVEMENTS IN MANITOBA.

FROM the addresses of Messrs. Macdonald and Punshon, delivered at the annual meeting of the Missionary Board at Brockville, as given in the preceding chapter, it will be seen that the establishment of an educational institute in Winnipeg at an early day had received their careful consideration, and was regarded with special favor. Mr. Macdonald had secured a promise from Hon. Donald A. Smith, then Governor of the Hudson Bay Company, of a suitable lot on which to place college buildings, and subscriptions amounting to a large sum were called for and received at the Brockville meeting. As I was reminded by Mr. Macdonald of this promise, I applied to Mr. Smith, requesting him to kindly locate the lot thus promised, and was assured that this should be done as soon as we were prepared to commence the building or buildings in question and proceed with the contemplated college. But inasmuch as we were not in the possession of funds sufficient to warrant our entering upon what would necessarily involve a heavy outlay, and also as the number and circumstances of our adherents in Manitoba were not such as to promise the patronage requisite for the sustentation of such an effort, we felt that for us to enter thereupon, until our Methodist community should be considerably increased, would be decidedly injudicious. The fulfilment of the promise was not realized, for the reason indicated. I make this record chiefly to relieve the minds of any who may have expressed surprise at my having allowed the promise of Mr. Smith to lapse, thereby missing a gift that would have been of great value to the Church at a later period. I was as unable to comply with the condition on which the gift was offered as I was to proceed to the erection of college buildings—or to do any other impossible thing. In the spring of 1873, however, there came into existence what seemed a sufficient reason for the commencement of a movement, though on a very small scale, for the twofold purpose of safeguarding our youth from error and adverse influence, and also to secure for them better educational advantages than those hitherto enjoyed. The Winnipeg *Free Press* of the 10th of May contained the following criticism of the public school facilities of the town: "The common school system, as our legislators have left it, has not yet done much for the country, and the present state of things (educationally) is far from satisfactory.

"We have the public school of the district, and the Roman Catholic school, recognized by law as a separate common school. The first of these has never received the united support of Protestants which it needed to put it on a proper basis.

"We hear of a good deal of dissatisfaction in relation to it, and that the children are not advancing, etc.

"The Roman Catholic school has profited from the misfortune of the school of the majority, etc."

Under the condition of things, of which a glimpse is afforded in these quotations, a considerable number of the Protestant children of the village were being sent to the institution opened by the "Sisters of Charity" in Notre Dame Street East, and among them several of the Sabbath-school scholars of Grace Church. The parents of some of these, finding that they were learning and adopting some un-Protestant notions and customs, such as crossing themselves before meals, etc., complained to their pastor, asking if something could not be done to protect them from such teaching, whereupon I offered to meet the case at once by building, without cost to them, a small school house on the church lot, and employing a competent lady teacher, if they would promise to sustain the school by sending their children and by paying a reasonable fee. This was readily and cheerfully agreed to—the building was erected, and in a few days Mrs. D. L. Clink, who had been accustomed to teach in Ontario, was placed in charge. The school soon became so popular, and the attendance so large, that the building was found quite too small to accommodate all desiring admission.

In June, 1873, I attended Conference in London, after an absence therefrom of six years, when the needs of my distant parish were duly considered, and it was recommended that my stay in the country should be so prolonged as to enable me to visit the principal towns and cities, and solicit funds for the two-fold object of aiding in the building of small chapels in some of the outposts; and also in the erection of a suitable building in Winnipeg as our Wesleyan Institute. My work began forthwith, the ministers at the Conference and many kind friends in London subscribing very liberally to the fund. During the next two months I visited Brantford, Hamilton, Toronto, Oakville, Port Hope, Peterboro', Belleville, Picton, Kingston, Ottawa, Montreal and Quebec, with encouraging results—the subscriptions amounting to about $3,000, which in addition to what Dr. Punshon and Mr Macdonald had secured in subscriptions at Brockville, a good deal of which I collected, totalled nearly $6,000. My summer's work was not by any means a light one. Early in September I returned to Winnipeg, bringing with me a somewhat expensive outfit for the Institute, in maps, charts, globes, and apparatus, as well as books for library reference, etc. On the 27th of September, our Winnipeg newspaper reported that "The frame of the Wesleyan Institute was now up" and that the building was of two stories and would be very commodious, and later on the report given was that "the opening of the Wesleyan Institute took place on the 3rd of November, and that the building had been erected on the corner of Main and Water Streets, on the same lot as that occupied by the parsonage and Grace Church." The cost of the buildings and equipment was nearly $3,000. A portion of the balance of the collections made as referred to, was used in aiding in the erection of the first Zion Church in the North Ward, and also in aiding the people in building small places of worship at Rockwood, Poplar Point, High Bluff, Palestine, and near the third crossing of the White Mud River. By the balance remaining, the excess of expenditures over receipts in the running of the Institute, which unavoidably amounted to a considerable annual deficit, was in most part paid, aid being afforded us from the Educational Fund of the Church in small grants for a short time, until in 1877, when, the fund being exhausted and in association with another reason I will mention, it was deemed advisable to suspend operations for a season. That suspension was all the less regretable in view of the greatly improved condition of our public schools, and the fact that those who had hitherto supported the Institute found that the "school tax," which they had to pay in common with those who were profiting therefrom, together with the fees of the Institute, amounted to more than they were able to pay. In connection with the opening on the 3rd of November the following circular was issued:

"MANITOBA WESLEYAN INSTITUTE.

"1873–4.

"On the occasion of the opening of the new building and the beginning of advanced classes, the Board of Management desires to call attention to some of the advantages of this School of Higher Education.

"Its central position, on Main Street, near Grace

Church and the new Post Office, makes it of easy access from all parts of the town and vicinity.

"The building is commodious, school-rooms large and well lighted, ceilings high, and in heating and ventilation as well as in the arrangements of desks, seats, blackboards, etc., special care has been taken to have everything in accordance with the most approved designs. Ample accommodation is thus afforded for more than one hundred pupils.

"The apparatus is, probably, the best of the kind in the Province, having been specially selected from the Educational Depository of Ontario, and consists of maps, charts, globes, philosophical apparatus and general school-room outfit.

"The Institute will be in charge of Rev. A. Bowerman, B.A., assisted by a staff of competent and experienced teachers."

The number of pupils whose names were entered in the register for the first month after the opening was forty-seven. Arrangements were also made for evening classes in a commercial course and in modern languages.

At the close of the session of 1875-6, the Principal presented the following report:—

"*To the Board of Management of the Wesleyan Institute*:

"The attendance has been considerably in advance of any previous year, and with a more promising class of pupils. This is, no doubt, owing in a great measure to the increase in the staff of teachers as well as to an increase of population. The following is a classification of the attendance:

"The Higher Department, Ancient and Modern Languages, Higher Mathematics, etc.—18.

"Intermediate Department, the English branches of the Ontario High School Course.—13.

"Primary Department, consisting of all below the standard of entrance to a High School in Ontario.—40. Total 71.

"The evening classes of Mr. Morden in German and Shorthand have been fairly attended. The character of the work done is very evident from the marked progress of his pupils. The class in Vocal Music has been of great value to the Institute during the past year.

"The Primary Department has been well attended and has already furnished a number of pupils for the higher departments.

"In regularity and punctuality on the part of the pupils and interest on the part of the parents, there has been a marked improvement. Two young men are just completing their preparation for the University of Victoria College. This one item, small as it seems, is the best possible evidence of the value and necessity of the Institute to Methodism. No student from the other denominational schools (and we will have nothing else here for several years) will go to Victoria. The apparatus, though scanty, is sufficient for the present need; one globe, a full set of maps, a magic lantern with several hundred views, a case of chemicals, a lot of charts of various kinds, and a variety of books very good for prizes, with a number of educational works, complete the list. A few text-books also remain on hand.

"Respectfully submitted,
(Signed) "A. BOWERMAN.
"Winnipeg, May 11th, 1876."

I have pleasure in acknowledging my indebtedness for what follows, in relation to both the Wesleyan

Institute and to Wesley College, to the Rev. T. E. Morden, B.A. The chapter as a whole will indicate, I judge, that the Institute was the College in embryo.

"Principal Bowerman continued his work, with an assistant in the Preparatory department, until May, 1876, when he returned to Ontario. The work of that year was completed by Rev. T. E. Morden, B.A., Miss Fraser, of High Bluff, Man., conducting the Primary department for part of the time, and Miss Spencer (afterwards Mrs. Large, of Japan) continuing it until its close about a year later. The growth of the city and the improvement of the Public School system had by this time removed the necessity for the maintenance by the Methodist Church of a separate elementary or a preparatory school; and the city and country did not seem prepared as yet to sustain a college. The patronage would have been too limited, and funds could not have been secured from Manitoba or Ontario for its sustenance.

"THE ESTABLISHMENT OF WESLEY COLLEGE.

"For some years previous to the founding of the Manitoba Wesleyan Institute, the Church of England had had St. John's College; the Roman Catholic Church, St. Boniface College; and the Presbyterian Church, Manitoba College, engaged in doing the educational work of those denominations. These institutions did not then conduct many students beyond university matriculation; and there was no degree-conferring body in the Province. In 1877 the Manitoba Legislature established the University of Manitoba, with the three colleges named in affiliation; at the same time a charter was granted to 'Wesley College,' with provision made for its affiliation as soon as it should be established as a teaching institution with a certain number of professors, and become possessed of a suitable building. No further progress was made towards meeting the educational requirements of Methodism in Manitoba and the North-West until 1886, when an amended charter was granted by the Legislature to Wesley College. The question of providing training for candidates for the ministry was, however, often discussed in conferences and district meetings, and resolutions were passed, accompanied in some instances with offers of subscriptions of considerable sums.

"The actual work of teaching was begun in the fall of 1888, the appointment of the Principal, Rev. J. W. Sparling, D.D., dating from August of that year, and the commencement of lectures by the first professors, R. R. Cochrane, M.A., and G. J. Laird, M.A., Ph.D., a few months later. Steps were soon afterwards taken to secure the affiliation of the College with the University of Manitoba, which result was effected before the close of the academic year. The Department of Theology was instituted at the beginning of the second year, when the Principal began to devote his full time to his College duties, his position as President of the Montreal Methodist Conference and pastor of a large church in the City of Kingston, Ont., having retained him in Eastern Canada during the greater part of the first year.

"The teaching of the first year was done in the class rooms of Grace Church. For the second and third years a building on Albert Street was rented. The constantly increasing attendance then made it absolutely necessary to remove to a third place, and fortunately the Board succeeded in securing premises more commodious and fairly suitable for the purpose, which are still occupied by the college, namely a three-storey brick veneered building at the corner of Broadway and Edmonton Streets. These, though far superior in accommodation to the quarters previously

occupied, have long since become too small, and are otherwise unsuitable, thus making it highly necessary that the college should have a building of its own erected.

"The attendance of the first year numbered only seven students, the decision to open classes having been reached too late in the year to admit of sufficient publicity being given to the fact throughout the country. For the past two years there have been over seventy in the classes, which is certainly a highly creditable showing for a history of practically little more than four years.

"At the end of the first year there were no graduates to present themselves at the University convocation for degrees; at the end of the second year two received the degree of B.A., namely, Miss Earle and Mr. J. D. Hunt; the third year three, Messrs. Garratt, Shipley and Tufts, were sent up for similar parchments; the fourth year saw the number increased to five; the fifth year it had grown to six; and it is expected that the convocation of next June will see about twelve come forward to bow at the feet of the Chancellor and receive their B.A. hoods, thereby swelling the number of graduates to the respectable total of thirty.

"Besides the Principal, and Professors Cochrane and Laird, the first College staff included, as tutor of French, Mons. Le Chevalier de la Mothe. Subsequently Rev. A. Stewart, B.D., was appointed a tutor, and at the end of a year he was made a professor. Mr. Ed. Bourgeois, LL.B., succeeded M. de la Mothe as tutor in French. Mr. T. J. McCrossan, B.A., was the next to occupy a position on the College staff; he served very efficiently for two years as tutor in Classics, while pursuing at the same time his B.D. course under Prof. Stewart. His successor was Rev. J. H. Riddell, B.A., B.D., who still performs the work required in this department. The latest addition to the staff is Mr. W. F. Osborne, B.A., who recently graduated with high honors from Toronto University, after pursuing his course of study at Victoria College. He has charge of the Department of Moderns. The names mentioned comprise the staff as it now is, by whom the work is done with some occasional assistance from student-tutors.

"Though laboring under many inconveniences and disadvantages, the students of Wesley College have upheld the honor of their *alma mater* in carrying off their fair share of the medals and scholarships of the University.

"Financially, Wesley College is sustained chiefly by the liberality of the people of Manitoba and the North-West, who, in an unexampled way, undertook to bear the heavy burden because of their conviction of the absolute necessity of the establishment of such an institution in the interests of the Methodist Church. The annual givings of the people to this cause, together with a grant from the Educational Fund of the Church, amount to about $10,000. The Bursar, Rev. Dr. Sparling, visits all parts of the country in presenting the claims of the College; and the remarkable success in sustaining its interests is due to his untiring energy and the hearty co-operation of the ministers of the denomination and the loyalty of the people throughout the bounds of the Manitoba and North-West Conference.

"The College also commends itself to the sympathy and support of the Church in Eastern Canada, seeing that its work is to a great extent of a missionary character. One of its graduates is now a missionary in China, and many other missionaries will be found in both the foreign and domestic fields who will have received their training here.

"The affairs of Wesley College are under the able

OUR EARLY EDUCATIONAL MOVEMENTS. 279

management of a Board of thirty-six members, of whom eighteen resident in Winnipeg constitute the Executive. The officers of the Board are: Mr. J. A. M. Aikins, Q.C., Chairman; Mr. J. H. Ashdown, Vice-Chairman; Rev. Principal Sparling, Bursar; Mr. G. H. Campbell, Secretary; Dr. Laird, Assistant Secretary.

"Wesley College, including the site and building, cost in round figures $100,000—something over rather than under that sum. The subscription list amounts to between $94,000 and $95,000, of which about $67,000 is already paid in. With improvements made and increase of value of the land, the property is considered to be worth at present about $125,000.

"The registered attendance of students this year is 127. There are 49 graduates in Arts and 2 in Divinity. The students in attendance last year numbered 121; those of the year before, 83. There are out in the work of the ministry 35 who have attended the College, of whom 13 are graduates; and there are 28 probationers now attending."

CHAPTER XVIII.

TWO MISSIONARY JOURNEYS INTO THE INTERIOR.

IN June, 1874, a strong detachment of the Mounted Police Force, under the command of Colonel French, left Winnipeg for Fort Pelly and Swan River, where they were to have their headquarters, at least for a time. I presume it was in view of the line of the C. P. R. passing through that region on its way to the Rockies and the Pacific Coast that the Government of the day decided to centralize the force at that point; but as the route was soon changed so as to pass through the country a long way to the south and through a prairie instead of a thickly wooded and often swampy region, this most unsuitable place was abandoned, and great loss incurred by the heavy expenditures made in surveying the line and in building a steam saw-mill, stables and barracks, and officers' quarters, etc., at Swan River.

At the date referred to it was thought that large settlements would soon spring up in that region, and that these incoming settlers, together with those already there, as well as the police and a large band of Indians near by, would render it the duty of the Church to establish a mission among them, and so bring Gospel ordinances within their reach. As yet the place was far distant from any mission and had not been visited by a missionary.

It was in order that I might be able to come to an intelligent conclusion as to our duty as a Church to these far away people that I decided on a journey thither. In an interview with Colonel French in regard to the matter, I received a very kind invitation to accompany the force and to share "pot luck" with the officers and men during their journey. Accordingly I started from Winnipeg on the 18th of June, and overtaking them in camp near Portage la Prairie, I held service and preached at 11 a.m., and then preached again in the church in the village in the evening. On Monday evening we camped at Totogan, near where the "White Mud River" enters Lake Manitoba, and proceeding during the week, crossed that crooked little stream at no less than three crossings, and also the Little Saskatchewan River, and made our way over the Riding Mountain and across the prairies until we reached Shoal Lake on Saturday, the 26th, where we camped for several days while a depot for supplies was being built, and where a number of the men and horses were left for a time. On the Sabbath I preached once or twice to an attentive audience. On the 30th we struck our tents again and moved on toward our destination, crossing many leagues of beautiful farming prairie land and fording several streams—such as Bird Tail and Shell Rivers and others—and clambering up and down many high banks, which seemed as we viewed them at first well-nigh insurmountable, until at length, weary with travelling, we reached and looked in upon Fort Pelly, and then pushing on twelve miles farther we came to Swan River barracks, where we found a resting place on the 6th of July.

Fort Pelly was simply a Hudson Bay Company's trading post, consisting of a store, dwelling and certain stores and outhouses, the premises surrounded by a stockade, which was connected with a small farm under cultivation, and all in charge of a very kind Presbyterian, a Mr. McBeth, from whom I obtained much information. Colonel French, and in fact all the officers and men, treated me with much respect and kindness throughout the journey; Dr. Kitson and Inspector Dickens, son of the great novelist, sharing their tent accommodations with me.

Several of the young men of the force were graduates of European universities; but unsteady habits, in most cases, had resulted as never anticipated by their parents or themselves.

Captain John French, a brother of the Colonel, poor kind-hearted, impulsive fellow, lost his life at Batoche in 1885, through incautiously exposing himself from a window after the battle was over, when a miserable half-breed rebel shot and killed him instantly. It was some satisfaction that his slayer, being seen by one of our volunteers, was in turn shot and killed only a few moments later.

After such a survey of the surrounding country as was practicable, and after visiting the few settlers, I arranged my three appointments for the following

Sabbath thus: Barracks at ten o'clock, Pelly at two, and then Chief Cotie's, twenty miles distant, at seven; but I was unable to fill the last appointment through failing to have present an interpreter, a disappointment which I very much regretted. At my service at the fort I baptized several Indian children.

A SNAKE STORY.

The barracks at Swan River were located on a rocky hill which was specially noted for the multitudes of snakes, said to be harmless, which were known for years to have infested the place. In the early spring they were wont to crawl from their winter quarters in the crevices of the rocks, and seek more warmth and comfort in the sunshine, where, in masses often of almost incredible size and numbers, they coiled and wriggled until by an increasing vitality they should feel themselves ready for their accustomed summer pursuits. The sight was not a pleasant one to the police, who, after consultation, decided upon a war of extermination. The attack was to be made on the Queen's birthday, and in this wise: Two detachments of fifteen men each were matched for a snake-killing game, which was to occupy just half an hour. A number of empty flour barrels were placed in convenient positions, into which the captured ones were to be thrown, whether living or dead, and then at the close of the half hour, the detachment having the largest showing would be proclaimed and rewarded as per agreement. The result of this sanguinary attack upon their snakeships, as I was assured by an officer present on the occasion, was that there were eleven thousand fewer snakes on that stony hill than before it began—a very good showing for that half hour's slaughter. The same officer also estimated that not less than twenty thousand of these reptiles were killed during that spring. They were decidedly scarce at the date of our arrival.

This round trip, as I made it, extended to about seven hundred miles, and during the journey out, which occupied over twenty days, I held services and preached on four Sabbaths. Returning with my kind and good roadster, "Nechie," I made the run in six days, but we were homeward bound, and the trails being in good condition, and leaving each morning at 4.30, we were able to make, without injury to horse or driver, an exceptionally good run. Before parting with Colonel French I had arranged for accommodations for a missionary to be sent on my return home. In due course, the brother, accompanying another party of men going out to join the force, reached his post and entered upon his duties. He was charged with the responsibility not only of giving ministerial attention to the Police and of preaching to them, but also of visiting the settlers and the Indians and of making special efforts for their evangelization. His mission, I am sorry to say, proved a failure. He was poorly adapted to the position, the Police did not take kindly to him, and so after about three months he became discouraged and left the mission. The results were very disappointing to me, but I trust we were both instrumental to some extent at least, in doing good to those to whom we preached "the everlasting Gospel."

Soon after my return a sore trial came to our home. Our son was stricken down with the prevailing Red River fever, and for nearly two months vibrated 'twixt life and death. On two occasions we were forced to regard him as having passed away, but the Lord's "good hand was upon him and upon us for good," and after distressing solicitude on our part and inexpressible suffering on his, his health was restored. In the latter part of September I attended the first General Conference in Toronto, which consummated the union of the following Conferences: The Wesleyan Conference of Canada, The Wesleyan Conference of Eastern British America, and the Methodist New Connexion of Canada; the uniting bodies to be henceforth known as "The Methodist Church of Canada."

My second missionary journey into the interior was very unlike the first, and I will avail myself of the report I made thereof to the "Mission Rooms," and which Dr. Wood published in due course in the *Missionary Notices*, and which may instruct or interest some who have not before read it.

"On the 7th December last, it was my privilege to assist in the opening services of a new church on the High Bluff Mission, about forty-eight miles west of Winnipeg. My good Brother Fawcett has cause for rejoicing in the completion of so comfortable a church at a point where it was so much needed. Mr. W.

Gowler, whom I found, on my first visit in 1868, more than ready to give me a hearing, and to show kind hospitality, has by the power of grace become a happy, consistent and zealous Christian, and as the Lord has prospered him in worldly pursuits, he has evinced a commendable liberality in giving several acres of land near his residence for church premises, besides a considerable sum in contributions, and a good deal of labor on the building. The opening services were attended by large and seemingly devout congregations, upon whom gracious influences rested during the day, as a result of which special services were commenced. On my return home, Monday evening, I found the Rev. E. R. Young waiting, with Indians, dogs and sleds, to take me to Berens River, on my long trip to visit the Indian missions of the north. I was led to decide on making this trip by a conviction, long felt, that I could not discharge aright my duties either to the Missionary Committee, or the missionaries, without such a knowledge of the field and the work as can be secured only by actual observation. My purpose had been to make the journey during the summer, but I chose the winter instead, from a wish to get in my report before next Conference, because of a saving of time in making the trip— larger numbers of Indians to be met at certain points, and greater press of duties in Manitoba in the summer; besides which, I desired, as a means to an end, a just appreciation of the toils, privations, exposures and expenses inseparably connected with the long winter trips in this 'Wild North Land,' which are being made by my brethren in the prosecution of the great work of evangelization. To be the more systematic in my statement, I shall group my observations in the following order: The journey made, the country passed through, the missions visited.

"The journey extended to a distance of well nigh

REV. J. H. RUTTAN.   REV. E. R. YOUNG.   REV. J. SEMMENS.   REV. GEO. YOUNG.
            REV. O. GERMAN.   MRS. GEO. YOUNG.

A MISSIONARY PARTY, WITH DOG-TRAIN AND SLED.

one thousand two hundred miles, occupied twenty-eight travelling days, and was performed by some walking, and a good deal of riding in dog-sleds. The sixteen dogs, four sleds, four Indians, and two missionaries made up such a procession, as we left in the early morn of December 9th, as would have brought to the front a crowd of spectators had it appeared on King Street, Toronto, instead of the Red River of the North. Let me describe. Foremost of all was the 'runner,' Jake Savanas, or Southwind, a fat young Indian, a good runner, a still better feeder. Then came the Rev. E. R. Young, with his valuable train of dogs, and a sled, heavily laden with supplies needed at home. Next in order, my cariole, with its one hundred and eighty pounds, more or less, of humanity; and how much of bedding, clothing, pemmican, etc., I know not; and then two other trains, loaded with flour, pork and fish, either for use on the trip or to meet the wants of the people at Berens River. Two of the four teams of dogs and sleds were required for my use, the other two were independent though 'attached,' for reasons sufficiently apparent. The dog-sled, used as a cariole, is made of thin oak, about an inch thick, fourteen or eighteen inches wide, and about ten or twelve feet long; with the front end turned up like a skate, while the sides and back are made of parchment drawn tightly around a framework, and so hinged to the bottom of the sled as to yield a little when it runs against blocks of ice or trees, and thereby escape being wrecked, even though the passenger experiences an unpleasant squeeze from the collision. The whole thing is very light, and runs easily and rides smoothly on smooth ice, or a well-beaten road; otherwise, not. My experience in dog-sledding was of the following order: First period—quite amusing; the thinness of the oak bottom and the pliability of the sides render it a springy sort of thing; and as it runs over an uneven surface, the bottom changing quickly from the straight to the convex, and then to the concave, and back to the straight again—the sides meanwhile working like the leather sides of a bellows—it seems almost a thing of life, and might easily suggest to a half-awake passenger the idea of his being a sort of second Jonah, who by some hook or crook had got inside some monster, who, though on the ice, was making desperate strides toward an opening, through which to plunge with his victim into his native element, the 'vasty deep.' Two months before this, to a day, I was enjoying a ride on one of the beautiful and comfortable Pullman cars, between Chicago and St. Paul. Between that ride and this there was but little semblance, save that in each one is conscious of being strangely jerked, feet foremost, toward some place, he scarcely knows where. The second period —barely enjoyable, with interruptions; sitting for hours, not as in a chair, but after the fashion of a jack-knife half open, with an occasional let down, when the sled drops from a cake of ice or log, while the dogs are at a trot, or to be capsized and find one's self as helpless as an Indian babe in a 'moss-bag,' to say nothing of the cool attentions of Jack Frost, when thermometers indicate forty or fifty degrees below zero. These things act as interruptions to the barely enjoyable in a dog-sledder's experience. The third period is one of desire to have done with dog-sledding for ever. This I reached while yet far away from the home-side end of my journey. The dog-train is managed by a driver running behind without any reins, but with many words of which 'yee,' 'chaugh' and 'march' are among the most important, and in some instances the least objectionable; to these words are added certain persuasive measures in which a whip, often loaded with shot, is brought into painful requisition. Unlike the horse or ox, the dog speaks out his feelings in relation to these passing matters. By 'running' in this connection I do not mean that either Indians or dogs literally run; nor do they walk much; both take a kind of 'shack,' a sort of nondescript gait, which they can do very well, even to the extent of sixty or seventy miles per day, on a pinch. In that case they set off from camp at two or three in the morning, and deducting simply brief rests, during which two meals are taken by the men, they continue running until sunsetting, or even late in the evening when the end of the journey is to be reached. These long day journeys can only be made with good dogs, and on smooth ice or roads. To those who have not witnessed it, the statement that these men can travel so far in a day seems incredible; but so much for use. And let no one imagine that all this is done quite easily; not so, these achievements are the results of straining, fatiguing and wearing efforts, which in many cases are followed by an early breakdown.

"The camp for the night is quickly made by all hands setting to work—some scraping back snow, some cutting spruce boughs and carpeting the place, building up a back wall with them about three feet high, and others getting fuel for the fire. Thawing fish for the dogs, getting supper, getting frost and ice from clothes, preparing flat cakes and cooking pork for the next day, constituted the work of the evening around the camp-fire. Then after our evening hymn and prayer the weary ones retired for rest in the open wild, sometimes with snow falling thickly and wind blowing sharply, with 'spruce feathers' under them and a blanket or two over them, to sleep comfortably sometimes. I found that as long as I could avoid turning in bed I could keep warm, but to turn or to strike a match to see my watch, for I kept time for the men, was to give the cold an entrance, and then to sleep or to shiver became the question. Among the last things done before sleep, and the first on waking by most of the men, was to drink strong tea and smoke tobacco, large quantities of which had to be supplied them. Nor can such exertions be sustained, and such intense cold endured, without frequent replenishings with nourishing food. Four meals a day are requisite; a strong tea, pemmican, or pork, or venison, or fish, with flat cakes often baked in fat, seem necessary. In these almost Arctic regions such a head of steam as is requisite can be kept up only by a heavy supply of fuel. This will account for the fact that the supplies for one of these trips in the land of 'magnificent distances' and high prices, run up to an amount that cannot but astonish the uninitiated. The different stages in my journey were: from Winnipeg to Berens River, about five days; thence to Norway House, four days; thence to Oxford House, five days; the return trip occupying about the same time. During these twenty-eight days I camped out some twenty-three or twenty-four nights, some of which were colder than any I had ever before experienced. My aim was to walk about five or six miles a day, but in crossing a long rough portage I made one day about fifteen miles, and suffered for it too.

"The country through which I passed is one in whose praise I cannot say much. From Winnipeg to the last house in the lower settlement, about thirty-five miles, the land resembles the other portions of Manitoba, rather flat, some timber, but generally prairie; the soil, however, of the richest description. From that point to Lake Winnipeg, about fifteen miles, we passed over a marshy, muskegy region. The beach at the lake is high, made up of sand and flat stones. Once on the ice of this great lake, which is nearly three hundred miles long, and of peculiar shape, we struck for the western shore, along which we found for a long distance large quantities of timber, mostly poplar, which may yet serve us in Manitoba for building purposes and for fuel. The soil here is no doubt very good.

"Our day's run brought us to the region of evergreen trees—spruce, Norway pines, all too small to be of much value except for fuel or fences. Here I had my first night in a winter camp. From that point until I came back to it, excepting barely portions of country near Berens River, I saw very little affording any encouragement to the agriculturist. In fact, there are two things which would discourage any farmer, and which must be met all through this northern region—want of soil and want of season; soil in *depth* and of season in *length*. As a general thing the soil barely covers the rocks to a depth sufficient to grow shrubs or small trees, whose roots often strike down into the clefts of the rocks. In the lake there are two large islands, on which timber large enough for saw logs, or for small frames, can be obtained. On one of these a steam saw-mill has been recently erected, and from the other Mr. E. R. Young obtained the timber used in the buildings he had erected on his mission premises, drawing it with dogs across the ice, a distance of ten or twelve miles. From Norway House to Oxford House the country seemed to have no higher destiny than to be what it now is, the roaming, feeding and hiding ground of game and fur-bearing animals, and the home of those who hunt, trap, fish, or 'trip' for a living. The soil is thin and poor, the timber fit only for fuel, or to supply poles for the Indian's cabin, or for his use in making the traps or dead-falls wherewith he kills his game. Small lakes, rivers, marshy grounds, tamarac swamps and rocky hills—these make up the variety between those two points. Unless valuable minerals should be discovered, I should think that fifty years hence a thousand acres of this land might be worth a thousand cents.

"On the east shore of Lake Winnipeg there are large quantities of iron sand, which the magnet takes up readily; what this may betoken I know not. The tracks of game and fur-bearing animals, however, all through the northern region, abound, while in the lakes and the rivers the finest fish in the world are to be found. Fish is the main dependence of the people as food for themselves and dogs. During the trapping season the Indians are obliged to scatter in every direction. We saw the wood traps all along the shores of the lakes and rivers as we passed, and the number of skins of beaver, otter, mink, fox, lynx, bear, etc., which these hunters bring into the Hudson Bay Company stores at the different trading posts, all tell of their success.

"The missions I visited belong to the Methodist Church; no other denomination has ever occupied this ground.

"The Rossville Mission is very pleasantly situated on the shore of a beautiful little lake, within two miles of Norway House post, and is the oldest and by far the strongest of our Indian missions in the North-West. It was established in 1840 by the Rev. Mr. Rundle, Wesleyan missionary from London. The church was built by Rev. Mr. Evans in 1844, and enlarged by Rev. G. McDougall in 1861-2. In looking over the register of baptisms and marriages, which has been carefully kept from the first, I found the first baptism recorded on May 28th, 1840, by Mr. Rundle, and the last on January 3rd, 1875, by myself; between these dates one thousand five hundred and sixty baptisms were registered. Mr. Rundle was succeeded by the late Rev. James Evans, who, in labors and travels and successes, was 'more abundant,' and whose name is ever mentioned by these Christian Indians with profoundest respect and gratitude. Probably one thousand Indians or more consider this place, and neighborhoods adjacent, their home. The mission itself embraces a large number of families who live in very comfortable and clean-looking little houses, not far from the church and school and mission house. . . .

"Since the Rev. Mr. Evans, the mission has been occupied by Rev. Messrs. Hurlburt, Brooking, George McDougall, Stringfellow, E. R. Young, and their present pastor, Mr. Ruttan, all of whom have been made great blessings to this once benighted people. At present there is a membership of three hundred and eighty-one, of whom forty-seven are on trial, making a net increase this year of sixty-four. There are eighteen classes with leaders and assistant leaders, one day-school and one Sabbath-school at Rossville, and one day-school and a Sabbath-school at 'Crooked Turn,' about eight miles away. In these schools there are about one hundred and fifty scholars.

"At the love-feast there were present three hundred people, while nearly two hundred came to the Lord's table, among whom one was over one hundred years of age, and one came one hundred miles to attend the services.

"New Year's day was 'a high day' with the Indians of Rossville, over five hundred of whom feasted on 'fat things,' all of which were gratis to the feasters. From morn till even the eating went briskly on amid indication of good appetites, and great enjoyment, and but little weariness. I reached the mission on my return trip from Oxford, about 10 a.m., just in time for the feast. In the evening they had the public meeting with ' Big Tom ' for a chairman, who, by the way, is a good man and true, but oh, so slow in getting up to speak, and, in speaking, exceedingly slow. Just imagine a great tall man getting up an inch at a time, and waiting between the inches. But he got all the way up at last, and spoke, I presume, very sensibly, which is more than many a white man does who gets up with less hesitancy. A number of speeches were made, and a very enjoyable meeting indeed terminated in good time. I visited both schools, and while pleased with the appearance of the children, regret that I cannot report more favorably of their study of the English language. . . .

"The Rev. Mr. Ruttan has succeeded admirably at this post; his kind, prudent and Christian walk, and his zealous and faithful ministry have borne fruit abundantly, while his excellent young wife, right from the Wesleyan Ladies' College, Hamilton, only a few weeks elapsing from the day she left her studies till she entered upon her duties in this far-off mission, has been 'a helper indeed' to her husband. Long may these devoted servants of Christ be spared to each other, the Church, and the great work they are now so heartily and so cheerfully prosecuting.

"At Norway House I received the most kind and considerate attention from the Chief Factor, Mr. Ross, and also from Messrs. Sinclair and McTavish; in fact, this holds good of all the officials of the Hudson Bay Company at every post I visited. They are all manifestly interested in the mission work, and in sympathy with our missionaries, of whom they spoke to me in the kindest and most commendatory terms.

"The mission at Jackson's Bay, near Oxford House, and about two hundred miles north-east from Norway House, was established at a more recent period, and has been occupied by Rev. Messrs. Steinhauer, Brooking, Stringfellow, Sinclair and the present missionary, Mr. German.

"At the outset, premises as mission and school houses and a church were erected, and, I understand, paid for by the Missionary Society in England. The expenditure must have been very heavy. At the present time the tendency of the settlement seems towards the fort, which is about fourteen miles from the mission house at the bay. The decision to build a church near the fort was a wise one. Here large numbers collect every season for trading purposes, and several families reside permanently, who, with the officers and servants of the company, will make a good congregation throughout the year. A beautiful site has been selected and a comfortable church erected, and is now in use, though not quite finished. The mission house at the bay is occupied by Mr. German, our bachelor missionary, who has his interpreter and family residing in a portion of the building, by whom he gets his 'house-keeping' managed. A comfortable building, comparatively new, is used both for the school and the place of worship. It seems necessary to keep these two extreme ends of an awkwardly shaped mission, as many families will continue to reside at the bay on account of an excellent fishery there, while others will reside near the fort as employees of the Company. In working the mission, Mr. German gives one Sabbath at the old fort, and the next at the old mission, holding two services at each place, with prayer-meeting, and class and Bible-class during the week, as he can get them together. During the summer a school is kept open at the bay, with about forty children, but in winter the families scatter, as elsewhere, to their hunting-grounds, and the school is interrupted. The membership when Mr. G. went there in September, 1873, consisted of about sixty. Since that date he has received fifty-seven on trial, and the membership is now one hundred and seventeen. He also visits an outpost about one hundred and fifty miles away, where he has instructed and baptized a large number who were unevangelized prior to the above-given date. I was greatly pleased with the heartiness and cheerful spirit manifested by Brother German in the prosecution of his work, notwithstanding his lonely position and hard field. 'The Lord loveth a cheerful giver,' whether the gift be in money or in service.

"We reached the mission on the evening of Christmas day, after a very fatiguing day's run, from early morn till long after dark. On Sabbath I preached and gave the Sacrament, and baptized a child at 10 a.m. at the bay, and then we crossed over to the fort, fourteen miles, and held service there. The night was the coldest I had ever experienced, and when we set off next morning before sunrise to cross the lake— a distance of about forty miles, it is said—with wind sharp ahead, neither present experience nor future prospects for that day were very pleasing. The Indians with me froze cheeks and ears in a very general way, but said very little about it, while I felt the cold very much with all my mummy-like wrappings, till finally I had to get out and run to keep my feet from freezing. The thermometer at the fort was useless in such intense cold—I have no doubt it should have gone down to fifty degrees below zero. I mention this to show under what circumstances of discomfort and peril our devoted missionaries are often placed. Dr. Taylor once in his life endured the almost purgatorial sufferings occasioned by the swarms of mosquitoes, which gave him such a warm reception in this same region, and glowingly did he depict his sufferings. Once in my life, for a little while, I have felt the discomfort and faced the peril, and endured the toil of a trip through there in midwinter. But what is all this in either case to what our dear brethren stationed out here have to meet with every summer and every winter—and are they not equally susceptible to suffering as either of us?

"Let our good brethren in the more comfortable home-work bear them up in their prayers, and use all allowable means to secure to them the most liberal 'appropriations.' These are the toilers who earn and really need the highest salaries going. High prices prevail, hungry Indians clamor, and perquisites and presents are unknown—these are noteworthy facts.

"The Nelson River Mission is situated about two hundred miles north from Norway House, and is the most northerly point of our mission field. The work of instructing these poor pagans was commenced by Rev. E. R. Young during the occupancy of Rossville, and by him a large number were baptized. Through his representations and influence mainly, the authorities of the Church were led to open a mission there, and to appoint the Rev. J. Semmens as their first missionary. Upon him rests the heavy responsibility of making, if possible, this mission a success, and his will be the honor in that case from the Church of the future. As I understood that the Indians were generally away to their hunting-grounds, I decided not to extend my long and tedious and costly trip to that point; but, during my visit to Oxford House, the missionary arrived at Norway House, so that on my return I met him there, and received from him a full statement of the work done and of his plans for the future. During the last few months he has baptized fifty-five persons, and conducted services regularly on the Sabbath, with congregations not very large, but attentive, some seven of whom have become communicants. According to the returns made to the Hudson Bay Company's officer, Mr. Ross, the Indians in that vicinity numbered in 1872, fifty-five husbands, having among them sixty-eight wives, ninety children, and fifteen widows and several orphans; but I believe that there are other bands near by, so that Mr. Semmens reckons about five hundred Indians as placed under his pastoral care. According to the judgment of Chief Factor Ross, as well as Rev. E. R. Young, this field is a central and very important one, which should be worked with energy and true faith.

"The new mission at Berens River is situated on the shore of a pleasant little bay which puts in from Lake Winnipeg, on the east side of the lake, and about midway from the mouth of Red River and Norway House. The mission was opened by Rev. E. R. Young in 1873. When the statement of Rev. John Ryerson, as published in his book of travels through this land in 1854, is remembered, that this point ought to be made a mission, that the Indians and the Company's officials desired it, and that missionaries in passing had promised that they should have a missionary, and then the fact noted that, despite all this importunity and recommendation and promise, no missionary was sent until 1873, the old adage, 'large bodies move slowly,' will be apt to occur to the mind. On Sabbath, the 13th of December, I reached this pleasantly-situated mission in time to enjoy a service in the 'tabernacle,' as they call it, erected a few months ago. Our arrival was followed by no small stir among the natives, who, on the call of the beautiful bell given by Jas. Ferrier, Esq., assembled, and gave earnest attention to my message from 'Behold, I bring you glad tidings,' etc. Each Sabbath services are conducted in the Tabernacle at 11 a.m., in Indian, through an interpreter, and at 6 p.m., at the fort, in English. Class and prayer-meetings and a Bible-class are conducted in the afternoon or during the week. At the three services I attended the congregations were very encouraging—about twenty received the Sacrament and three were baptized.

"As a centre, the mission is of great importance. Large bands of Indians yet unchristianized can be easily reached, as at Poplar River, Jack's Head, Sandy Bar, Pigeon River and Grand Rapids, many of whom will probably settle near the mission ere long.

"The fisheries and hunting-grounds are the best, I suppose, on the lake. Being about midway between Norway House and Red River, it will afford our missionaries, as they pass to and fro, a much needed and quiet resting-place, securing to the mission a visit, and to the weary travellers a home and a Sabbath rest. To my mind the field here is attractive, and the prospects of the mission are cheering. Mr. and Mrs. E. R. Young are toiling hard, and even with weeping, to scatter 'precious seed.' May they soon realize the promise fulfilled, and 'come again with rejoicing, bringing their sheaves with them.' I felt it my duty here and elsewhere to speak with plainness on the real mission of a missionary, informing the Indians that it was not to scatter presents, either of food or clothing, so much as to teach them the way to the Saviour. The idea of some of them seems to be that a missionary must be a sort of unweariable giver, and with such I am sure I must have made myself very unpopular. In my judgment our missionaries will have to insist on a little more of 'self-help' among them. During my journey I had several conversations with uninstructed pagans, all of whom professed to feel dissatisfied with their position, and to desire more light, and to be anxious for instruction in the doctrines of Christianity. From several I got a promise that they would pray to the Great and Good Spirit to lead them into the true light. Polygamy, a superstitious dread of their medicine-men and conjurers, wandering habits, and an idea that he who would teach them ought to feed them to a considerable extent—these are obstacles in the way of their Christianization, but they are surmountable, and have been surmounted in thousands of instances. The difficulty of mastering their miserable language so as to preach in it, or of getting the truth properly before them through an interpreter, is felt by all our missionaries. From them we need fear neither violence nor opposition. The term 'savages,' if by any applied to the Indians of this country, whether Christian or pagan, is a misnomer. Openings for schools and missionaries abound—'The fields are white unto the harvest'—the laborers are comparatively few, and the funds are not as plentiful as they should be in the treasury of a Church bought with the Redeemer's blood.

"After parting with the kind people of Berens River on the 11th of January, I reached home on Friday the 16th, weary and sore indeed, better as I supposed in health, and yet after the services of Sabbath the reaction came, and for several days it seemed uncertain whether an attack of fever or inflammatory rheumatism awaited me. However, deliverance came, as has been usual with me, through the infinite mercy and goodness of God. I am thankful that I have been enabled to make the trip in the winter, but this one, with its fatigue and exposure, must suffice for me. Were I possessed of the vigor and activity and endurance and lightness which were mine thirty years ago, I might decide otherwise. Providence permitting, I hope to start in a day or two for the extreme limit of our Province to the westward, and to visit the missions in that direction. This journey over, I shall have visited each mission on this large District since December 9th, excepting barely that at Nelson River, and travelled one thousand two hundred miles with dogs, and five hundred with my horses."

CHAPTER XIX.

MY LAST HAND-SHAKE WITH AN HEROIC MISSIONARY.

BEFORE entering upon the subject indicated by the above heading, I will make, by way of introduction, brief references to the circumstances under which, and to two or three consecrated men by whom, the early missions of Methodism were established among the aboriginal peoples of these great lone lands.

In the same year in which I was converted, and at about the same time, now fifty-seven years ago, the authorities of British Methodism, having decided upon establishing certain missions in these Territories, appointed the following brethren as missionaries to the following places, viz.: Norway House, Lake Winnipeg, James Evans; Moose Factory, etc., George Barnley; Lac-la-Pluie and Fort Alexander, William Mason; Edmonton and Rocky Mountain House, Joseph Rundle; *James Evans, General Superintendent*. Thus we trace up to its source a stream, small indeed at the first, which has, nevertheless, flowed on and on, ever widening and deepening as it flowed, till it has become as a mighty river bearing offers of life and salvation with manifold and great benefits to tens of thousands of redeemed and immortal men. The "day of small things" which some despised has become a day of great things not now to be despised even by our enemies. As we look over this "list of stations" we may well be struck with the vastness of that District over which they extended, of which Mr. Evans was appointed Chairman, and the work throughout which he was to supervise; and yet right well did he accomplish the work given him to do in that he visited every mission in his District, and journeyed far into "regions beyond," preaching the "everlasting Gospel." Thus this man of great resources in himself, and of never failing courage, and with his great heart all aflame with love to God and humanity; this heroic and zealous and successful apostle to the Indians and Hudson Bay Company officials as well, literally rushed, now by canoe of his own construction, and now by train of dogs of his own training, from point to point in this country of magnificent distances, proclaiming "the unsearchable riches of Christ," and declaring the way of salvation to all from whom he might gain a hearing. The dangers he faced, the toils and hardships he endured, and the privations and vexatious trials which he suffered were far beyond any that fell to the lot of any of his associates or successors in this great work of evangelization. Yet his faith failed not, and not fearing "the wrath of man," he unflinchingly pressed on in his work until relieved of his heavy responsibilities, first by the authorities by whom he was appointed to his difficult mission, and then by the ever-observant and sympathizing Head of the Church, who said, "It is enough; come up higher."

It has been thought by some (perhaps uncharitably) that missionaries sometimes have trenched rather closely on the extravagant and the imaginative in their reports given through the press and on the platform, of scenes witnessed, perils braved, and achievements effected by themselves. Be that as it may, I have never read or heard of any such accusation against our sainted brother. He was too great a man and too good a Christian to indulge in exaggeration in order to self-laudation, or to gain popular applause, while recounting the Lord's doings where he toiled. In his Master's good time this worker " was not, for God took him." The Lord of the great harvest "can bury His workmen, and yet carry on His work."

Of this band of pioneer missionaries there are other names which should be held in grateful remembrance by all who rejoice in the progress of the work of grace among the Indians of the North-West. First and foremost, next to that of Mr. Evans, is that of Robert Rundle. His appointment was to "Edmonton and Rocky Mountain House," a field fully one thousand miles distant from any of his brother missionaries, where, in the midst of the then wandering, warring, and superstitious Crees and Stonies, he was to "lift high" the blood-stained banner, and seek both to teach the children and persuade these braves of the plains to be at peace with each other and to be reconciled unto God. The bearing of the teaching and example and efforts of Mr. Rundle and his successors in this work on the safety of property and life, in the case of many a traveller and trader, has been most direct and influential for good. The rights, and even lives, of the "pale faces" were not always accounted very sacred by those who, having been often wronged by the white man, sometimes avenged themselves terribly, even upon the innocent, until the missionary visited and taught and influenced them. Thus these holy men, with trust in God, and yet, as men say, "with their lives in their hands," ofttimes stood up between imperilled ones and these avengers of blood, rescuing those about to perish; and yet, in many cases, they have received but little, if any, credit for it.

Many of the fruits of the labors of Mr. Rundle remain to this day. Among both Crees and Stonies are those—long ago converted through his instrumentality—who testify with gratitude and deep feeling to the light and blessedness of salvation which came to them through his faithful and loving ministry. Mr. Rundle, I take it, was rather an evangelizer than an organizer. Perhaps there was but little opportunity for organizing in his day, and so without any seeming centre of operation, he moved as the Indians moved, following them to the buffalo hunt or wherever they might roam, in order to have opportunities of teaching their children and preaching to and evangelizing their adults. A truly and fully consecrated life was his, and not unworthy the distinction conferred upon him by the giving of his name to a grand mountain with snow-clad peak in the immediate neighborhood of Banff, which he ascended, guided by an Indian convert (and, I judge, was the first white man who ever did so), and which is still called " Rundle Mountain," an everlasting monument, seen from afar, as is another great mountain nearer Morley, appropriately called " McDougall Mountain," in well deserved honor of the heroic and now sainted George McDougall.

Mr. Rundle, after several years of toil in these vast and wild regions, returned to England, where, for many years, he rendered very efficient service in the home work. After a season of superannuation, he was only recently called from labor to reward.

It would be inexcusable in me to pass over the name of another in this "bright succession," who was one of my early friends in the ministry, and is, by all who know him, highly esteemed and honored for his godly character and his "works of faith and labors of love." I refer to Rev. Thomas Woolsey, the successor of Mr. Rundle. I received from officers of the Hudson Bay Company's service, more than a score of years ago, most gratifying testimonies to his Christian deportment and his self-sacrificing zeal as a missionary. Like Rundle, he traversed the great plains with his pastoral charge, ever acting the part of a good under-shepherd, even though perils had to be braved and hardships endured. I met godly Indians at Morley, quite recently, who gratefully and lovingly remembered the good missionary and his work. Like Evans and Rundle, Thomas Woolsey also has left it, to others to proclaim his exploits in the days gone by, while with the Psalmist he ever exclaimed, "Not unto us, O Lord, but unto thy name be all the praise."

He, like his friend and predecessor, Mr. Rundle, has but recently entered upon his everlasting rest. The name of the missionary hero to whom the remainder of this chapter will relate, and who was a worthy successor of Evans, Rundle, and Woolsey, will be readily anticipated. Dr. Chalmers has been credited with the affirmation, "Methodism is Christianity in earnest." He might have added, very truthfully, that whenever that ceases to be true of Methodism, there will be but little left worthy of extension or preservation. What wonders have been accomplished through the instrumentality of an "earnest ministry and a working Church;" and what opportunities, more than golden, have been lost forever—aye, criminally lost—through the dilatoriness of an un-earnest ministry, and an inactive, ease-loving Church?

George McDougall was a man of intense earnestness from the date of his "second birth," until he "ceased at once to work and live." Having given himself to the mission work, "he counted not his life dear unto himself" from that hour forward, but heroically, and with full trust in God, set himself to face whatever might threaten to obstruct his way, or hinder him in the prosecution of that work.

"Send us a good swimmer; our last preacher was drowned in trying to reach one of his appointments," was the earnest message sent to Bishop Asbury by a hardy pioneer, when petitioning for a missionary adapted to the requirements and difficulties of a new field. It was well, both for himself and many others, that George McDougall was a "good swimmer"—he had need to be. Many a rushing and unbridged stream was crossed by him, both in making and fulfilling his appointments, without either boat or raft or float of any kind, and thus for long years, not alone by driving or riding or walking over roadless prairies, but frequently by swimming unfordable rivers and streams, he carried the "glad tidings" to the un-Christianized humanity of the North-West. Brave, earnest man,

> "Whose living like I shall not find,
> Whose faith and works were bells of full accord."

Concerning him and a host of others, who have vanished out of our view, we cherish the hope

> "That we shall meet,
> In life complete,
> At Jesus' feet,
> And say a glad good morning, in a higher, brighter, happier clime than this."

The Rev. George McDougall was born in Kingston, 1820; was born again in his nineteenth year; was received on trial for the work of the ministry in 1850, and owing to the special need of an ordained man where he was laboring and also to his special fitness for it, he was ordained in 1852. The various fields of labor occupied by him, as the years went by, were:

Alderville, Garden River, Rama, Norway House, Victoria, Edmonton House, and Morleyville.

In July, 1875, after long years of acquaintance and close friendship, the Rev. Dr. Wood and he met in our little parsonage, Winnipeg, and after three days spent in conferring with each other and myself, parted for the last time.

On Monday Dr. Wood arrived by steamer from the

REV. GEORGE M'DOUGALL.

south, and in the evening he preached and ordained a missionary in Grace Church. During the three days of his stay with us we had consultations relating to the management and prospects of the "Wesleyan Institute," and the appointment of the Rev. Mr. Manning, then with us in Winnipeg, to the Saskatchewan District, and other important matters. I was, very unwillingly, in the minority in regard to Mr.

Manning, for he was proving a great blessing in our work on my District, to which he was specially adapted, but of course the minority had to yield, and Brother Manning went west. Dr. Wood took steamer for home on the 21st of July.

On Sabbath, 1st of August, Mr. McDougall preached in Grace Church and joined us in the Holy Communion, and on the following Sabbath he took three services in Winnipeg, while I ministered to the scores of railroad men at Rat River and other points along the line on the east side of the Red River.

Just then, when Mr. McDougall was preparing for his return journey, exciting rumors came from Carlton and still farther west, to the effect that the Indians were threatening to give serious trouble. Surveyors had been laying out the line of the railroad and blocking out the land where they claimed ownership, prior to any explanation of matters such as should have been given them, and to any treaty being entered into. This certainly was an unaccountable oversight. It was a fortunate circumstance that Mr. McDougall was then within reach, and Lieutenant-Governor Morris, sending for him forthwith, urged him to undertake a journey among these distant and much agitated tribes for their pacification and to secure promises from them to meet a Government Commission in the following summer, to arrange and sign treaties, etc. But he was anxious to push on at once, by the shortest and quickest route, for his distant mission-home, from which he had been so long absent, and so, hesitating to comply with the Governor's request, he conferred with me on the subject. My judgment was, that as the circumstances were alarming, he should consent to go as requested, if the Government would furnish a sufficient outfit of carts, horses and provisions for the long journey, and for a wise distribution of presents to the needy ones, and also give him positive assurance that the Indians should not be disappointed in the following summer, by the non-arrival of the Commission. He thereupon gave his consent, and in a few days all needful authority from Ottawa was received, and all arrangements requisite were made and he was ready to begin his journey.

On the 9th of August we grasped hands for the last time, when I was much surprised by his saying, " Brother Young, we will not likely ever meet again in this world. You are going back to the work in Ontario, and I am undertaking a difficult and perilous journey and task in order to pacify these excited Indians, and I know not what may befall me; and besides that, I am frequently suffering from a sharp pain about my heart, which came upon me while addressing large meetings so often in Canada and England, together with irregularities as to diet and hours of retirement which seemed unavoidable. This pain has troubled me a good deal during the last few days, but I hope when I shall get out on the plains again, that the change will bring me all right." I tried to utter a few encouraging words, and we parted with a solemn " Good-bye." His reference to that pain in the region of the heart came forcibly to my mind when I received the sad intelligence of his sudden and mysterious decease on the western prairies.

Leaving Winnipeg, he struck first for Carlton and thence to Prince Albert, and having interviewed the natives at these points and by the route taken, he started out westward for the big plains. Travelling from camp to camp and meeting large numbers of the already disturbed Indians, he explained to them the matters in question, assuring them, according to his instructions, that in the following summer Commissioners would be sent into their country to treat with them. He was received everywhere with confidence, and his words being believed, the Indian mind all over the country was set at rest, despite the efforts of agitators and the prophesying of the envious.

In due course the Commissioners put in their appearance, and after a good deal of speech-making and distributing of presents, the treaties were signed. In January, 1876, it was found that the food supplies with the mission families at Morley were running short, and there being no parties available to employ as buffalo hunters, he and his son and nephew left home on a hunting expedition to secure the needed supply of buffalo meat. On the 23rd of January, after a successful but very hard day's work, they started at nightfall to retrace their steps toward the camp, which was about eight miles distant; and when within two miles of the place, Mr. McDougall proposed that his son, then walking and weary, should take the pony he was riding, and proceed to the camp and make ready the supper. To this John demurred, requesting his father to continue riding, while he would follow the loaded sleighs as he had been doing; whereupon, directing attention to a certain star toward which they were to move, he set off, galloping his pony in the direction indicated. They never saw him again in life. "By a mysterious providence, never to be revealed in this life, he failed to reach the camp and perished on the plains. Diligent search was made at once by his son, and then by a large number of anxious friends, but it was not until the thirteenth day that the frozen body was found, uninjured, and as if laid out by loving hands for burial." His son, the Rev. John McDougall, states in a beautiful memorial volume: "As I looked at him and beheld his features, I said, Whatever may have happened my father, he was conscious at the last, and feeling that death was upon him, he picked out a level spot and laid himself out straight and crossed his hands and thus prepared to die. His face was perfectly natural, bearing an expression of conscious satisfaction. Reverently the body was lifted to the sleigh, and we started that Sunday afternoon on our homeward journey." He also adds, in reference to the sad occurrence, about the cause of which there were so many differing opinions: "My own theory is that some disease affecting either his heart or his brain so acted upon him that for the time being he was rendered unconscious of his surroundings, otherwise I cannot explain his being lost."

As soon as the report reached me at Winnipeg, I

wired Dr. Sutherland in relation to it, and received the following reply: "I fear there is absolutely no hope. Thus has fallen one of the noblest and most self-sacrificing missionaries that ever entered the work. I feel as though in this calamity I had lost a brother."

On the following Sabbath evening I preached a memorial sermon in Grace Church, from the text (Genesis v. 24): "He was not, for God took him." In the concluding part of the discourse I remarked as follows: "Our departed brother was a man of wonderful resources, possessing more of what is called 'self-help' than any one I had previously known. His courage and presence of mind never failed him, even amid scenes of greatest danger. Circumstanced as we are to-day, with but few facts before us, we can scarcely avoid asking questions which must remain unanswered, at least for the present. What became the agency used in his dismissal from the toils and trials of this life? Was it what is now so often reported as the cause of sudden death—'heart failure'? Those of us who knew him well cannot bring ourselves to believe that George McDougall perished as an ordinary wanderer who had missed his way perishes. And did he, suffering the loss of consciousness for a time, regain it when near his last moments; and as he sank amid the whirling clouds of frost and snow, did he realize the presence and helping hand of an Almighty Saviour, who so transfigured the driving snow-clouds as to cause them to seem but as the chariots and horses of light which were commissioned to bear his ransomed and released spirit away to the glorious presence of Elijah's God? Let all this be as it may, we are confident that the seeming severity and desolation by which the external circumstances attending his decease were characterized, were in striking contrast with what was internal to the departing servant of his Lord. All there was calm, peaceful, blissful and heavenly. 'He was not'—that is, to those who sought him, an embodied being. His body, once so full of life and vigor, was near, and it may be that his spirit, then separated from that body, looked down upon them as they prosecuted their search, while he was in blessed companionship with many whom he had instructed and led to Christ, including some even of his own loved ones who had passed on before, he and they alike enjoying the 'beatific vision.'" All that was mortal of our sainted brother rests in the cemetery at Morley, where a substantial and appropriate monument has been reared by those who are following after. On the occasion of each of my two visits to that beautifully situated mission, in 1892 and 1893, I spent some time at the grave of my former associate in the work of the Master, while my thoughts went forth to some period in the future when I hope to meet him on the Mount of God.

It seems appropriate that this chapter should close with the following brief sketch, written by the late Rev. Dr. Stafford in 1883:

"ENOCH WOOD SKINNER.

"Among those who accompanied the mission party from Toronto to the North-West in 1868, was the lad whose name heads this brief notice. For several years he resided with the late Rev. George McDougall, where he saw and heard much of missionary life, learned the Cree language, and with the zealous missionary travelled extensively through that great country. After his return to Toronto to his parents he was converted to Christ, and immediately his heart was drawn toward the poor unevangelized aborigines of the far west, whose habits, language and needs he knew so well. Consulting frequently and prayerfully with the Rev. Drs. Wood, Sutherland and Young in relation to the matter, he finally obtained permission to enter upon what he intended to be his great life work, and started for the field of toil he so greatly desired to occupy. His outfit was secured at Winnipeg, and several hundreds of miles journeyed over with his ponies and carts, and then Enoch 'was not, for God took him.' Alone on the wild prairie, from an accidental discharge of his gun, his young life was instantly terminated. How very mysterious that he, as well as his sainted friend McDougall, should have passed out of life, like Moses, with no earthly friend near. It cannot be doubted but that in his case the will was accepted, by the Master, for the deed, and that in the great reaping and rewarding day, Enoch Wood Skinner will 'stand in his lot' among that great multitude of earnest workers, who, having sown 'precious seed' weeping, shall come again with rejoicing, bringing their sheaves with them. The grave of this zealous young missionary is at Prince Albert, where a Methodist mission was subsequently established."

CHAPTER XX.

RETURNING TO ONTARIO.

I WAS led to decide in favor of this return by three considerations, which I shall specify as follows:

First, my belief was then, as it is now, that, except in the case of remote missions, our Methodist system of itinerancy is far better adapted to the needs of the people and to promote the edification and extension of the Church, than is a settled pastorate. This consideration seemed to me to be of special force in my case, in 1876, because of the interblending of educational with evangelistic interests in Winnipeg.

For eight years I had ministered to the congregation there, and for three years had been closely connected with the management of the Wesleyan Institute; a position which I deeply felt implied and needed a scholarship and an experience such as I could not lay any claim to. In view of these combined interests, I felt certain that the Conference could easily select from among its university graduates a successor who should more efficiently discharge these multiform duties than I could hope to do. In order that such a turn in the great wheel of our itinerancy might take place, I forwarded my request for the double transfer—myself to the work in Ontario, and some more competent brother to Winnipeg.

A second consideration which influenced me in making the request was what I may designate as an increasing weariness of "serving tables." My position in that centre of communication with the remote Indian missions of two Districts had rendered it seemingly necessary for me to take on, with my other duties, that of making purchases for the missionaries and their families, such as might be ordered, making payments out of the proceeds of their "authorized bills" from the Mission Rooms, and then securing their transportation by carts or boats to their distant destinations. All this required more attention to bookkeeping and more labor in selecting and sending off the required supplies than was compatible with my other responsibilities, and became exceedingly irksome and tiring, especially when the requisitions called for more than appeared to the credit of the requisitionist.

A third consideration was a conviction that the transfer sought would afford me greater opportunities than I could otherwise enjoy of advocating the claims of our missions in the North-West in committees and at missionary anniversaries.

In connection with our making arrangements to leave Winnipeg, the following testimonial addresses were presented to me, the one by the late Chief Justice Wood, and the other by the late Sir John C. Schultz, afterwards Lieutenant-Governor of Manitoba:

"Reverend and Dear Sir,—It becomes us to acquiesce in the decrees of Providence, and yet it is no less becoming at times to manifest regret at the substance of these decrees as they specially affect us.

"Your removal from this wide field of usefulness, where you have so long endured hardship as a good soldier of Jesus Christ, maintaining a character without reproach, and in the zealous and discreet exercise of your sacred calling, gaining the good-will and respect of all classes without distinction of creed, may be (as we trust it will) for the benefit of the Church with which you are immediately connected, for the Church generally, and for yourself particularly, nevertheless the present loss is ours, and we can not but express our sense of it. We part with you, therefore, as one parts with a friend.

"Be assured you carry with you our best wishes for your future welfare and happiness, and that in your new sphere of usefulness you may be blessed with abundant success as a faithful husbandman in the Lord's vineyard.

"We cannot close this address without expressing our deep sense of the obligation the citizens of Red River Settlement are under to you for the patriotic course taken by you during the troubles of 1869 and '70, in this country.

"In connection with this address we beg to present you with the accompanying purse as a small testimonial of our respect and esteem.

"Signed on behalf of the citizens of Winnipeg,

"E. B. Wood,
"Chairman of Committee, Chief Justice of Manitoba.

"To Rev. Geo. Young,
" Wesleyan Methodist Minister.

" Winnipeg, Man., 26th May, 1876."

"*To Rev. George Young, Pastor of Grace Church, Winnipeg:*

"SIR,—Remembering your connection with the events of the Red River rebellion; willingly giving your only son to aid those who strove to maintain law and order and to defend the flag of their country; your ministering care of those who languished in prison, and of him who was put to a cruel death; and the fearless discharge of your duties at all times at great personal risk:—those who were witnesses of your conduct and the recipients of your ministrations have thought it well to offer you a slight testimonial on the occasion of your departure from among us.

"A meeting of the prisoners of 1869-70 have accordingly instructed us to express to you their high appreciation of your conduct as a minister of the Gospel and a patriotic man during these trying times; to tender their thanks for your zealous, kindly and sympathizing attention to them while in prison; and to say to you that, among the many who are now publicly testifying their appreciation of the services you have rendered this country, there are none who more deeply regret your departure, or who will longer hold you in grateful remembrance.

"JOHN SCHULTZ, *Chairman.*
"JAMES STEWART, *Secretary.*

" Winnipeg, Man, 25th May, 1876."

Our return to the work in Ontario was facilitated and made all the more pleasant by the fact that two important charges, which I had previously ministered to, intimated, as soon as they knew of my purpose, that their "gates were ajar" for our re-entrance. A sense of obligation to the officiary and friends of

RETURNING TO ONTARIO.

the Richmond Street Church, in view of their exceeding liberality in the support of the little Red River mission, and the encouraging kindness which they had shown by word and deed through the eight years, influenced me, not a little, in my decision in favor of their "call" should the Conference approve. Our *outgoing* from Winnipeg at that date, as may be imagined, was in striking contrast with our *ingoing* in 1868. Numerous kind friends accompanied us to the steamer, prayerfully asking for us all needful guidance, protection and blessing for coming days. Our route was by steamer to "Fisher's Landing" on the Red Lake River, thence by cars to St. Paul, Chicago, Detroit and Toronto, where a deputation was waiting our arrival at the depot, and we were conducted to the pleasant home of my faithful friend, the late H. E. Clarke, M.P.P., where we were most kindly entertained until the parsonage was ready for our occupancy. Pursuant to the request from the Official Board of Richmond Street Church, the Conference appointed me to that charge, and to the Chairmanship of the Toronto District, in June, 1876.

Very noticeable changes had taken place both in the arrangements of the building and in the congregation since I left the charge in 1868. The order of things in the interior of the church had been, at a heavy outlay, so modernized as to involve a complete reversal of pulpit and pews—the former removed from the front to the rear end of the auditorium, while the south end of the all-around gallery had been cut down to make room for the pulpit and platform, and the pews changed to face the pulpit in its altered position. Several other changes had been made in order to rejuvenate the old, out-of-fashion structure, and make it attractive as far as practicable. I do not think the expenditure was warranted. It did not arrest the manifest down-town tendencies of the locality, nor diminish the absorbing power of the great central and in every way attractive Metropolitan Church, then at its very best in its newness, and by reason of its popular ministry and choir, and the social status of its leading officials and members. It was not at all marvellous, therefore, that the crowded congregations of the old church of 1850, 1864 and on to 1870 were not there in 1876. Families by the dozen and hearers by the score had transferred themselves to the newest and most magnificent church home in the city.

The depletion of the Richmond Street Church congregation did not result from any failure of the Conference to send to the charge ministers whose abilities and faithfulness were most likely to prevent such a result.

The Rev. T. W. Jeffrey, who was my immediate predecessor, was by no means an easy man to follow. He was a gifted brother, and though somewhat peculiar in his style and eccentric in his manner, with views on many profound subjects that were somewhat startling to his hearers—yet in his best moods he was a really brilliant and attractive, as well as impressive preacher. He was, as a pastor, a general favorite and especially with the young people, to whom his influence was stimulative and his addresses inspiring, even when, through no fault of his, they failed to instruct. Mrs. Jeffrey was a great help to her husband in his pastoral work, and no one can overestimate the value, to him and his charges, of her holy life and counsels and prayers. Though afflicted for years with a distressing ailment, yet to her and to the Church death came suddenly at length. While her husband was engaged in his Sabbath morning service in the sanctuary, she was released, and doubtless through the ministry of holy angels she entered the upper sanctuary and engaged in the "nobler worship there" ere he returned.

The hour of Brother Jeffrey's return to God came several years later. After languishing for months from an incurable heart-ailment ending in dropsy and dissolution, he also received the summons on a Sabbath—and while his congregation were worshipping in the Berkeley Street Church at the evening service. With only his little daughter and a domestic in the house, he passed out of the "earthly tabernacle" to enter the "house not made with hands." "Blessed are the dead which die in the Lord."

To be associated again in Christian fellowship and service with so many whom I had ministered to and worked with on my former term in this charge, was to me a source of much enjoyment, but it was only by our united and persistent efforts in Sabbath-school and pastoral work and evangelistic services that we succeeded in holding our own from quarter to quarter. And no pastor ever enjoyed a heartier co-operation from his officiary and membership than I did. The energy, wisdom, and faith of Mr. Pearson, our popular Sabbath-school superintendent, so guarded and guided the interests of the school as to secure an advancement that, under the circumstances, was really marvellous; while as leader of the largest society class he was equally successful. Mr. H. E. Clarke, afterwards M.P.P., was one of the most instructive Bible-class teachers as well as the best Recording Steward I have ever known.

These earnest and gifted brethren, in association with Rev. Dr. Withrow, J. J. Withrow, H. Walton, Richard Clarke, and many others, stood by us nobly even while the absorption process was going steadily on. The result, by the Divine blessing, was a slight increase, during our first year, in membership and connexional funds.

At the Conference of June, 1877, my brethren did me the unearned honor of appointing me to the presidential office, thereby assigning me responsibilities which hitherto I had not been called to sustain In this, I take it, they had respect, not so much to any special fitness for the position, as to my eight years' service in the mission field. In their generosity, by a proportionate assessment of their charges, they provided for the support of an assistant for the year, in order that I might be able to visit throughout the Conference as circumstances might require, and assist by sermons and addresses in missionary and other anniversaries. Their selection of my assistant was a very wise one and in every respect acceptable to the church as well as helpful to myself. The Rev. Dr. Wallace, now of Victoria University, proved himself to be the right man for the position. His ordination, as ordered by the Conference, took place in our church early in the year. His rapid progress in ministerial service and professional work in the University have given him a prominent place in the ministry as well as in the affections of the many students who have had the good fortune to attend his classes. At the end of my term of office I was glad to be released of all presidential responsibilities and to welcome to the chair as my successor the Rev. E. B. Harper, D.D.

My third year, which was really my fifth in the pastorate of this church, was decidedly one of much hard work, for Brother Wallace was no longer my assistant, and the full measure of pulpit and pastoral duties fell to my lot. But notwithstanding the predictions of a few, ever ready to act the part of alarmists, and to declare that this old "down town" church was on the "down grade," at the summing up at the end of the year our membership and finances showed that the work had been well sustained. The Conference of 1879 appointed the Rev. I. Tovell as my successor, and I was placed in charge of the Berkeley Street Church.

Ere my term in Richmond Street closed, the following notice appeared in the New York *Christian Advocate*, at whose instance I never knew:

"Cornell College, Iowa, conferred the degree of Doctor of Divinity on Rev. George Young, President of the Toronto Conference of the Methodist Church of Canada. Dr. Young has for thirty-six years proved himself a man of unsullied character and worthy scholarship. For eight years the great mission work in Manitoba flourished under his superintendence, while as President of this honored Conference he has secured to himself a lasting hold on the affections of his brethren."

This was an honor to which I have never felt myself on any imaginable account entitled.

The Official Meeting of the Richmond Street Church I was leaving entered upon its records the following resolution, which was forwarded to me in due course:

"At the last Official Meeting of the Richmond Street Methodist Church, the following resolution was unanimously adopted: 'That in view of the near approach of the time when our pastor, Rev. Dr. Young, will by the disciplinary arrangements of our Church be removed from us to some other field of labor, we, the members of the Official Board, desire to record our high appreciation of his unvarying deportment as a Christian gentleman, his earnest and efficient ministrations, and wise government of the affairs of the Church, and would hereby assure him and his estimable partner of our warmest love and esteem, and of our earnest prayers that they may have both temporal and spiritual prosperity, and that the Divine blessing may rest upon their efforts wherever their lot may be cast.'"

My term of service in the Berkeley Street Church terminated with the first half of 1879. As the result of a great deal of house to house visiting as well as earnest pulpit work, and the co-operation of the church, a gratifying increase in the congregation and class services was manifest, and the prospect for a successful year seemed very encouraging; but just then "a Macedonian cry" was heard at the Mission Rooms. A considerable number of our people had established themselves in business in a small village on the boundary between Minnesota and Manitoba, about seventy miles south of Winnipeg. At that date a new line of railway, from St. Vincent to Winnipeg, had just been opened, and as several small villages were springing up along the line, and many new settlements were being formed in the section of which Emerson was seemingly a promising centre, the urgent request of our friends for the immediate opening of a mission in that locality seemed but reasonable, and the decision of the Board accorded therewith.

As in 1868, I offered my services, and in a very short time, being relieved of my responsibilities both in the Berkeley Street Church and the Toronto District, and my successors duly appointed, we made ready for our journey to what seemed in that booming time a most inviting field.

The ministers of the Toronto District assembled immediately after my leaving and passed the following resolution, which reached me in due course:

"Moved by Dr. Sutherland, seconded by Dr. Ryerson, That this meeting hereby records its sincere appreciation of the fidelity and efficiency with which the Rev. G. Young, D.D., has discharged the duties of his office as Chairman while on this District, and that whilst regretting his departure, we do earnestly pray that his return to the Province of Manitoba may be signally owned of God for good." Carried unanimously.

CHAPTER XXI.

MY SECOND APPOINTMENT TO MISSION WORK IN MANITOBA.

THE reason for that appointment, and the circumstances under which it was made, are given in the preceding chapter.

The winter of 1879-'80 in the North-West was very much more severe in its cold and wind-storms than were any I had hitherto experienced in the country; so that the occupants of cheaply built and unplastered frame dwellings, and especially travellers and unhoused animals, suffered greatly. And then each cold snap seemed but the precursor of a relentless blizzard, which rendered travelling over trackless, houseless and treeless prairies exceedingly hazardous. Of this my son, Captain G. H. Young, had ample proof. While engaged in Customs duties along the United States boundary between Wood Mountain and the Rockies, and especially while crossing the prairies from Wood Mountain to Fort Qu'Appelle, a distance of two hundred miles, in the coldest and stormiest season of that severe winter, he with two or three assistants experienced a notable escape from death by freezing. The snow was deep, and in the ravines badly drifted, and fuel hard to find, while their only shelter was a tent. The great marvel is that they did not all perish during the same intensely cold night when seven or eight of their hardy ponies were frozen to death. As a last resort, when nearly helpless from the cold and want of fuel and proper food, but fortunately when near their destination, they were compelled to make fuel of their sled and to pack the few necessaries of life still remaining on their well-nigh exhausted ponies, and in this plight they reached a settlement where their wants were supplied. To us it was a time of intense solicitude, for while we had reason to fear peril and suffering, we could afford them no assistance, nor for many weeks get any tidings concerning them. As may be imagined, it was with special thanksgiving that we received a telegram from Portage la Prairie announcing their arrival in the settlement. The good hand of God was upon them, and upon us, for good.

On our arrival at Emerson on the 19th of December, 1879, a small, poorly-furnished hall was rented as a place of worship *pro tem.*

As soon as practicable the trustees secured a fine large lot in a desirable locality as a site for a parsonage and church. There were on the lot two small buildings intended for dwellings, which, being joined together, formed for us a parsonage sufficiently large for our requirements, and thus a mission home was very quickly made ready for our occupancy.

After a brief delay a cheap, rough, unplastered building was erected to be our "house of prayer," and henceforth known as "The Tabernacle." From the date of its opening our congregations increased very considerably. The Trustees of Grace Church, Winnipeg, generously donated to me personally the bell which had already become somewhat historic, and which they did not require, as the first Grace Church had given place to the Wesley Hall block. The good old bell was duly loaned by me to the Board in Emerson for use until such time as required elsewhere. For the last seventeen years the loan has been continued, but I think the time has now fully come when it is more fitting that it should be returned to Winnipeg to become a portion of the equipment of Wesley College, where I trust it may long be regarded as a suggestive memento of former times.

I quote from an Emerson paper the following interesting history of the Tabernacle bell:

"In our last issue we were slightly in error in stating that the Trust Board of Grace Church, Winnipeg, had donated the bell, which had been used in their church until quite recently, to the Trust Board of the Methodist Church of Canada in Emerson. The gift was made to the Rev. Dr. Young, pastor of the Tabernacle, to be used in any way he might direct, but still to remain his property. As he is now loaning it to his congregation in Emerson, it is presumable that it will do service here for a considerable term. The bell was cast in Troy, N.Y., in 1869, in fulfilment of an order from the Sabbath-school in Oshawa, of which the Hon. W. H. Gibbs was superintendent, and it bears an inscription to that effect. At the suggestion of John Macdonald, Esq., of Toronto, Mr. Gibbs and his Sabbath-school made this appropriate gift 'To the first Methodist Church in Red

River country,' not then a portion of the Dominion. Its weight is about two hundred and fifty pounds, it is artistic in its appearance, and has a clear, musical ringing tone which all will admire. In 1869 it was freighted out from St. Cloud, then the terminus of railroad communication, in this direction, on an ox cart. For the first two or three years it was rung for service chiefly by the missionary, Dr. Young, who discharged the duties of pastor and sexton at the same time, and never did he ring it more heartily and energetically, we are told, than on the morning when Colonel Wolseley and the troops passed through the village and disturbed Riel and his tatterdemalion army in Fort Garry. That day has long since passed away, but those who were here during that nondescript reign are not likely to forget the unpleasant experiences which were theirs. All will feel that the Board of Trustees did a very nice thing in a most appropriate way when they unanimously passed the resolution, and directed their Secretary to prepare the letter, which we have been permitted to subjoin:

"WINNIPEG, April 15, 1881.

"*Rev. Geo. Young, D.D., Emerson, Man.:*

"REVEREND AND DEAR SIR,—It is my pleasing duty as Secretary of the Board of Trustees of Grace Church to inform you that, at a meeting of that Board, a resolution was unanimously adopted that, in recognition of your valuable services in times past in connection with our church in Winnipeg, there should be presented to you the bell and belfry of old Grace Church, to be used in whatever place you may desire. We are now only commencing to realize the extent of those services not only as a pastor but as one who had the material interests of the church in view. To your foresight and judgment we are much indebted for the valuable property now owned by the church in this city.

"We trust you will accept this gift, which, although of little intrinsic value, will be a souvenir to you of the incidents of the eventful years during which you took so prominent a part in the history of our young Province. I am also instructed to express to you the sorrow of the members of the Board at your great bereavement, and to assure you that you have their deepest sympathy. I am, dear sir, respectfully yours,

"J. S. AIKINS, *Secretary of Board.*"

Our little village soon became the head of a Circuit embracing several small neighborhoods adjacent thereto. One, more remote than the others, was a settlement of Prince Edward Islanders in Minnesota, U. S., who were entirely destitute of the means of grace. Years after, while attending missionary anniversary services on the Island, I met with their near relatives and received hearty thanks for having visited and ministered to their distant friends in advance of any missionary from any Church in their adopted country. Dominion City, so called, where I established week-evening services at first, soon became the head of a pleasant mission, and is now, I judge, a self-supporting charge. West Lynne, at the first an exceedingly promising village just across the Assiniboine from Emerson, became a Sabbath appointment, where we built a small but neat place of worship, and enjoyed a season of revival. In the history of this place we met with a sore disappointment. Its booming days were of brief continuance, and were followed by a disastrous collapse. Inundated and desolated by the great overflow of the river in 1882, its population became so utterly discouraged (fearing subsequent liability to similar calamities), that they very generally moved away from scenes which must continually remind them of their disappointment and loss, and established homes in more promising localities. The flood was a great calamity to Emerson and its surroundings in that section of the country. The rushing waters bore with them immense masses of ice which, though broken, remained quite firm, and which, as they crushed over the banks of the river, speedily swept away the costly bridges which had been but recently erected, and with them the storehouses and landings belonging to the merchants and forwarders of the town. The streets, especially in the lower portions of the place, were flooded to the depth of eight or ten feet, necessitating a hasty removal of the goods in the stores and of the families as well, to the higher stories or to higher grounds until the flood should subside. A steamer unloaded its freight of lumber, etc., in one of the principal streets, while sidewalks and crossings were generally destroyed. Making "a virtue of necessity," each householder became a boat owner in very quick time. Marketing had to be done by means of boats. I found it necessary to learn to manage my little craft in order to visit the butcher and baker and store, or even the Tabernacle. Fortunately our little parsonage was built on a slight elevation, so that the rising water simply filled the cellar and reached within an inch of the floor of the house before it began to abate. Union services were held in the Baptist Church, which stood on higher ground, while our Tabernacle, with four or five feet of water covering the floor, might have served for the immersing of the people had it been so required.

Great as was this calamity to us in 1882, the following extract will show that the Red River settlements in earlier days had suffered greater losses from the same cause:

"In this connection we might mention the following extracts from an old diary, which were made some time ago by Mr. A. McDermot. In 1826 the flood began early in May. May 14th, water came into the upper church (St. John's). The people removed to Snake Indian Hills (Stony Mountain), where they remained until June 12th. Only three houses were left standing in the settlement. 1852, the ice broke on the 28th April. The winter had been fine until the end of February, and there had been much snow during March. May 2nd, water rising; people alarmed; snow and sleet. May 9th, water at the corner of the churchyard, St. John's. May 12th, house still dry; water entering hall. May 19th, water at a stand-still. Highest point reached, 40 inches in the bishop's house. May 21st, water receding. May 26th, water down to 20 inches in the bishop's house. June 1st, flood abated in the upper church; weather very hot. The church was closed altogether five weeks. The people went out to Little Stony Mountain, and St. James (Silver Heights), the latter locality being dry, as well as the former."

I deeply regret that at the time of this writing (April, 1897), Emerson is reported as again inundated by the overflow of the Red River.

MY SECOND APPOINTMENT TO MANITOBA. 335

From these representations it will be seen that the church which still exists in Emerson was founded, by the blessing of God, in trying times and amid manifold discouragements. And yet I have to refer to a still darker shadow which was projected across my pathway while I was prosecuting the work the Church had given me to do. In less than a year after we entered our little parsonage already referred to, the wife of my youth, who for thirty-two years had been my wise counsellor and most devoted and efficient helper in the service of the Church, after a brief and distressing illness, was stricken out of the life that now is, and advanced to an infinitely higher life among the immortals. The following kindly *in memoriam* references by Dr. Wood, and an obituary notice, both of which appeared in the *Guardian* shortly after her decease, will not, I trust, by any, be deemed inappropriate in this connection:

From the Methodist Mission Rooms, for the " Christian Guardian."

" To identify and perpetuate the memory of Sister Young 'as a servant of the Church,' in carrying on the work assigned to the Methodist Missionary Society, we place her obituary in the columns assigned to missionary intelligence. She was the first of our sisters to accompany her husband to Fort Garry, now the City of Winnipeg, and hers is the first grave that has opened to receive all that was mortal of a faithful and devoted laborer in the Lord's vineyard. Forty years have passed since the first Wesleyan missionaries began their missions among the Indians some three hundred miles north of Dr. Young's first station; of these laborers Mr. and Mrs. James Evans, Mr. and Mrs. Thomas Hurlburt, and Mrs. Brooking have gone to rest; but Mrs. Young belongs to the foundation of a colony, and with it the establishment of the Methodist Church at the entrance of a magnificent country containing all the elements for national greatness and homes for millions. Called by the Church, she willingly gave up her happy associations

THE LATE MRS. (DR.) YOUNG.

in Ontario, and though unaccustomed to the rough and exposed travel attendant upon camp life, cheerfully contended with its inconveniences, blending her energies and knowledge of domestic wants to promote the comfort of her fellow-travellers. The first two or three years at Fort Garry were accompanied by many trials; but before leaving that newly-formed mission she had to rejoice in the success attendant upon her husband's ministry, having succeeded in the erection of a sanctuary, a mission house, and the ingathering of a living Church, to the formation of which she consecrated her time and influence.

"Our esteemed and lamented sister was distinguished for her diligence, love of order, and punctuality, courteous hospitality, and an intelligent spiritual-mindedness. She both pointed to heaven by her instructions, and led the way by her example. Nor has she been alone in this work; for verily we think too little of Methodist ministers' wives, both at home and abroad, who, by their sacrifices and efforts contribute largely to their husbands' success, and the prosperity of the varied institutions of the Church. We need more of the spirit and remembrance of St. Paul, as shown in his last chapter to the Romans."

THE OBITUARY.

Mary Alsy Homes, the beloved wife of the writer, was born October, A.D. 1822, and entered into rest on the 2nd day of December, 1880. Hers was a godly ancestry. Her father, the late Rev. Ninian Holmes, was one of the pioneer Methodist missionaries who did such good service for their blessed Master in the wilds of Canada during the period of its early settlement, and a worthy associate of the apostolic Dr. Nathan Bangs, whose achievements in various fields of Christian usefulness the Methodists of Canada and of the United States will never forget. Two events of untold importance to the subject of this notice, and to many others, transpired during her childhood-days, viz., the sudden death of her saintly father and her own conversion to God. The genuineness of that conversion and the practicability of a true and enduring Christianity in association with the well-known characteristics of early youth, were fully demonstrated by her subsequent life. Realizing continually that she was Christ's, she steadily aimed at unreserved consecration to His service, sought and experienced the cleansing and healing which the "precious blood" only can accomplish, and daily studied and planned to do good from love to the world's Redeemer. Her experience in the deep things of the faith and inner life of the Christian as related by her in love-feasts, class and fellowship meetings, led many to feel that she had been much with Jesus, and had received rich baptism from His hand. She possessed a large measure of the true missionary spirit. And all that she did and endured during the eight years from 1868 to 1876, and especially in March, 1870, in connection with the opening and organization of the Methodist missions in the Red River country, can never be made known to the Church whose interests she so earnestly strove to promote. Yet when the way opened in December, 1879, for a return to the mission work in Manitoba, she rejoiced exceedingly, for she desired most to work where workers were most needed. In her little book for "Memos" the following record appears, which was made on the train which bore her towards her new field of labor: "December 19th, 1879. Left Toronto to-day for Emerson, to help commence a work for the blessed Master. Lord help us." Words which indicate her life aim—which was "to help" in every good word and work to the extent of her ability. Quebec, Ontario and Manitoba can testify that she was indeed a very efficient helper. While she saw nothing that was attractive in the merely frivolous, whether in society or amusements or literature, she specially delighted in the study of the Word, in the ordinances of God's house, in close communion with God, in the society of the godly, and in energetic action for the glory of Christ and the salvation of souls. In fact, her ruling passion was to work for the salvation of souls; and this feeling seemed to deepen and become intensified as her years increased, and even when death drew near, for when told of the fears of her medical adviser she promptly expressed her belief that "God had some more work for her to do here." And so he had, but it was to be accomplished by means of her peaceful and confident death, rather than by her loving, earnest entreaties and prayers. Her health had been uniformly good since her return to this country until within a few days of her decease, when the disease which struck her down so quickly (pleurisy) seemed to fasten upon her at the outset with a death-grip which was never relaxed for a moment until the silver cord was loosed and the golden bowl broken. When asked if the intimation that she was nearing the world of spirits startled her, she replied instantly, "Certainly not." "Have you any fear?" "Not in the least," was the prompt response. "Is Jesus present with you in your great suffering?" "Oh, yes, He is very near to me all the time," was the comforting answer. After such a life of trust and consecration, and with such a testimony borne within a few minutes of her departure, what more could have been reasonably required? Our son, having arrived from

Winnipeg, was recognized at once, to our great joy, and having looked her love and blessing, for she could do no more, she rested her weary head on the pillow gently and "was not, for God took her." As we bowed in that death chamber, amid tears and sobs, and asked the Father of spirits to minister an entrance abundantly to her dear departing spirit into the celestial city, we all felt that all of heaven, at least, was not very remote.

It is a noteworthy fact that a considerable number of young persons, for whose conversion she had earnestly labored and prayed, many of them members of her Bible class, have been led to accept the Saviour's grace since her decease, attributing their conversion mainly to her influence and prayers and the Divine blessing which attended the deeply-mysterious and afflictive dispensation.

The following is a portion of a testimony borne to Mrs. Young's useful life, as it was published in a Winnipeg paper:

"Her consecrated life and untiring endeavors in the Church were signally instrumental in gathering many into the fold of the Good Shepherd. None made greater sacrifices in the interests of the Methodist Church in Manitoba than did she, and her deep solicitude for the safety of her husband and son, during the long weary months of the rebellion, in 1869 and 1870, will never be fully known."

And yet another of the little family circle of three individuals who entered the parsonage home in 1880, was called from suffering to rest ere my third year in

Emerson had ended. For nearly ten years Miss Linton, formerly of Kingston, was closely associated with Mrs. Young in household cares, and in earnest Sabbath-school work. In the providence of God they were not long separated, and their graves may be seen in the same family plot in the cemetery near the city of Winnipeg. Thus I alone remained of the little circle so broken into by death.

At the close of my term in Emerson an exceedingly well written address, accompanied by a beautiful album containing the photos of many friends, was presented me on my leaving for Ontario. The Conference of 1882, yielding to my request, allowed me a year without an appointment. It was my privilege to accompany my friends, Rev. Dr. and Mrs. Douglas, on a tour to the Maritime Provinces, in order to visit the Nova Scotia and New Brunswick Conferences. To me this was a season of special interest and enjoyment. I had opportunities of addressing, from platform and pulpit, large numbers whom I had not met before, and of becoming acquainted with many of the elect brotherhood of these two Conferences. Parting with Dr. and Mrs. Douglas at St. John, N.B., I went on to Prince Edward Island, where I also had many opportunities of preaching and of associating with the ministers and membership of our Church in that pleasant and interesting country. During my stay on the Island I took board for a time near the sea-shore, not far from Rustico, with a kind family in whose house my eloquent brother of former years, the Rev. Lachlan Taylor, D.D., "finished his course" and passed over into the great spirit world.

During the next few months, after voyaging in the Gulf, staying for a little at Cacouna, and at Brantford, I visited Chautauqua, and enjoyed the only opportunity I ever had of hearing that prince of preachers, Bishop Simpson, on the text, "The morning stars sang together, and the sons of God shouted for joy"—a wonderful sermon. In the autumn of 1882 I attended the General Conference in the city of Hamilton. One of the many important decisions of that Conference was the organization of "The Manitoba and North-West Conference" and the appointment of a Superintendent of Missions for the North-West, whose duty it should be to organize the Conference in 1883 and act as its first President. The selection of that official was relegated to the Board of Missions, which was called to meet at once after the close of the Conference. The next day I received notice by a telegram of my appointment, and a request to meet the Board as soon as practicable.

CHAPTER XXII.

MY THIRD APPOINTMENT TO MISSION WORK IN THE NORTH-WEST.

THE *Missionary Notices* for October, 1882, issued soon after the appointment was announced, and I was duly "certificated" with the accustomed cordiality of the General Secretary, contained the following reference:

"The announcement that the Rev. Dr. Young has been chosen to fill the arduous and responsible post of Superintendent of Missions in the North-West, will, we are sure, be received with lively satisfaction by the whole Church. Dr. Young's long experience in that country will be of immense service in the work to which he is now called, while his whole record will carry the fullest confidence that the task of laying foundations will be conducted alike with prudence and vigor. Immediately after receiving his appointment, Dr. Young started for Manitoba, where he will spend the present month in the work assigned him. He will then return eastward, and spend some time in missionary anniversaries, and in promoting the interests of the Church and Parsonage Aid Fund. We need not bespeak for him a cordial reception; he is sure to get that wherever he goes."

In accordance with this notice my appointment was made on the 29th of September. On the 2nd of

October I started on my journey to the North-West to engage in the work assigned me. Reaching Winnipeg, I proceeded at once to visit certain points which required early attention. Regina, now the capital of the North-West Territories, but then only six weeks old, belonged to that class. At that date it was represented as containing eight hotels, eighteen stores, two blacksmith's shops, one saddler's shop, two livery stables, two tin shops, two laundries, three billiard halls, two bakeries, one drug store, one jeweller's shop, two doctors, six lawyers, and four lumber yards, and a population of between eight and nine hundred souls.

On returning to Winnipeg an interviewer from the office of the *Free Press* drew from me such replies as enabled him to produce the following report:

"REV. DR. YOUNG'S WESTERN TOUR.

"Rev. Dr. Young, Superintendent of Missions, Methodist Church of Canada, arrived here on Tuesday evening from the west, after having paid his first official visit to various points in this Province and the North-West Territories. He left Winnipeg on Saturday, 7th inst., and arrived at Millford by way of Brandon the same evening. The following morning he conducted the services in connection with the opening of a new church at Millford, and in the afternoon returned to Brandon, where he preached that evening. He found the church at Brandon in a flourishing state. The congregation at the evening service numbered some five hundred people, and about filled the church. An enlargement of the building is projected, to come into effect next spring.

"Leaving Brandon on Tuesday, 10th inst., Dr.

Young continued on his journey westward and reached Regina on Wednesday. On Friday he went, in company with Rev. Mr. Hewitt, of Regina, to Moose Jaw Creek, and then on to Old Wives' Lake. The regular passenger trains running only as far as Regina, it was necessary to travel the remainder of the distance, nearly a hundred miles, in a caboose attached to a construction train, carrying rails, ties, etc. The track was laid about eighteen miles beyond Old Wives' Lake, but the latter point was the terminus, so far as the construction train was concerned. Its distance from Winnipeg is a little over 470 miles.

"Regina was found to be progressing very rapidly. Several frame buildings were in course of erection, so that henceforth the place is not likely to consist, as during some time past, entirely of tents. There were already in existence hotels and business places of various kinds, and small buildings, for use as such, were rapidly going up. The people might be said to be in reality merely squatters who had taken possession in the expectation of being able to purchase as soon as the land should come into the market, but having no certainty as yet as to their ownership.

"On Sunday, 15th instant, service was held by Rev. Dr. Young twice at Regina, a large tent, capable of accommodating two or three hundred people, being used for the purpose. The congregation was estimated to number about fifty. The circulation of a subscription was commenced, with the object of providing for the erection of a place of worship. The sum of $250 was subscribed, but it is expected that this amount will be considerably increased. With this result of local effort, together with some assistance from the Church Extension Fund, it is expected that the tent, which has been in use during the summer, will be replaced this fall by a place of worship more suitable for winter occupancy."

On the 23rd of October, having visited seven or eight of these recently occupied fields of missionary effort and travelled 4,322 miles in twenty-four days, I left Manitoba for the remote east, and reaching Charlottetown, Prince Edward Island, on the 3rd of November, I began the work assigned me by preaching missionary sermons in that town on the day following, and arranging for a series of meetings during the week on several of the more important charges in that very pleasant country. On the following Sabbath I took full work in Windsor, Nova Scotia; and thenceforward, in city, town, or neighborhood, in both Nova Scotia and New Brunswick, on Sabbath and week-day evenings, I tried to fulfil my mission, until my campaign in the Maritime Provinces ended on the 20th of December, 1882. During the first six weeks of the new year, I was similarly engaged in various parts of Ontario, but unfortunately, as the result of this overtaxing of voice and strength and of undue exposure, I was compelled to cancel many other engagements, by a sharp attack of bronchitis which shut me in for a month, necessitating medical treatment as well as absolute rest. Convalescing, however, I was enabled to return in March to the North-West, and to take up the line of work I had left in the preceding October, and to visit many inviting openings both in Manitoba and the adjoining territory, and preach and render such other aid as opportunity afforded until June, when I returned to Ontario in time for the Toronto Conference at Peterboro', where I hoped to secure more volunteers for earnest work in these rapidly extending mission fields. On July 3rd I left, *via* the lakes, for Winnipeg, in order to make such arrangements as seemed needful prior to the assembling of the brethren as ordered by the General Conference, for the purpose of organizing an Annual Conference for Manitoba and the North-West. The proceedings of the Conference, which were full of interest, were admirably reported for the *Free Press*, but want of space will prevent me from giving more than a few selections from these reports:

"THE NEW CONFERENCE.

"The Manitoba and North-West Conference of the Methodist Church of Canada met for organization yesterday morning in Wesley Hall, Rev. George Young, D.D., first President, taking the chair, in accordance with the appointment of the General Conference.

"The first hour, beginning at ten o'clock, was spent in singing, reading of the Scripture and prayer, Rev. S. D. Rice, D.D., President of the General Conference; and Rev. Messrs. Halstead, Bristol, Betts, Hewitt and Colpitts taking part.

"THE PRESIDENT'S INAUGURAL ADDRESS.

"The prayer-meeting having closed, the President, Rev. Dr. Young, delivered the following address:

"My dear brethren, we meet this hour under circumstances quite unique, and exceedingly interesting. As a section of the Church in this land, we have before us, in some respects, a new departure. We are about to inaugurate a new era in our church work by organizing an Annual Conference, thereby bringing the number up to seven, which will be further increased very soon to nine or ten such Conferences in our Dominion. In 1872 a Conference was held near this spot, in the Grace Church of that period, which was presided over by the late Dr. Punshon and attended by Rev. Dr. Wood and missionaries of that time in the North-West, but while it involved consultation and decisions on many matters of importance, and was followed by important results, yet it did not involve organization.

"You are all aware that the General Conference of last September authorized the organization of a Conference at this date and in this place, for Manitoba and the North-West, and also, whether wisely or unwisely, it is not for me to say, appointed the Superintendent of Missions in this country to preside and to continue in the presidency for one year.

"Your first duty to-day will not be, therefore, as in the ordinary Annual Conference, to elect a President, but to proceed at once to the appointment of a Secretary for the year before us. I need not remind you, brethren, that during our different sessions you will be called upon to deliberate carefully and prayerfully upon a variety of questions, which have most important practical bearings. The duty of outlining work in the committee room, and of accepting or rejecting or modifying the various reports and resolutions that may be submitted, of adopting measures for the sustenance of the connexional funds, for the extension of our mission work, and for the promotion of great educational interests, will demand much prayerful consideration.

"We do not feel that we have fallen behind any of the Churches in our efforts, during the last fifteen years, to supply both the aborigines and the new settlers with the ordinances, and yet we have cause for regret that more has not been done, and ought to feel the obligation pressing to still more earnest endeavors. In order to reach the more remote settlements as quickly as possible, it will be necessary for us to imitate as closely as may be the early Methodist itinerants of Ontario in performing frequent and long journeys, and in visiting scattered settlers during the week when it cannot be accomplished on Sabbaths. Forty sermons in four weeks, with journeys of hundreds of miles on the saddle, was no very uncommon achievement in those days. Under existing circumstances the Master requires a consecration of all our energies. This Conference session will doubtless be brief, and yet it may be to us all a memorable and profitable season. Soon we shall separate, and possibly not meet in Conference again. Let us, therefore, strive together in our prayers and godly councils, that we may go forth all the wiser and holier for the privileges we now enjoy.

"ROLL OF CONFERENCE.

"At the conclusion of the President's address, the roll of the Conference members was called, and Conference Secretary appointed, when the President then introduced Rev. S. D. Rice, D.D., President of the General Conference, who gave a brief address. He explained that he found himself unexpectedly able to be present after having written to the effect that he could not come, owing to other duties. He spoke of the peculiar interest which he felt in everything connected with the North-West, and which was shared by everyone who had anything to do with this country. He regarded this as prophetic of what was to be in this North-West prairie land. He had found the eastern climate very trying, but felt himself greatly invigorated on reaching the prairies again. He had hardly supposed it possible that he would look into the faces of so many that he did not know,

He contrasted the number of ministers here with that of the very few who were here three years ago when he first arrived. He considered that the responsibilities of the work here were such that they could hardly be overestimated. Those who had been here but a short time could form no conception of the responsibilities and the glory to be associated with laying the foundations of this country if rightly laid; though those who had been here longer might somewhat appreciate them. These responsibilities were such as belonged to no other part of the world that he had seen or known, and they could only be looked upon in the most serious light. He was very glad to meet his brethren again, both those whom he knew and those whom he did not know. (Laughter.)"

The report of the Committee on Statistics, as then presented, and as compared with the statement made by a similar committee at the Conference of 1896, will indicate a wonderful progress realized during those years.

"There are at present sixty-eight missions and circuits in connection with this Conference, of which five are self-sustaining; forty-six missions to the white settlers, and seventeen to the Indians. Our missionaries traverse an area of 175,000 square miles, containing two hundred and sixty-nine preaching-stations where regular services are maintained, forty-eight churches, thirty-two parsonages, and twelve rented houses.

"The services are attended by thirteen thousand, eight hundred and seventy-five hearers. There are two thousand, eight hundred and eighty-three members, and one thousand, seven hundred and sixty-seven families in connection with our Church.

"For ministerial support there was raised last year

$13,085, which amount will be largely increased during the current year. The society classes number eighty-two, the Sunday-schools sixty-eight, two hundred and thirty-six officers and teachers, and not less than three thousand scholars."

The following comparative statement, showing the progress made since the Conference was organized, will, I am sure, be most gratifying to all who have in any way contributed to results so unspeakably important:

	1883.	1896.
Number of preaching-places	269	548
" members	2,883	16,131
" Sabbath-schools	68	245
" Scholars	3,000	14,241
Paid by circuits for ministerial support	$13,085	$59,433
" " sustentation of College	....	$7,030
" " all purposes	....	$170,731

On the last day of its sessions the members of the Conference were favored with a visit and an address from one of world-wide celebrity, who at that date was giving a series of lectures in the city. The following is a brief synopsis of the address:

"A DISTINGUISHED VISITOR.

"Rev. Henry Ward Beecher at this stage of the proceedings entered the room, accompanied by the Rev. Mr. Stafford, who introduced him to the President of the Conference. The President welcomed the reverend gentleman in cordial terms, and introduced him to the Conference, all the members rising and loudly manifesting their applause.

"Rev. Mr. Beecher said he perceived that most of the assembly were young men, not having yet reached the meridian of life. The fact brought back to him reminiscences of his own early ministry, for he, too, had been a pioneer preacher. He had labored in Indiana when all the northern part of the State was an Indian possession. He remembered to have ridden over Illinois, and, looking upon the prairies without stone, coal or wood, except a ribbon of forest along the river, concluded that it would never be settled; that there might be a few farms along the river, but that the great interior of the State would never be settled. But the railroad had changed all that, and now there were great and flourishing cities there. He had received all his early inspirations for the ministry in the mission-field, performing just such work as had fallen to the most of his hearers, and he therefore had sympathy for those who were beginning their ministry, and for those of any age who were laying foundations upon which other men would build when they were gone. This was the most honorable work of the whole Christian ministry—the original creative work of going where no man had gone, of which Paul had boasted. It was laying a foundation, the superstructure of which they would see only when looking out from Heaven's window, and it was the manliest and most Christian work that man was called to. In later life he had seen a great deal of work, both in Europe and America, so that he might say the experience of his later years was as directly opposed to his early experience as could be imagined. Yet he could bear witness that he could be glad to go back again to the ministry with which he had begun his work among the poor, outlying districts, and suffer, if need be, as he had done, poverty and ill-health. One of the most commanding words of Sacred Writ to him, and one that ought to knock at the door of every man that had scanned the word of inspiration, was this, 'To you it is given to suffer with Him.' There were degrees of enjoyment that were never attained by prosperity, that belonged to a magnanimous life, and a self-sacrificing life. The depth, height, breadth and length of the love of Christ was shown in His suffering for the objects of His love. All love, deep and eternal, was to be measured by what one would suffer for love's sake. He honored their vocation, he might almost say he envied it. By-and-by, when these scenes were over, and they were drawn by the heart of God to stand around their beloved Saviour, it would matter very little whether they labored on the prairies of the North-West, the middle regions or the populous cities. Their joy would be to see Christ and find they were like Him, and to be eternally satisfied. He thanked them for their greeting, and trusted they would have more and more the joy of bringing in the sheaves and reporting what the Lord had done through their instrumentality. He looked forward to the time when this Conference would become so unwieldy that it would have to be divided. The reverend gentleman was loudly applauded as he resumed his seat."

In reporting the adjournment of the Conference of 1883, the Winnipeg *Free Press* made the following appropriate reference to the occasion, which I have much pleasure in reproducing:

"The meeting of the North-Western Conference of the Methodist Church of Canada, which has just adjourned its first session in this city, marks a momentous era in the religious history of the Dominion. It also marks an important stage in the progress of the North-West. Hitherto this section of the Church has been under the supervision of the

Toronto Conference; but, having grown with the country, it has attained sufficient importance to justify the handing over of its interests into its own keeping.

"The progress of development of the Methodist Church in the North-West has been truly wonderful. A great work has been already accomplished by it; and, so much having been done while its matin beams are but just beginning to shine above the boundless horizon of our great north-western prairies, what may we not anticipate when its meridian glory shall have been attained? Forty years ago its labor of love was begun among the aborigines of this country. In 1868 Rev. Dr. Young, now Superintendent of Missions and first President of the first North-Western Conference, arrived and laid the foundations of the prosperity which the Church has since attained among the then small, though now large and rapidly increasing white population. There are at present about seventy clergymen in connection with the Church in the North-West, most of whom are young, vigorous men, thoroughly alive to the importance of the interests committed to their care, and anxious to promote them to the full extent of their ability. With such an army of workers, a great future is necessarily in store for the Methodist Church in this country.

"This first session of the new Conference was worthy of such a body. It was marked throughout by the greatest unanimity and energy of action. Business of the highest importance was transacted with a promptitude and a freedom from petty dissensions and bickerings which older bodies would do well to take a pattern from."

Immediately after the close of this interesting season of conferences, I visited Brandon and also a recently formed mission in the Souris country, in charge of Brother Harrison. On Sabbath a round trip was made of twenty miles, in a day more than ordinarily warm, and because urged to do so, I imprudently preached three times, and then on the following evening attended and gave an address at a tea-meeting, resulting, so far as I was concerned, in an illness which would have proved more serious but for the prompt and skilful treatment of my kind friend, Dr. Fleming, of Brandon, who attended me night and day until I reached convalescence. I shall never forget the distress I endured during the drive from Souris to the comfortable home of Mr. and Mrs. Sifton, where I was cared for in the kindest manner until I recovered.

On the 29th of August following I reached Belleville, where the General Conference assembled, at which, after very able and prolonged debating, the "Union" was consummated. On the Sabbath I enjoyed the privilege of hearing an excellent sermon by my friend the Rev. Chancellor Nelles, the last I was permitted to hear from him. In the evening of the same day I preached in the Methodist Episcopal Tabernacle. On the 26th of September I was again on my way, *via* Chicago and St. Paul, to our great Canadian North-West, reaching Winnipeg on the 29th. Sabbath, the 30th September, was a day of special interest to Methodism in Winnipeg, inasmuch as the new and costly and commodious Grace Church No. 2 was then opened for worship. By request, I preached at 11 a.m., and conducted the dedicatory service. The Rev. Dr. Gordon (Presbyterian) preached at 3 p.m., and Dr. Stafford, the pastor, gave an admirable discourse in the evening. The congregations were very large and the offerings liberal, amounting to over $400. What a change in our circumstances from the Sabbath in September, 1871, when I preached the opening sermon in Grace Church No. 1. On the 3rd of October I left for Medicine Hat, stopping over at Brandon and Moose Jaw on official duties.

SECOND "GRACE CHURCH."

The following extracts from my letters to the Mission Rooms, reporting progress at various points, will be in order here:

EXTRACTS FROM LETTERS.

"WINNIPEG, Oct. 24, 1883.

"I am glad to be able to report myself in good health and quite ready for any reasonable amount of work. . . . My visit to the western missions was very satisfactory, to myself at least.

MY THIRD APPOINTMENT TO THE NORTH-WEST.

"At Medicine Hat, where Brother Bridgman has been less than three months, I opened a new church 24 x 40, and preached to good congregations. He conducts service each Sabbath at the coal mines, eight miles distant, to upwards of eighty miners and clerks, and in the village at 'The Hat' he is the only resident missionary.

"At Broadview Brother Joslyn has opened a very large mission. He goes one Sabbath in the month to Crescent City, forty-five miles distant, where he has a class of about fifteen members, and good congregations. Then along the railroad he has appointments about thirty miles, and south and south-west he has several others. He has built a parsonage and church by aid of a loan of $500. He has secured good lots, and is doing nobly—all in three months.

"At Qu'Appelle Brother Lawson has two new churches, aided by a loan of $500, the last to be opened next Sabbath. At Virden a good building for parsonage, with hall for church purposes, is nearly completed. The brethren are doing nobly. But the reduced grants under such circumstances cause me great sadness."

Returning I visited Regina and Qu'Appelle and Broadview also, where I found our zealous missionary, Brother Joslyn, carpentering in a new church in order to have it ready for the opening services on Sabbath, when I preached twice to full congregations, and we rejoiced in hope of brighter days in the near future. At 4 p.m. next day I took cars for Portage la Prairie and Winnipeg.

In looking over my journals and reckoning up distances, I find that from October 2nd, 1882, to October 16th, 1883, I had travelled a distance of

20,900 miles, by rail or steam or buggy, in the Provinces and adjoining Territory of our great Dominion.

After preaching missionary sermons on Sabbath at Brandon, and speaking at the meeting Monday evening, and then doing the same at Portage la Prairie on the following Sunday and Monday, and again engaging in similar services in Emerson, I left for Ontario, to enter upon another winter's missionary campaign at the several points for which I was booked by the General Secretary, which in the good providence of God were all reached in due course. Among these were Scarboro, Queen and Elm Street Churches (Toronto), St. Catharines, Drummondville, Welland, St. Thomas, Aylmer, Sparta, Tilsonburg, London Circuit, Sarnia, Petrolia, Meaford, Mitchell, Clinton, Owen Sound, Markdale, Flesherton, Streetsville, Meadowvale, Port Hope, Cobourg, Belleville, and Brantford.

Returning to Manitoba in May, I preached twice in Winnipeg, also in Portage la Prairie, at Neepawa and Minnedosa, and at Prospect and Burnside. On Saturday, 7th of June, I was taken violently ill with congestion of the liver, which brought me very low in a few days. Fortunately I was at the parsonage in Portage la Prairie, and enjoyed the kind and thoughtful care of Rev. Mr. and Mrs. Woodsworth, and Mrs. Young, who was with me on this trip. In consequence of this illness, I was unable to join in the opening of the Conference of 1884, at Brandon, when Dr. Stafford was elected my successor in the presidency. Being advised by my physician that I must

MY THIRD APPOINTMENT TO THE NORTH-WEST. 359

seek rest for some time, or imperil my life, I asked the Conference upon my arrival, shortly before its close, for a superannuated relation for one year. My case was submitted to the Committee on Church Relations, with the following result:

"A report from the Committee on Church Relations was read, submitting in the case of Rev. Dr. Young that he was temporarily unable, owing to illness, to engage in regular work.

"Rev. Dr. Young was heard in reference to his own case. With deep feeling he referred to his past work in this country and spoke of his continued interest in the welfare of the Church here, and his joy in the success of its great prosperity. His physician, however, advised that he must be set free from all responsibility, and he himself felt the necessity of this for the present. He therefore asked that he be placed in the position of a superannuated minister for one year, though hoping still to help forward the work.

"Rev. Jas. Woodsworth moved, Rev. John McDougall seconding, that the request be granted. Both mover and seconder spoke in terms of the deepest regret that Dr. Young's temporary retirement, even for a short period, should be necessary.

"Rev. Messrs. Rutledge, Halstead, Dyer, Ruttan, Betts, and the President spoke with evident emotion in reference to Dr. Young's work, and the occasion was felt to be the most solemn one during the session of the Conference. The motion was carried, all the members of the Conference rising.

"Rev. Messrs. Stewart and Woodsworth were appointed a committee to draft a suitable resolution to be inserted in the published Minutes, expressing the feelings of the Conference in reference to the retirement of Dr Young."

The following is the resolution thus prepared, and which was subsequently published in the *Christian Guardian*:

"Moved by Rev. J. Woodsworth, seconded by Rev. John McDougall, and unanimously resolved, That we as a Conference do hereby express to Rev. Dr. Young our sense of joy at seeing him with us once again—a joy that is mingled with great sadness because of his being compelled, by reason of failing health, to ask for a superannuated relation. We cannot allow this opportunity to pass without expressing our high appreciation of the value of Dr. Young's labors as the pioneer missionary of the Methodist Church to the white settlers of the North-West. We glorify God for what He hath wrought through the instrumentality of His servant, and join in the earnest prayer that, being restored to health, the Church may for many years enjoy the benefit of his godly example and wise counsels."

As already intimated, I became an itinerant Methodist preacher in June, 1842. The month of June, 1892, therefore, brought me to the fiftieth anniversary of that event. In view of that fact, my ministerial brethren of the Manitoba Conference who had been appointed a committee to arrange for the services to be held during its sessions in Winnipeg, gave me a very cordial invitation to preach my Jubilee sermon on the Conference Sabbath. My acceptance of the invitation was followed by a severe attack of la grippe just prior to that date, which, although it did not seem to justify the cancelling of the engagement, did nevertheless so affect me as to

MY THIRD APPOINTMENT TO THE NORTH-WEST. 361

make the duty a more than ordinarily difficult task. My brethren of the Conference and the large congregation present gave me a patient and prayerful hearing while I preached from the text, "The Lord hath done great things for us, whereof we are glad;" and reminded them of a few of the many "great things" which the Lord had done for us as a Church and as individuals, for which we should be glad before Him with no ordinary gladness. During the five years which have elapsed since then, I have had many opportunities of preaching the Word in different parts of the Dominion. But the end draweth nigh.

I have referred before in these pages to the devoted native missionary, Rev. H. B. Steinhauer, now passed to his reward, and I cannot bring myself to close these reminiscences without giving my readers the following synopsis of an exceedingly interesting address delivered by him at the Conference missionary meeting, and which appeared in the Brandon papers at that date:

"Being introduced and received with applause, Mr. Steinhauer said that he was an example of the fruit of missionary labor. He referred to his experience during the last forty-four years. Men now came to the North-West in a sleeping-car, and sighed to heaven over the great hardships they had to undergo. (Laughter.) He came with Rev. James Evans by way of Fort William, whence they had to paddle their own canoes and carry them on their shoulders across portages. Mr. Evans went first to Norway House, and the speaker to Fort

Frances, whence, however, he was soon called by Mr. Evans to act as interpreter and school teacher. He continued in this capacity some time with Mr. Evans, until the latter finished his invention of the syllabic characters, when the speaker began translating the Scriptures into these characters. The characters were very simple and easily learned by the Indians. On being given them in the morning, an Indian would sometimes be able to read the same night. He had been given the Book of Job to translate, and thence to the end of the Prophets, and from the Acts of the Apostles to the end of the New Testament; and, as was known, these were hard portions to translate. Although difficult for one man, yet by the help of God the work was done; and now, he was glad to be able to say, these Scriptures were being read by the Indians. On the mission where he had spent a long time there was hardly a man, woman or child but could read the Scriptures in these characters. In their religious gatherings, every Indian was to be seen having under his arm his Bible and hymn-book; and they would search out the texts of the sermons and follow the preacher as he read. This was what had been accomplished by missionary labor, and the Indians would be benefited by it as long as they lived. About twenty-nine years ago he had been sent to the Saskatchewan country, after having spent already fourteen years in service on missions. He had opened up the Oxford House Mission, where Rev. Enos Langford had been a missionary for four years. From there he had been sent to open a mission at White Fish Lake, in the Saskatchewan country. The beginnings were small. Besides the occupants of his own tent and that of another, there was no human being near. They never forgot to assemble for worship, although they were so few. After a while the Indians came around, but were very shy. By handing around the pipe of peace, he caught them with guile, and gained the opportunity of firing upon them the Gospel gun. After that a great many came to the ground, and he commenced preaching the Gospel among them. God blessing his labors, he did some good to some of them, and they felt the converting power of the Gospel. At present there were about four hundred Indians there professing Christianity. When they commenced imitating the white man in making their living out of the ground they had no hoes, so they made wooden spades with which they broke some ground. After a while the missionary got what was called a Scotch plough; but they could not make their ponies work, as, instead of going ahead, they came back. (Laughter.) Not willing to be beaten, he took some shaganapi and hitched up twelve Indians, by which means he broke up a small piece of ground. On this he sowed some barley, and thus farming was commenced at White Fish Lake. He was glad to say that every family, almost, had now a yoke of oxen, cows, pigs, etc. Before they embraced Christianity the poor women did all the work, but now the men shared the burdens and no longer treated the women as slaves. They were poor people and could not have everything they wanted, yet, notwithstanding, they were trying to imitate the white man as far as they were able. The women would like to dress something like the white women. Formerly it took only two yards of cloth to dress an Indian woman, so they did not have long trains. In the early days there was a fashion among the women which they had since given up; but he saw that among the white ladies it was becoming resuscitated; they called it banging, he thought. (Cheers and laughter.) If the fashion continued it might come to that of the Blackfeet, who wore a bunch of hair coming down under the nose and then turned up. (Laughter.) Traders had wanted to establish posts there, but he would not allow it. If he had done so at first, there would have been no mission; but their Indians were now somewhat established in Christian knowledge. They were very zealous in attending the means of grace. They had two local preachers who led the service in his absence, five classes, two day-schools, and one flourishing Sabbath school. (Applause.) Some of the children were beginning to read the Word of God in English, and they learned thirty to fifty verses at a time to recite in Sunday-school. They were very fond of singing, and it was delightful in travelling over the plains on a buffalo hunt to hear them sing their beautiful hymns. Formerly, before the missionary came, only the war-song was heard. He gave an illustration of this singing, and by way of contrast sang a hymn in Indian to the tune, 'Hold the Fort,' and was applauded with spirit on concluding. He expressed his pleasure in the kind reception given him; thought that the same feelings would not be given to the pagan Indians seen on the streets of the town, and said that the difference in his favor was due to missionary labor. But for this and the treatment bestowed by the Hudson Bay Company, the white people would not have got up here so easily and possessed themselves of the heritage of the Indians. It was not the redcoats who had secured this peace, though he would not speak disrespectfully of them; it was Christianity. He hoped his hearers would be more than ever for the spread of this cause, that every Indian in the North-West 'might know the only true God, and Jesus Christ whom He has sent.'" (Applause.)

www.ingramcontent.com/pod-product-compliance
Lightning Source LLC
Chambersburg PA
CBHW020310240426
43673CB00039B/758